MUSIC
& PSYCHE

MUSIC & PSYCHE

Edited by
Paul W. Ashton and Stephen Bloch

Preface by
Paul W. Ashton and Stephen Bloch

Spring Journal Books
New Orleans, Louisiana

Published by
Spring Journal, Inc.
627 Ursulines Street #7
New Orleans, Louisiana 70116
Tel.: (504) 524-5117
Website: www.springjournalandbooks.com

Cover design:
Michael Caplan

Cover photograph:
"Town Crier"
by Chidi Okoye
Used by permission of Chidi Okoye
www.chidi.com

Printed in Canada
Text printed on acid-free paper

Library of Congress Cataloging-in-Publication Data Pending

Grateful acknowledgment is made to the following publishers, persons, and institutions for permission to reproduce the following:

Introduction: Wordsworth Editions Ltd gave permission to publish verbatim the story "The Golden Key" from *The Complete Illustrated Fairy Tales of the Brothers Grimm*. Nicholas Abbott's family gave permission to use the recording of "The Golden Key" by Nicholas and his brother Simon.

Chapter 1: Robert Hinshaw of Daimon Verlag in Switzerland consented to our use of Melinda Haas's essay "The Third in Mahler's Ninth," originally published in *Barcelona 2004: The Edges of Experience: Memory and Emergence: Proceedings of the Sixteenth International Congress for Analytical Psychology* (2006). EMI/Virgin Music in Canada gave permission to reproduce excerpts from *Mahler: Symphony No.9. Richard Strauss: Metamorphosen, Tod und Verklärung*, Simon Rattle conducting the Vienna Philharmonic Orchestra, Angel Records, 1998.

Chapter 2: Permission to use lyrics from "Why Was I Born," words by Oscar Hammerstein II, music by Jerome Kern, granted by Hal Leonard Corporation. Permission to use lyrics from "Experiment," words and music by Cole Porter, has been granted by Alfred Publishing. Permission to use lyrics from "A Sleepin' Bee," words by Truman Capote, music by Harold Arlen, has been granted by Hal Leonard Corporation. Permission to use lyrics from "Once Upon a Time," words by Lee Adams, music by Charles Strouse, has been granted by Williamson Music. Permission to use lyrics from "Ten Cents a Dance," words by Lorenz Hart, music by Richard Rodgers, been granted by Alfred Publishing and Williamson Music. Permission to use lyrics from "Me and the Blues," words by Ted Koehler, music by Harry Warren, has been granted by Alfred Publishing. Lyric reprint for "Sweet Kentucky Ham" licensed under permission, (c) 1981 Swiftwater Music (ASCAP) administered by Kohaw Music (ASCAP), c/o The Bicycle Music Company.

Harry Fox Agency and Sony Music granted permission to use Lee Wiley's recording of "The Memphis Blues," music by W. C. Handy, words by George A. Norton. The Harry Fox Agency granted permission to use Connee Boswell's recording of "On the Isle of May" by Andre Kostelanetz, music based on the "Andante Cantabile" from *Tchaikovsky's String Quartet No. 1* in D Major, words by Mack David.

Chapter 3: Artwork used by kind permission of the artist, Gillian Mathew, and the owners of the original work, Michael Oak Waldorf School in Cape Town, represented by Ann Kantey. EMI/Virgin Music in Canada gave permission to reproduce excerpts from Beethoven's *Piano Sonata No 31 in A Flat Major* on *Piotr Anderszewski Plays Bach: English Suite BWV 811/Beethoven: Piano Sonata Op. 110/ Webern: Variations Op. 27* (24354 56322).

Chapter 4: Nancy Cater of Spring Journal Books consented to our use of material from a 2008 interview with Mario Jacoby by Robert Henderson, which originally appeared in *Living with Jung*, vol. 2, *"Enterviews" with Jungian Analysts* (2008).

Chapter 6: Robert Hinshaw of Daimon Verlag in Switzerland consented to our use of Laurel Morris's essay "Creative Torment or Tormented Creativity," originally published in *Cambridge 2001: Proceedings of the Fifteenth International Congress for Analytical Psychology.* The piano music that accompanies Laurel Morris's article was especially recorded by Steven Masi for *Music and Psyche.*

Chapter 12: Lyrics from "To God in God's Absence" on *The Iron Stone* reproduced with the kind permission of Robin Williamson.

Chapter 15: Chiron Publications permitted the use of the article "Abandonment, Wish, and Hope in the Blues" by William Willeford, first published by Chiron in 1985.

Chapter 17: "The Song of Wandering Aengus" performed by Nóirín Ní Riain is taken from the album *Sanctuary,* sales of which support victims of domestic violence. Used with the kind consent of Fr. Joseph McGilloway, producer of *Sanctuary.* See www.myspace.com/sanctuaryalbum.

*In memory of Nicholas and with love and
gratitude to Cathy, Charles, Simon, and Lyndall. (PWA)*

In memory of my parents. (SB)

Contents

Acknowledgments

Thanks to my friend and colleague Stephen Bloch for all his assistance and good humor during the at-times-tedious process of editing this book. We complemented each other well, his intuitive ability enabling me to see the bigger picture and my sensate attention to concrete detail helping him formulate his ideas accessibly. The contributors to this collection of essays have mostly been a pleasure to work with and accepted our editing with a preponderance of good humor, and I am immensely grateful to them for producing work of such a high and creative standard while remaining cooperatively themselves. Thanks also to Charles Abbott for sharing his publishing and computer expertise with me and remaining calm in the face of my near-hysteria when hours of work disappeared or I could not transfer an image from Picasa to Word.

Helise and Frances tolerated my bent back, hunched shoulders, and furrowed brow with minimal murmurings and suffered my pessimistic outbursts as well as my grandiose elaborations with resignation but also support. Thank you both; you are enormously dear to me.

I have received strong support and much information from a host of other individuals. I would like to thank particularly Lucy Norton, Helen Anderson, my cello teacher Sarah Acres, Dizu Plaatjies and Peter Klatzow from the College of Music, as well as some of the staff of St Luke's Hospice. All the above have been of assistance in one way or another and given me of their time, attention, and knowledge. Enormous thanks go to Lance Field for his putting together the master copy of our CD from disparate bits of recording and for his thoughtful ad hominem advice.

—Paul W. Ashton

Acknowledgments

I would like to acknowledge and thank the following people who supported me in my contribution to this project: my co-editor Paul Ashton for his vision, experience, and determination. I am glad our relationship survived times where there were differences of opinion. Lois for her many kinds of support and backup, and Leila, Nina, Rafi, and Joni for being here. Chris Wildman always gave of his joy in and knowledge of music, and Paul Whelan showed how listening to music can be a creative act in itself. Thanks also to the rest of our music listening group: Mike Cope, Rod Gurzynski, Terry Volbrecht, and Michael Toye. My gratitude to Dr. Yvonne Blake for her sustaining presence. I would also like to thank Dr. Tina Stromsted for her encouragement and feedback and Rod Anderson and Dr. John Gosling for helpful comments.

—Stephen Bloch

We would both like to acknowledge the perspicacity and dedication to detail of our copyeditor Kate Babbitt (to whom we apologize for adding to her gray hairs) and the encouragement of our publisher Nancy Cater at Spring.

Preface

PAUL W. ASHTON
STEPHEN BLOCH

Reaching for meaning while keeping an image alive is a challenge within analysis and when writing about psychoanalysis. This is particularly true when approaching creative arts. The danger is always that a reductionist approach can deaden the subject while the writer is trying to engage with it.

In collecting and editing these essays, we were conscious of this challenge. Our hope was to create a deepening experience by approaching music with a (psycho)analytic understanding. By doing this we hoped that the two areas—of psychoanalysis and of music—would be mutually expanded, and we deliberately sought for a range of perspectives and musical genres.

In order to keep the area alive our initial aim was to provide extensive musical examples. This proved difficult, mainly due to copyright issues. We therefore had to modify our aim, and, in the end, were able to provide musical excerpts and examples for only about half the papers. However, the music referred to in all the papers is available easily through online stores and in some cases YouTube clips are also accessible. Most chapters include a list of recordings.

We have ordered the chapters in rather a loose way, but we start with essays that explore the way that musicians, both composers and performers, have created music that fosters individual growth or transformation, sometimes in a work, sometimes during a lifetime. Next is Paul Ashton's essay "Music, Mind and Psyche," which focuses on music and the brain. This is followed by essays and an interview that delineate (mostly from an extra-Jungian perspective) current thinking on music and "primitive" states. Thereafter come three chapters that focus on the healing of groups or communities through music. Stephen Bloch's paper on mercy starts the ascent from the chthonic to the spiritual that is completed by Nóirín Ni Riain's chapter.

Paul W. Ashton
Stephen Bloch
Cape Town, 2010

Introduction

PAUL W. ASHTON

Nicholas was a young friend of mine in his early twenties who studied music at the University of Cape Town. Composition was his major, but he also played piano, flute, and piccolo. One weekend while he was exploring a route up Devil's Peak, an extension of the famous Table Mountain in Cape Town, Nicholas fell and sustained multiple injuries. He was airlifted to a local hospital, where he died some hours later.

It seemed impossible that someone with so much energy, life force, libido could die, and the only way that I could make sense of it to myself was to think that he had to transcend his individuality, his ego, and submit to what Schopenhauer has called "the Will" (but that could also be termed the Self, God, the unconscious, the void, or the deep empty world) and enter the unknown.

About eighteen months before he died, Nicholas composed a short piece of music entitled "The Golden Key." This was his response to a Grimm's fairy tale of the same name that I quote in full. It is the shortest in the Grimm brothers' collection and goes like this:

> In the wintertime, when deep snow lay on the ground, a poor boy was forced to go out on a sledge to fetch wood. When he had gathered it together, and packed it, he wished, as he was so frozen with cold, not to go home at once, but to light a fire

and warm himself a little. So he scraped away the snow, and as he was thus clearing the ground, he found a tiny, golden key. Hereupon he thought that where the key was, the lock must be also, and dug in the ground and found an iron chest. "If the key does but fit it!" thought he; "no doubt there are precious things in that little box." He searched, but no keyhole was there. At last he discovered one, but so small that it was hardly visible. He tried it, and the key fitted it exactly. Then he turned it once round.

And now we must wait until he has quite unlocked it and opened the lid, and then we shall learn what wonderful things were lying in that box.

I first heard a performance of "The Golden Key" at a pre-Christmas family get-together at my home. Nicholas played on a prepared piano while his brother Simon accompanied him on a violin. The prepared piano was simply opened in the front and some strings labeled so that they could, at the ordained times, be plucked by hand. This gave rise to a harp-like effect. The attached recording, Track 1 on the CD that accompanies this volume, was not done professionally but does give one a flavor of the piece.

On the evening that Nicholas and Simon played for us, I found myself wet-eyed and wondering whether this piece represented an intimation that Nicholas had had of his own mortality. The ending particularly reminded me of the ending of Mahler's *Symphony No. 9* that Melinda Haas writes so movingly about (see chapter 1). There is a clear sense of the ego submitting to the Will and disappearing into Great Silence or emptiness.

Neither the Grimms' story nor the music impose answers on us, whether those answers would have been satisfactory or unsatisfactory. Rather, they introduce us to a space that is not limited by the preconceptions of either the storyteller or the composer, and out of that limitless space our own truths may appear.

Stephen Bloch and I came to collaborate on this book via different routes, although we were on paths that often crossed. My drive came from my interest in void states, which I articulated in a monograph entitled *From the Brink,*[2] and we first joined forces when Stephen contributed an essay on minimalist music, "Music as Dreaming," to a collection that I edited titled *Evocations of Absence.*[3] "Evocations of Absence" was also the title of a group presentation at the seventeenth congress of the International Association for Analytical Psychology (IAAP) held in Cape Town in 2007, where Stephen was able to illustrate his ideas with musical examples.

For Stephen, the experience that music gives rise to is itself important because music evokes a particular feeling or affect, but also of significance for him is the way that music can metabolize experience. In developing this understanding Stephen draws on the work of Michael Eigen.

Michael Eigen uses the *idea* of music rather than actual music in the elaboration of his understanding of the analytic encounter. He encourages us to listen to what occurs behind the actual meaning of the words in the encounter between the analyst and his or her analysand. There is something inchoate there; it is not quite formed nor elaborated, but it can take the process beyond what is consciously experienced. There may not be words for it but there will be rhythm, tempo and melody, feelings of coherence or incoherence, harmony or discord, and a constant interplay between sound and silence. Words or language, as Lawrence Wetzler suggests in his chapter "The Music of Unthinkable Anxiety and Nameless Dread" (chapter 11), may come between an analyst and his or her analysand, and words may even separate a person from his or her self,[4] but music has the potential to be Self-enhancing.

We thought that Michael Eigen would be rewarding to interview, as he has worked in this area for so long, hence the "Interview with Michael Eigen" (chapter 13). Most of the questions he was asked were generated by Stephen.

In Cape Town in 2008, Stephen presented a paper he had written on "The Music of the Black Sun," choosing music that gave an auditory expression to the concepts elaborated by Stanton Marlan in his book.[5] This paper has been developed into a chapter for this book (chapter 12). Stephen articulates in auditory terms what Marlan describes in a visual way, and in this process Stephen makes possible a more felt experience of the Black Sun. Marlan has been criticized for making his exposition too beautiful and in this way protecting his readers from the depth of the anguish that experiencing the Black Sun can evoke. Stephen does not let us off the hook so easily, and in listening to the music he has chosen we are forced to know the pain yet experience the possibility of the greater joy that Marlan intuits. Unfortunately we have been unable to include that music on the CD, but a list of recordings is included for the interested reader to explore.

Stephen's other essay has been written expressly for this book and is a searching exposition of a little-explored analytic theme, that of mercy. In "Mercy: The Unbearable in Eigen's Writings and John Tavener's *Prayer of the Heart*" (chapter 16), Stephen describes in some detail the pain of the confrontation with what has been called "the unthinkable" (as in Winnicott's unthinkable anxieties) and "the nameless" (as in Bion's nameless dread), and he suggests that an understandable response is reaching for mercy. He takes as a musical exposition of this concept John Tavener's *Prayer of the Heart*. This is a modern version of the "Kyrie eleison" ("Lord have mercy") that is sung by the Icelandic singer Björk. This work captures the feeling of someone small and powerless before the might not of righteousness but of a kind of amoral and naïve power. It evokes in psychological terms the appropriate attitude of the human ego faced with the enormity and ultimate unknowability of the Self. Again the music is accessible via the list of recordings.

We did not direct our contributors to write about a particular topic but trusted in the idea that each individual should write about what was of interest or concern to him or her and that the products of that writing would somehow fit together. We have chosen contributors on the basis of our knowledge of them or their work, particularly because of their interest in both music and psyche. Of note is that each contributor thinks about music and its relation to analysis or to healing in a different way. And sometimes these ways are quite contrary to each other. For example, Helen Anderson will never choose music for a patient but waits for the choice to spring from him or her, whereas Lawrence Wetzler describes the powerful effect of music that he chose for a particular patient (see chapters 3 and 6, respectively). Helen waits for psyche to speak—that is, to send an image —whereas Lawrence uses his intuition and musical knowledge to inform him as to how to "nudge" psyche. As editors we may not agree with everything that is presented here, but we do feel that everything that is presented is of significance.

One of the ways that Nicholas thought about the different types of music was as "music from below" and "music from above." He had split them in this way, I think, to separate earthly or physical music from spiritual or mind music, but he did not value one above the other. I feel sure that had he lived longer, he would, like Beethoven (see Helen Anderson's chapter), have found a way to bring these "musics" together. He was as happy performing wildly on the dance floor, penetrated "physically" by the rhythmic thump of a rock band, as he was when listening in stillness to the distant silence of a "feather on the breath of God" evoked by the music of Hildegard of Bingen or Arvo Pärt. He was moved by the chthonic and the spiritual both.

For Nicholas the "music from above" was an expression of what I would call one pole of the archetype of music. It was something like a platonic ideal that existed in the sublimated realm of pure spirit, and it could take on some substantiality, be made manifest, only through the efforts of a composer. For him, the composer's task was to attempt to give form to the ethereal or unmanifest—in other words, to make the unmanifest manifest or the inaudible music audible. To use Keats's image, he wanted to give tone to the "spirit ditties of no tone."[6] So the title of the chapter written by Kevin O'Connell, "I wrote what I heard," which is a quotation from Stravinsky about his composition of *The Rite of Spring*, makes sound sense to me. And so does Kevin's concept of Stravinsky's refusal to entertain us or ornament the work but rather to leave it "vacuous" (see chapter 7). We do need space in which to "co-construct" any artistic experience, whether it be music, art, or literature. That is, we do if we are to be part of the creation of something new. And it is in the experience of "the new," especially if we have been part of its creation, that we feel more at one with ourselves, with our whole selves.

There are different ways in which music engages one. Perhaps we can attribute that to different types of consciousness being stimulated. Above and below are two extremes, the spiritual and the physical, and they are stirred by different types of music. Spiritual consciousness is stimulated by the sort of music that evokes space, vacuousness, void; one might call that "meditative music." It is the sort of music that a mystic might choose to meditate on and is a combination of structure and emptiness, form and formlessness. The structure or form helps hold you while you drift into the formless, listen to God, hear the silent hum of the universe. In order to experience what Lacan called "the Real" one has to let go of the usual structures that defend us against chaos, but if all of one is adrift in chaos, then there is nothing left to bring back what has been learned or experienced. As John Dourley has written, the descent into the "nothing" is valueless unless there is also a conscious return from it.[7]

The exquisite harmonies of Palestrina or the careful structure of J. S. Bach's music may console us with the experience that it all fits in the way that we know that it should. But the spiritual, as defined as something other, something new, something previously unknown, may be evoked in quite another way. The spaciousness of some of Mahler, for example his Ninth Symphony (see chapter 1), the vacuousness of some Stravinsky (see chapter 7), or the silence evoked by Arvo Pärt or John Tavener (who uses a drone to symbolize the great silence that is the unknown God) may all lead to a previously undreamed-of experience of unitary reality,[8] whether that be called an experience of God or the Self or the Unconscious or the Real.

But, as suggested above, there are other forms of consciousness too, each of which can be stimulated or enhanced by music. Sometimes it is the type of music that is important in this process, but it can also be the way that it is listened to, and this may have more to do with the typology of the listener. For example, someone whose superior function is thinking may approach a performance in an analytic way, gaining pleasure from that process, whereas a more feeling type may listen to the same music in a predominantly right-brain way and feel into its emotional qualities. The clear marching rhythms of, for example, "Mars" in Holst's *The Planets,* the stimulating beat of Vangelis's "Chariots of Fire," or the driving punctuations of much modern dance music all activate the motor system of the listener. And sensory consciousness may be aroused by the timbre of particular instruments, the "color" of the melody or harmony, the overall "flavor" of a piece.

Lawrence Wetzler, who is both musician and psychoanalyst, uses the ideas of Lacan as well as those of Bion, Zizek, and Winnicott to give a theoretical background to his musical and analytic exploration of the psyche of his patients. Sometimes they have been wounded by incest and family violence, but sometimes they remain "catastrophically unborn" because of the incapacity of their primary objects to contain them. Wetzler has written two chapters for this collection from his non-Jungian viewpoint. They are aptly named "The Music of Unthinkable Anxiety and Nameless Dread" and "In You More Than You: The Lacanian Real, Music, and Bearing Witness."

Wetzler attempts to recreate in the reader, through his writing, some of the "nameless dread" and "unthinkable anxiety" that his patients are heir to and that renders them seemingly unreachable. But he does not leave us in a state of hopelessness; rather, he demonstrates how a musical sensitivity to our clients and what they are going through may help us access them and in fact helps them to access themselves. This accessing of themselves will lead to a sense of connection with their interiors. It is as though the right music "recognizes" an aspect of the person and the person feels recognized, feels seen, as though by another, and that "feeling seen" facilitates her dealing with "unthinkable anxiety," especially the anxiety of falling forever or of being absolutely alone.[9]

Some of the chapters have been published before. William Willeford's chapter was originally published in *Chiron* in 1985 and then a version of it was used as a chapter in his book *Feeling, Imagination, and the Self,* published in 1987. Laurel Morris's chapter was originally presented at the Cambridge IAAP congress in 2001 and published in the proceedings thereof. Melinda Haas's papers have both been presented as lectures: "The Third in Mahler's Ninth" at the IAAP congress in Barcelona in 2004 and "Can Music Save the World?" at the 2008 conference of the Council of

North American Societies of Jungian Analysts. And Kevin O'Connell's chapter was originally given as a paper at the 2008 C. G. Jung Conference in Zurich, held at the Swiss Federal Institute of Technology.

Music can be intensely individual—it often seems to speak "only to me"—and yet music can be broadly collective, linking individuals or groups or whole societies, perhaps uniting or saving the world. Saidie Kahn, a music teacher, worked very successfully with the inmates of a psychiatric hospital in South Africa, bringing long-term patients out of their "cocoons" and teaching them to sing as soloists and members of a choir.[10] She felt that her patients/ pupils should be protected from certain aspects of music or words of songs that might be detrimental to them. Thus she would remove or change words that she felt might be depressing, for example deleting "death" and substituting "love" in a song. She worked from a base of "knowing" what patients needed and was extremely effective in fostering their growth. I wonder whether she was fostering the growth of the ego rather than the Self, which, particularly in these patients, was sorely needed.

Helen Anderson, a music therapist, seems to work from a very different perspective where she honors Psyche as being the one who knows. She sees herself as the facilitator of that knowledge on behalf of the whole personality. I think she is more closely attuned to the Self, which, because the Self is ultimately unknowable, requires an attitude of listening expectation rather than knowledgeable interpretation. And yet the ego may well need to have the unconscious aspects of the psyche interpreted to it as they become available. The focus of Helen's chapter ("The Innate Transformational Properties of Beethoven's Passion Music") is on the opposing aspects of Beethoven's composing, the spiritual and the chthonic, which relates back to Nicholas's ideas about music with which I began this introduction. Her idea of the musically expressed crucifixion, which lies inside Beethoven's Passion music, gives an inkling of the pain that is inherent in embracing her attitude.

Chris Wildman is another music therapist but one who extends his practice into the more public arena. Here the thrust of the work is to allow an individual or several individuals to express the traumata a community has suffered in order to facilitate collective healing. This is done through a version of playback theatre. Chris makes clear in his chapter "Bonfire of the Vanities" (chapter 14) that as musician, his task is a complex one that involves both listening to the "music" of the participants and translating that into performed music that evokes healing responses both in the audience as a whole and within the individual participants.

As I read his chapter I became aware of the complexity of his task, which is to be both "knowing" and yet absolutely open to hear what he did not know. And then somehow he must allow that to be expressed through the music he makes.

The idea of music being healing for a group is carried forward by William Willeford, whose chapter on the blues and blues performers as well as those who are "participant listeners" captures the idea of how a trauma can be worked through musically ("Abandonment, Wish, and Hope in the Blues"; chapter 15). His ideas again encompass both individual and group experience. Some sort of hardship leads to one suffering "the blues," and Willeford demonstrates convincingly how listening to the singing of the blues can be a healing experience. This is partly through the expressed irony in the lyrics, which allows performers and audience alike to hear and accept what is or has happened without taking it too seriously. Although Willeford does not say so, I wonder if part of the healing power of the blues stems from their steadfast refusal to satisfy the ear by returning to the tonic. They always fall short by using the seventh instead, thus leaving the melody unresolved; that is, the blues always leave the melody open. Completion has to be done by the listener herself.

Still on the theme of healing the group as well as (or through) healing the individual, Melinda Haas asks in her second chapter in this volume "Can Music Heal the World?" She uses the example of Venezuela's *el sistema* to suggest that it can. In this case it is the actual playing of the music as part of an orchestra that is healing or that aids psychological growth and the development of democratic values. Her argument—that playing music with others, apart from the hugely beneficial effects to the individual of learning an instrument, leads to greater tolerance of others and the acceptance and valuing of each member of the orchestra—is convincing. Not only does it lead to heightened self-esteem, but it also fosters greater cooperation. Would that the world's politicians played in orchestras or in some way worked together with the joint purpose of creating something beautiful.

The writing in this book is predominantly by Jungian analysts, but we are cognizant of the fact that depth psychotherapy is carried out in a verbal way by different psychoanalytic schools and that a host of other therapies touch our patients in many different ways. I think for example of movement therapies, voice work, art therapy, and music therapy, but it is music therapy that seems to work most profoundly and perhaps this is because music is so widely represented in the brain. My chapter on "Music, Mind, and Psyche" attempts to map out the different areas involved and the probable ways that different aspects of music give rise to different effects.

Melinda's other chapter, "The Third in Mahler's Ninth," takes a Jungian look at Mahler's great Ninth Symphony (chapter 1). She traces the significance of Mahler's time, place, and nature, demonstrating how that enabled him to articulate the feeling of being an individual on the edge of the collective. The fact that he, being Jewish, was not acceptable to the collective made his being-on-the-edge a source of profound conflict but also a source of wisdom. The end of her chapter, which articulates the end of the symphony, brings home to one the sense of the melting together of ego and Self in the unitary reality of the psyche. It is profoundly tragic but at the same time enormously hopeful. This is a lovely example of music as metaphor described in poetic terms.

Another example of music as metaphor is the chapter by Laurel Morris who, in "Creative Torment or Tormented Creativity: Robert Schumann and Nineteenth-Century German Romanticism" (chapter 6) uses examples of Schumann's music to demonstrate both his creative genius and the nature of his character. She connects Schumann's creativity with the concept of *Witz,* which she compares with the Jungian/alchemical metaphor of Mercurius. This chapter extends one's knowledge of music, of Schumann, and of Jungian psychology, which means that it deepens one's conscious awareness through associative channels.

Jungian analyst Patricia Skar describes her life journey from the musical matrix of her family home into the world of performance and teaching, a journey that eventually led to her use of musical improvisation as active imagination within the analytic container. So she has used music as metaphor, as tool and as container, and her chapter "The Matrix of Music and Analysis" (chapter 5) describes that journey and its usefulness for herself and others.

Interviewing Mario Jacoby, who is a musician and one of the "living ancestors" of Jungian psychology, was an enormous pleasure for me. He was so accessible, modest, and thoughtful that by the end of the process I felt that he had become a friend.

Generally speaking, the anima is sought for in figures of classical mythology or in the form of visual images, so the chapter "The Voice of the Anima in Popular Singing" by John Beebe is highly original (chapter 2). John explores the way each anima voice gives the anima a different acoustic face and each singer connects her listeners to the eternity of their emotions without sacrificing the ordinariness of her own personal origins. Thus John enlarges the realm of what "music" is and deepens our understanding of where it can take one, what it might foster in each of our psyches.

Music connects us body and soul, and beyond that it connects the chthonic with the spiritual. Nóirín Ní Riain is a theologian as well as a singer of Irish folk and spiritual songs. She coined the word "Theosony," which has to do with listening to the sound of God, and this brings out the idea that it is through really listening that we can "hear" God. Certainly, as those who have been lucky enough to hear her voice can attest, her singing constructs a stairway toward the ineffable beyond. In her chapter "Song and the Psyche: Whispers of the Mind" (chapter 17), Nóirín focuses on how the body produces sound, on listening, and on the significance of silence. She weaves together what have usually been seen as very different and disconnected aspects. Hers is certainly one of the voices of the anima, which demonstrates eros at work.

So, within the matrix of music that supports and enlarges us, we have been led through realms of knowing and not-knowing, pain and joy, the chthonic and the spiritual. And we end with the fragile purity of Nóirín's voice penetrating the silence that may be God. If we have turned the Golden Key and allowed you to open the iron chest of your awareness of Music and Psyche, your music, your psyche, we will be well pleased.

Notes

[1] Used verbatim with the consent of Wordsworth Editions from their edition of *The Complete Illustrated Fairy Tales of the Brothers Grimm* (1997; repr., Hertfordshire: Wordsworth Editions, 2007), p. 828.

[2] Paul W. Ashton, *From the Brink: A Depth Psychological Exploration of Void States* (London: Karnac Press, 2007).

[3] Stephen Bloch, "Music as Dreaming," in *Evocations of Absence: Multidisciplinary Perspectives on Void States,* ed. Paul W. Ashton (New Orleans: Spring Journal Books, 2007).

[4] See also Donald N. Stern, *The Interpersonal World of the Infant* (New York: Basic Books, 1985).

[5] Stanton Marlan, *The Black Sun: The Alchemy and Art of Darkness* (College Station: Texas A&M University Press, 2005).

[6] John Keats, "Ode on a Grecian Urn," in *Worldscapes,* ed. Robin Malan (Cape Town: Oxford University Press South Africa, 2001), p. 15.

[7] John Dourley, "Jung, Some Mystics, and the Void," in Ashton, *Evocations of Absence,* 51ff. Also John Dourley, "Memory and Emergence:

Jung and the Mystical Anamnesis of the Nothing," in *Barcelona 04—Edges of Experience: Memory and Emergence. Proceedings of the 16th IAAP Congress for Analytical Psychology*, ed. Lyn Cowan (Einsiedlen: Daimon Verlag, 2006).

[8] Kathryn Madden, *Dark Light of the Soul* (Great Barrington: Lindisfarne Books, 2008).

[9] Ashton, *From the Brink*, especially 214 ff.

[10] Saidie Smith, *They Shall Have Music: The Musical Achievements of Psychiatric Patients through Music Therapy* (Cape Town: Pretext Publishers, 1999).

Blues - Completion is done by the listener. Melodies are unresolven in the blues.

The voice of God in music.

1

The Third in Mahler's Ninth

Melinda Haas

I have always been mystified by the near-total absence of music in Jung's work. As a representation of culture, as a symbol system, it would seem the perfect vehicle for much of Jungian theory. What follows is my attempt to break that silence by looking at one glorious piece of music through a Jungian lens.

In 1956 Jung met with Margaret Tilly, a music therapist. At the end of their "session," sounding somewhat surprised, he said, "I feel that from now on music should be an essential part of every analysis. This reaches the deep archetypal material that we can only sometimes reach in our analytical work with patients. This is most remarkable."[1]

Gustav Mahler's *Symphony No. 9,* written during the summer of 1909, stands at the beginning edge of a century, at the ending edge of a composer's life, and at the border between music and culture as it had been built and known over the previous three centuries and as it would evolve in the course of the twentieth century. The music itself pushes the bounds of the known vis-à-vis tonality, form, and time. It hurtles into the twentieth century, stopping just short of Mahler's friend Arnold Schoenberg. In fact, in the last few days of Mahler's life he grew very anxious about Schoenberg. He worried: "If I go, he will have nobody left."[2] One wonders if that was a musical worry as well as a financial one.

Mahler experienced himself both *at* the edges and as a *product* of the edges. He was born in 1860 in a small town in Bohemia (now the Czech Republic), at the edge of what was the Austro-Hungarian Empire. His childhood was besieged by death. As the eldest child he witnessed the death of six brothers, leaving five remaining siblings. In his book *The Rest Is Noise* Alex Ross tells the following story:

> The family atmosphere was tense. Mahler recalled a time when he ran out of the house in order to escape an argument between his parents. On the street, he heard a barrel organ playing the tune "Ach, du lieber Augustin." He told this story to Sigmund Freud, in 1910, during a psychoanalytic session that took the form of a four-hour walk. "In Mahler's opinion," Freud noted, "the conjunction of high tragedy and light amusement was from then on inextricably fixed in his mind."[3]

Adding to that conjunction, Mahler's wife Alma quotes her husband's description of himself. "I am thrice homeless: as a native of Bohemia in Austria, as an Austrian among the Germans, and as a Jew throughout all the world; everywhere an intruder, never welcomed."[4] A prescient statement, as some forty years later his niece Alma Rosé would conduct the only women's orchestra in the Nazi camps before being killed in Auschwitz. He was baptized a Catholic in order to take up his appointment as conductor of the Vienna Opera. Although he was not religiously connected to his Jewish heritage, he carried it forever, as the outsider. His self-proclaimed identification with Ahasuerus, the Jewish figure from medieval Christian legend doomed to wander the earth for taunting Christ on his way to the Crucifixion, opens a window into his self-image and psyche.

Jung explains the eternal wanderer this way:

> Wotan is a restless wanderer who creates unrest and stirs up strife, now here, now there, and works magic. He was soon changed by Christianity into the devil. . . . In the Middle Ages the role of the restless wanderer was taken over by Ahasuerus, the Wandering Jew. . . . The motif of the wanderer who has not accepted Christ was projected on the Jews.[5]

This link between Wotan and Ahasuerus must have provided the archetypal underpinnings that made Mahler one of the greatest Wagner conductors the world has known. He even changed opera and concert audience etiquette, making latecomers wait outside, decreasing the amount of applause between movements and scenes, demanding silence with his icy glare. He wished to do for the symphony what Wagner had done for opera—trump everything that had gone before.

Mahler *was* a restless wanderer, like Wotan, moving from one conducting post to the next until achieving his ultimate goal, in anti-Semitic Vienna, as conductor of the Vienna Court Opera. Always he stirred up strife and worked magic, both as conductor and composer.

In Jungian understanding, the "third" refers to the "transcendent function." Jung's theory of the opposites is intimately connected to the development of consciousness. First one relates to a set of opposites by swinging back and forth between them. For example, one side is likely to be held in conscious awareness, while the other lies in the unconscious. Thus they are not both experienced at the same time. From there, one progresses to an awareness of the two poles at the same time, holding the opposites in the tension of consciousness. That tension creates the third, or the transcendent function.

It is my contention that Mahler's Ninth Symphony is built upon a multitude of opposites and that the sheer number of these sets of opposites seems to depolarize them. It puts us in a field of multiplicity much like the unhinging, illogical aspects of the analytic process. But also, like psyche herself, it breaks out of the binary ego-world of the opposites and thrusts us into a world outside ego that contains all, that leaves nothing out. At the beginning of this, the twenty-first century, the model of *a* set of opposites, *one* duality that produces *a* transcendent function, seems to be an oversimplification and no longer applicable.

Since Jung's discussion of the transcendent function in 1916, the complexity of the twentieth century has imposed its lasting imprint. The deconstruction of the old causal order took root. Mahler, straddling the edges, used the language of the past to intimate the future. Curiously, one does not hear this premonition in his previous works. The conjunction of personal and world events opened unexplored territory to him. He pushed his own familiar musical language to the edges of order, to the edge of what was permissible, forgivable, acceptable in 1909 Western Europe. If there is *a* "third" that comes out of the Ninth, I would say it might be beauty. But a beauty that is wrought from ugliness and sarcasm and a life lived as an outsider, constantly worried about money—a life full of illness and death, dashed hopes and betrayal, as well as an intimate connection to nature, the body in motion, the world of ideas, and meaningful relationships with people he chose to be close to. The music that emerges, *because* it encompasses all of these aspects, is exquisite, transcendent beauty. Put into psychological language, the music that emerges seems to flow directly from psyche, not from the constraints of the logical, goal-oriented, black-and-white world of the ego alone. In this excerpt you will hear first the raucous, almost hysterical pitch of music unleashed, no longer bound by the classical rules imposed by ego. This is the end of the third movement. It then tumbles into the wide-open spaces of the beginning of the fourth and final movement (Track 2 on the CD that accompanies this volume).[6]

Multiplicity and deconstruction produce one another and ultimately produce postmodernism. They are the ruling principles in today's world. Perhaps because 100 years ago they were still the exception, Mahler was able to make unified meaning of the disparate and various parts by creating a space expansive enough to contain them. I wonder if this music might serve as a model or at least an example of psyche's ability to contain multiplicity and in so doing allow the emergence of wholeness through that operation. If listened to with this in mind, I believe the music will elucidate Mahler's time, our time, and a path into the deep innermost parts of the human psyche that vibrate to something profoundly beautiful.

In 1935, at Tavistock, Jung spoke of multiplicity as he interpreted a visual image:

> This man, then, tries to gather in all the disparate elements into the vessel. The vessel is meant to be the receptacle for his whole being, for all the incompatible units. If he tried to gather them into his ego, it would be an impossible task, because the ego can be identical only with one part at a time. So he indicates by the symbol of the vessel that he is trying to find a container for everything.[7]

And I quote Mahler: "The symphony is the world. It must contain everything within it."[8]

That summer of 1909, Mahler had returned from his second season in New York, having conducted both the Metropolitan Opera and the New York Philharmonic. Clearly he was influenced by the energy of the "new world." He wrote to a friend: "The audiences here . . . are . . . unsophisticated, hungry for novelty, and in the highest degree eager to learn."[9] It is not merely coincidence that the resurgence of interest in Mahler in the 1970s and especially in the United States came at a time of unrest and protest. He had a profound ability to capture the complexity and energy of the contemporary world, to express the unconventional and still speak the recognizable language of the past. Pushing into new territory was not, however, a goal, a *Ding an sich* for Mahler. He was not a self-conscious composer but wrote from a deeply interior place. He wrote: "The need to express myself musically—in symphonic terms—begins only on the plane of *obscure* feelings, at the gate that opens into the 'other world.'"[10]

As with dream interpretation, the circumstances surrounding the creation of this work, the various discourses, find their way into the work but do not form its total interpretation or meaning. In 1909, the world was a tinderbox poised to ignite. Life and death were actively constellated as opposites. The dual monarchy of Austria-Hungary was fast becoming ineffectual, no longer able to contain the multiplicity of cultures in the empire. Anti-Semitism was becoming more politically entrenched in Vienna. Russia and France had formed an uneasy alliance. Even France and England had negotiated an entente, reeling in their centuries-old opposition in the face of the increasingly looming and expanding German empire. In that year a Spanish statesman said, "Either we make the revolution from above, or it will be made for us from below."[11] I wonder if that hints at revolution bubbling up from the deep interior, the psychological revolution, as well. Until this time, people had looked to religion for the answers to the impenetrable questions of life. Now those very same questions were being asked of psyche.

At the level of the personal, Mahler's beloved daughter had died at the age of four, two summers before. Immediately thereafter he had been diagnosed with a serious heart condition that circumscribed his life, limiting his ability to move freely in his beloved nature. He had finally succumbed to anti-Semitic pressure and resigned his Vienna Opera post and was once again homeless, wandering to America, emotionally unable to return to the country home where his daughter had died and where he had composed in previous summers. Whether he was superstitious or acutely aware of his internal clock, he tried to trick fate. The previous summer, while composing *Das Lied von der Erde* he refused to call it his ninth symphony because Beethoven, Schubert, Bruckner, and Dvorak had not lived past their ninth symphonies. When he approached *this* symphony he thought he was safe in calling it his ninth. But not even Mahler could cheat death. He died before finishing his tenth.

I do not agree with the many Mahler commentators who discuss the Ninth Symphony as his ethereal depiction of the afterlife, though he *was* processing the imminence of his own death. Rather, I am more inclined toward David Greene's comment: "Consciousness of the endness of existence doesn't diminish ecstasy of a world that is drunk with beauty and life. It creates a new kind of temporal process neither incomplete nor complete."[12] To the extent that Mahler succeeds in holding this tension of the awareness of life *and* death, he has formed a third, transcending a polarized experience of time. Through his action, Mahler's Ninth becomes one of the most profound statements about human possibility and capability that has ever been written. In this, he was fundamentally Jewish, expressing *this* life, not the next. The composer Alban Berg wrote this in 1912, upon hearing the first performance of the work:

> The first movement is the most heavenly thing M ever wrote. It is the expression of an unheard of love for this earth, the longing to live in peace upon her, Nature, still to enjoy her utterly, even to her deepest depths—before Death comes. For it comes irresistibly. This entire movement is based on a presentiment of death.[13]

Mahler stands at the far edge but still in his own time as he strives to create a "human-spiritual amalgam," to use David Tresan's term. If, as Tresan says, contemporary emergence theory means that "the concrete and the symbolic never blend together to form a third,"[14] then Mahler, though forward-looking, is not an example of this theory. For Mahler, the physicality of the sensory world is intimately linked with the spiritual. By pairing a flute with a double bass with nothing in between, he creates the "third," both as an experience of vast space and as the delineation of the edges of the sound container. By abruptly changing from raucous and *fortissimo* to *Schattenhaft* (shadowy) and barely perceptible, he confronts us with the "third"—a symbol that is able to hold our all-too-human fear.

He asks us to suspend our comfort with the familiar, inviting us on an uncharted journey through timbre, texture, and emotion. The outer movements are slow, surrounding the intense and fast middle movements. We have come to expect a declarative thematic statement at the opening of a first movement. Instead, the symphony opens with a barely perceptible heartbeat, drawing the listener in at an elemental level, pulse as sign of life, and the underpinning of music as it has come before, the *prima materia*. Slowly the first theme emerges from here. You will hear that in this excerpt from the first measures of the Ninth Symphony—from heartbeat to the emergence of the first theme (Track 3).[15]

The Classical and Romantic sonata form, with an expansive development section, a denouement, and a recapitulation that sews things up nicely, no longer holds. Mahler takes us now into his post-Romantic world: a world of small gestures and multiple climaxes, like the analytic process. The movement is loosely in rondo form (ABACADA). The Greek word *crusis,* or strong point, helps us better describe the shape of these episodes. As with life, the *anacrusis—ana* means before—collects and builds into the *crusis,* or we could even say crisis. The *metacrusis*—*meta* meaning after—is particularly interesting in this first movement. We expect a long logically devolving decrescendo that balances the slow building of the *anacrusis* that you heard part of. Instead the music quickly becomes disorganized, disoriented, diffuse, deconstructed—a complete *solutio.* Remember the calm and tenderness we heard moments ago in the opening of the first movement. Now listen to the mess he makes, several minutes later, still in the first movement (Track 4).[16]

And then the process begins again, *coagulatio* at its most difficult, scooping up the fragments and unintelligible mutterings, creating something that slowly accumulates meaning until it becomes recognizable as a distinguishable musical line. This is the section marked *Schattenhaft,* shadowy: still part of the first movement but now eerie, trying to gather the pieces (Track 5).[17]

Now we must look at the *third* in more detail. Since the Renaissance, diatonic music had consisted of a clear delineation of major and minor keys. In a major chord or scale, the interval of the third is major. It is comprised of two whole steps. In a minor chord or scale, the interval of the third is minor, made up of a whole step plus a half step, so it is smaller; the feeling is less open and less bright. We have come to think of one as light/happy, the other as dark/sad. Mahler plays with the two until all difference is blurred. He starts a theme in minor and ends it in major, or as Hefling describes:

> [The] first and second themes are bound together as brighter and darker polarities of the same tonic centre . . . B as the darker counterpart of A: the two thematic areas strongly linked, like the components of a syzygial pair,[18] and throughout the course of the movement they function as paired, interrelated opposites in rondo-like juxtaposition.[19]

Listen here for the melding of major and minor. Again this is near the opening of the first movement (Track 6).[20]

Instead of hearing them now as two distinct keys, the listener finds him/herself in a larger tonal field that contains both. At a simplistic level, we no longer seesaw between happy and sad as polarized. In our psychological language, we would say that we are no longer in between the poles or opposites, the binary thinking of ego consciousness. Instead, these formerly opposing qualities are now held equally and concurrently—in the field of human emotion, in psyche but outside ego. This mixing of major and minor thirds also pushes into the beginnings of chromaticism, thereby threatening the primacy of separateness and hierarchy. The two now function as "paired interrelated opposites" rather than polarized extremities. Thus Mahler forces the opposites not just into tension but into proximity. Because he makes only slight alterations to the familiar vocabulary, he is able to ask whether these pairs were really so opposed in the first place. Listen again to the conjunction of major and minor toward the end of the movement (Track 7).[21]

I have spent a great deal of time on the first movement. Mahler sets up all the rest of the movements through his particular use of form and vocabulary in this opening movement. The second movement is marked *Im Tempo eines gemächlichen Ländlers*. It is a folk dance. Listen to how it opens. You are almost transported back into Mahler's native hometown on the Czech border, but not quite (Track 8).[22] What a folk dance it is! He juxtaposes the rustic *Ländler* of the country with the sophisticated (Viennese) waltz. The *Ländler* turns grotesque and the waltz frenzied as he parodies both. As the frenzy breaks off, the hint of a minuet, the eighteenth-century antecedent to these folk dances, is exposed: the merest suggestion of an orderly time in the past that has been superseded by this present. As the excerpt opens you will hear first the frenzied waltz and then the delicate contained minuet (Track 9).[23]

He mediates between cultures, expressing his German and Jewish and Slavic heritage, and in so doing, to quote Henry Lea, he "exemplifies the tragically brief German Jewish symbiosis at its most intense."[24] The folk dance has become stripped of its nationality and its innocence. In its place is a dance of life with all its contemporary complexities.

The third movement, marked "Rondo. Burleske" (with the instruction *sehr trotzig:* very defiant, stubborn), is regarded as Mahler's most modern utterance. The sheer number of separate and, we could say, fugal voices piled one on top of the other places us in an extreme world of polytonality (more than one key at a time) as well as polyphony (more than one melodic voice at a time). He produces complex counterpoint with this technique. Hefling describes the third movement as "the most syntactically untraditional, contrapuntally complex, and riotously sardonic movement in all Mahler's oeuvre."[25] He achieves this by swallowing Bach whole, transplanting Bach's techniques of counterpoint into the twentieth century without the linear evolutional advantage of passing through Classicism and Romanticism. In so doing, he verges on both the postmodern and the emergent. His biographer Henri de la Grange comments, "Mahler never ventured further into nihilism than here."[26] Listen carefully to this section of the third movement, remembering that the first excerpt you heard was the raucous end of this same movement (Track 10).[27]

Each movement is in rondo form, which is most unusual for symphonic structure. To remind you about rondo form: theme A is the first theme. Then there is a contrasting theme, B, then there is a return to A, then there is the introduction of yet a third theme—C, and again back to A, then a fourth, and back, and so forth. Inherent in the form is a multiplicity of themes and of comings and goings. What does it mean that Mahler has chosen this form throughout? We are reminded of the other Mahler, Margaret Mahler the psychoanalyst, and her "rapprochement phase," a stage of development that occurs in the child at about eighteen months of age. The child has learned to walk and thus is far more separate and independent than before. Both the child and the first theme state themselves, go away, come back, check to see where home is, go away again, each time a little more daring. This is progressive movement, but it is not the linear progress of an ego product. It is more like a spiral, more a movement of psyche, for each time one leaves one is more separate and individual, and each time one returns, the experience of home is infused with the adventures of the journey.

Let us talk about home: in the key of D, for example, the note D is home, where one comes to rest, where the tension releases. Mahler has taken away a clear tonal center or home and the reassuring dichotomy of major and minor. He has pushed the form, the time, and even the orchestration to the outer edges of the familiar. We might say that all of these departures are within the natural order of things if one calls oneself Ahasuerus, because Ahasuerus is completely unmoored. He is, after all, the eternal wanderer. Rondo form inherently provides the touchstone that allows Mahler to keep wandering in this liminal world. These exquisite A themes, at one and the same time human and from this "other world," are the centering and homing function of Mahler's deepest creative force. They are the clear cries of a person living life with an excruciating awareness of the presence of death.

He started this journey with the heartbeat and ends without it, creating wider and wider spaces of silence, throwing our sense of time into another orbit. Alma Mahler observed that when her husband was conducting an adagio, a slow movement, if it "seemed to be lost on the audience he *slowed* the tempo down, rather than quickening it."[28]

Mellers describes Mahler's relationship to time at the end of this symphony thus:

> In the last movement of the Ninth, Mahler attains a translucent texture that evokes oriental rather than occidental modes of being. . . . The obsession with Time, by which Europe had been

dominated since the Renaissance, begins to dissolve into Asiatic immobility and the process is at once a laceration of spirit and an act of birth. Mahler lingers on those suspended dissonances, his last hold on the life he had lived with all his richly attuned senses.[29]

Using psychological language, we would say that this Western obsession with (Father) Time is an obsession with ego's linear, directed thinking. And the Eastern approach is the more feminine experience of psyche's ability to contain everything.

This symphony, then, is a postmodern deconstruction of the old order at every musical level. But it is not postmodern. It is not without hierarchy. Though everything is up for grabs, not everything is equal. Mahler is still able to leave us with a world-creating vessel that holds the fragments. That vessel, I maintain, is an aural manifestation of the all-containing nature of psyche. He has chosen chromaticism and the ethereal edge of the orchestra to express the final moments of his last complete symphonic statement. In so doing, he forces us to feel the horror of death as deprivation of our sensory life as we strain to hear the last notes, hoping they will never end. Listen now to the final moments of the Ninth Symphony. Just as you strained to hear the opening notes of the first movement, you will reach for the breaks in the ever-lengthening silence at the end of the last (Track 11).[30]

RECOMMENDED RECORDINGS OF MAHLER'S *SYMPHONY NO. 9*

Mahler, Gustav. *Symphony No. 9,* Claudio Abbado conducting the Berliner Philharmoniker, CD, Deutsche Grammophon, 2002.

———. *Symphony No. 9,* Leonard Bernstein conducting the New York Philharmonic, CD, SONY Classical, 1992.

———. *Symphonie No. 9,* Simon Rattle conducting the Vienna Philharmonic Orchestra. On *Mahler: Symphony No.9. Richard Strauss: Metamorphosen, Tod und Verklärung,* Simon Rattle conducting the Vienna Philharmonic Orchestra, 2 CDs, Angel Records, 1998.

———. *Symphony No. 9,* Benjamin Zander conducting the Philharmonia Orchestra, CD, Telarc, 1999.

NOTES

This chapter was first presented as a paper at the Sixteenth International Congress for Analytical Psychology in Barcelona, Spain, in 2004. The theme of the conference was Edges of Experience: Memory and Emergence.

[1] Margaret Tilly, "The Therapy of Music" (1956), in *C. G. Jung Speaking,* ed. William McGuire and R. F. C. Hull (Princeton, N.J.: Princeton University Press, 1977), p. 275.

[2] Alma Mahler, *Gustav Mahler: Memories and Letters* (Seattle: University of Washington Press, 1968), p. 182.

[3] Alex Ross, *The Rest Is Noise: Listening to the Twentieth Century* (New York: Farrar, Straus and Giroux, 2007), p. 19.

[4] Mahler, *Gustav Mahler: Memories and Letters,* p. 98.

[5] C. G. Jung, "Wotan" (1964), in *The Collected Works of C. G. Jung,* vol. 10, *Civilization in Transition,* trans. R. F. C. Hull (Princeton, N.J.: Princeton University Press, 1970), §374.

[6] In the score, this is Movement 3, measure 549 (four measures before rehearsal number 41) to Movement 4, measure 12. The score is available as *Symphony No. 9 (1908–1909)* (New York: Dover Publications Inc., 1993).

[7] C. G. Jung, "Tavistock Lectures: Lecture 5," in *The Collected Works of C. G. Jung,* vol. 18, *The Symbolic Life: Miscellaneous Writings,* trans. Gerhard Adler and R. F. C. Hull (Princeton, N.J.: Princeton University Press, 1976), §408.

[8] Quoted in R. Greenberg, *The Great Masters: Mahler—His Life and Music,* CD 4 (Chantilly, VA: The Teaching Company, 2001).

[9] Gustav Mahler to Alfred Roller, 20 January [1908], in *Selected Letters of Gustav Mahler,* ed. Knud Martner (New York: Farrar, Straus, Giroux, 1979), p. 309.

[10] *Ibid.*

[11] J. M. Roberts, *Twentieth Century: The History of the World, 1901–2000* (New York: Penguin, 1999), p. 158.

[12] David B. Greene, *Mahler, Consciousness and Temporality* (New York: Gordon and Breach, 1984), p. 267.

[13] Stephen E. Hefling, "Aspects of Mahler's Late Style," in *Mahler and His World,* ed. Karen Painter (Princeton, NJ: Princeton University Press, 2002), p. 204.

[14] David I. Tresan, "Jungian Metapsychology and Neurobiological Theory," *Journal of Analytical Psychology* 41 (1996): 411.

[15] Movement 1, measures 1 to 25.

[16] Movement 1, measures 174 (at rehearsal number 9) to 210.

[17] Movement 1, measures 254 (twelve measures after rehearsal number 13) to 276.

[18] In astronomy this means the conjunction or opposition of two heavenly bodies, especially of a planet with the sun or, in Jungian psychology, "a pair of opposites," as in Anima/Animus. Andrew Samuels, Bani Shorter, and Fred Plaut, *A Critical Dictionary of Jungian Analysis* (London: Routledge, 1986), p. 147.

[19] Stephen E. Hefling, "The Ninth Symphony," in *The Mahler Companion,* ed. D. Mitchell and A. Nicholson (Oxford: Oxford University Press, 1999), pp. 474–475.

[20] Movement 1, measures 21 (four measures after rehearsal number 2) to 30.

[21] Movement 1, measures 346 (nine measures before rehearsal number 16) to 369.

[22] Movement 2, measures 1 to 30.

[23] Movement 2, measures 168 (nine measures after rehearsal number 20) to 231.

[24] Henry A. Lea, *Gustav Mahler: Man on the Margin* (Bonn: Bouvier, 1985), p. 128.

[25] Hefling, "The Ninth Symphony," p. 484.

[26] *Ibid.,* pp. 483–484.

[27] Movement 3, measures 208 (at rehearsal number 33) to 265 (thirty measures before rehearsal number 35).

[28] Mahler, *Gustav Mahler: Memories and Letters,* p. 49.

[29] Wilfrid Mellers, "Mahler and the Great Tradition: Then and Now," in *The Mahler Companion,* ed. D. Mitchell and A. Nicholson (Oxford: Oxford University Press, 1999), pp. 570–571.

[30] Movement 4, measures 159 to 185.

2

The Voice of the Anima in Popular Singing

JOHN BEEBE

The *New Yorker*'s jazz critic Whitney Balliett once characterized America's greatest popular and jazz singers from the 1920s through the 1970s as having voices that were "homemade."[1]

I find this a perfect way to distinguish these traditions in singing, which we can recognize outside America too, from the trained voices of opera singers and singers of art songs, and not just musically but psychologically as well. What I want to secure in the remarks that follow is the preeminence of some of these singers in a particular psychological territory: the anima archetype as described by C. G. Jung and his followers.[2] The anima is the energy that drives our moods, the archetype of the tendency in the psyche to mull over life itself in the form of memories, reflections, or fantasies. Listening to music, which is so stimulating to memories, moods, fantasies, and reflections, lends itself well to evoking the anima. Singers who instinctively key into the importance of the anima in human experience often find ways of incarnating the archetype, even to the point of personifying it in their personal lives, and become adroit in simulating its effects in their art. I will call these performers in what follows *anima singers,* and I will attempt to verify this claim and unpack its meaning through my own listening experience. To make it easier to understand how a popular singer can manage to become an archetype of the feminine, which is how Jung understands the anima, I will focus just on women singers, although it is possible for a man, too, to perform the anima function. (Jimmy Scott and Chet Baker, at the high end of the male voice, are obvious examples of male singers who have succeeded in doing just this, and at the extreme other register of the male voice, the same could be claimed for Billy Eckstine and Johnny Hartman.)

Although I don't restrict the anima to the inner life of men only or assume that it is an archetype that can only be evoked by women, I will focus on women who have sung popular music in such a way as to perform the anima function for me. I will argue that it is precisely the homemade quality of their vocal art, its irrefutably individual character, that uniquely suited them to the job. While it is a commonplace that classically trained female voices often inspire listeners and in the art of bel canto singing frequently succeed in becoming a bridge to the beyond, a function of the anima figure in many mythologies, I have found that a classically trained voice, much as I admire its artistry, rarely performs the anima function for me because it does not also make the connection to the personal as convincingly. As the archetype that serves to reflect experience as it is actually lived,[3] the anima is uniquely positioned to bridge high and low, archetypal and personal, and the ego's less-developed aspect with the ideals and potential of the Self. It is best constellated within an earthbound frame that merely hints at the transcendent, the way some popular singers appreciate the moon and the stars with their homespun voices. The effect of the ordinary soul suddenly contacting the beyond is lost if the voice is already cultured beyond the ordinary from the start of the listening experience.

Part of the success of the popular singers I have gravitated to lies in the material the women recorded. Sometimes, as in Billie Holiday's case, this is inferior material that the singer somehow manages to make glamorous through her vocal presence, which shines through like a Cinderella in rags. When the same singers choose or are given superior material to sing, their voices never quite eradicate their awe of a great song's lyrics and musical phrases, which often has the effect of exalting the message of the song. What they don't do is simply render the song at its own degree of strength in a straightforward way. There's always a paradox, a tension between the anima quality of the performance and the level of the song. Without this paradox, the homemade quality of the singing disappears and an ego-based professionalism starts to take over that eradicates the anima effect. We see this phenomenon repeatedly in expensive-voiced singers with impeccable personas such as Ella Fitzgerald,

Doris Day, Julie Andrews, Barbra Streisand, and Celine Dion, none of whom can qualify as anima singers even when they have studied and drawn stylistic mannerisms and material from forbears who were. In her review of the movie *Star*, based on the life of Gertrude Lawrence, Pauline Kael noted how Julie Andrews's robust impersonation failed to do justice to the quavering complexity of Lawrence's actual singing. I would call this fragility its anima quality, which in Lawrence's case worked in counterpoint to the confidence of the music and lyrics of her great partner, Noel Coward, and later to the sophistication of Kurt Weill and Ira Gershwin's score to *Lady in the Dark*. Her vulnerable approach to delivering superior material served as an inspiration to the jazz singer Lee Wiley, a quintessential anima presence, who more than once recorded Lawrence's material in her own idiosyncratic voice with extraordinary results.[4]

Fragility, like vulnerability, is a key to recognizing the anima, and it works particularly well in the delivery of strong popular vocal materials. An anima voice is one that just might lose its way in a great song, not have enough breath, miss reaching the right pitch, wobble, lose control of its vibrato, possibly stumble on a word or a phrase or a vowel and even make an inappropriate substitution in a perfect lyric. Such a voice is perverse in what it can't seem to learn to do. For this reason, some of the greatest women popular singers who have sung the same songs, and sung them well—Sarah Vaughan, Peggy Lee, and Dinah Washington come to mind—are not anima singers: they are too much on top of the material for that. The anima, in Jungian psychology, is associated with the *inferior* function,[5] meaning that its consciousness is embarrassingly out of step, won't follow our will, and remains, as if incurably infantile, under the sway of the unconscious. Although Jungian psychology distinguishes the anima from the mother and suggests that there may be a link to the unconscious feminine side of the father in this particular archetype, it insists that however shaky, unsuitable, and unadapted her presentation may initially be, the anima deserves to be taken seriously by a man as his lifelong partner. With her capacity for vulnerability and her sincere desire for connection, she may even, paradoxically, complete the integrity his ego lacks by itself. And she is an archetype women find important in completing their identities as women. Under cultural conditions that are still, after so much social change, heavily patriarchal, this archetype is associated with the forgotten feminine, so that an ego adapted to the masculine world, whether belonging to a man or to a woman, is all too ready to leave the anima behind. It behooves the adapted "masculine" ego to listen to her.

That is what we do when we stop to listen to the "homemade" voices of the singers I describe here, those whose recordings I have collected and gravitated to since I first found many of their records in dusty used goods shops, often on 78 rpm shellac discs, worn from repeated playing with steel needles, part of a life that had become a discarded memory.

My own canon, which became more differentiated and wide-ranging during these searches through the used-record bins, began with three 78 records I purchased in 1954 at the age of fifteen from a favorite English teacher, who at the private high school I attended shaped the musical taste of some of us through his periodic sell-offs of records from his own collection, which had begun to be superseded by LP reissues that at that time few of us had the money to buy and even fewer the equipment to play. He sold me Billie Holiday's "My Old Flame"[6] with "I'm Yours" on the back, Ethel Waters's "Taking a Chance on Love" with "Cabin in the Sky" as the B side,[7] and Mildred Bailey's "Lover Come Back to Me" with "At Sundown" as its reverse side.[8] Not long after, at a specialty shop I somehow found in New York, I purchased a 78 album from 1940 in near-mint condition, *Lee Wiley Sings Cole Porter*,[9] one of the very first albums to feature a single vocalist singing a set of songs by one popular music composer. It was against the aesthetic and psychological standards set by these four vocalists that I came to measure every other singer I encountered. And I learned by listening to them to discriminate the voice of the anima in popular singing. I will now explore the basic ingredients of how the archetype expresses itself in a musical way. We start with how we can recognize that we are in fact dealing with the uncanny archetype of the anima rather than some aspect of personal style on the part of an interesting woman bent on using her voice to express her own individual view of life and love. Here's how I recognize the difference. In anima singing:

The voice shimmers but is not brilliant—the effect of moonlight, rather than sunlight. Doris Day, with her golden, sunny voice is well named: she is not an anima singer. Neither is Carmen McRae, who sounds rather like the setting sun. One of Billie Holiday's signature songs, "What a Little Moonlight Can Do,"[10] works as well as it does because the singer is reflecting on the role of Luna in shaping her peculiar form of vitality. The profound importance of the moon for the anima singer is brought out in Holiday's early "I Wished on the Moon,"[11] with its unironic lyric by Dorothy Parker, and in the singer's midlife expression of wonder, "If the Moon Turns Green" (recorded in 1952),[12] which conveys the alchemical possibility of transformation within a life spent under the spell of the moon, where little that is not psychological can be expected to grow.

The song "builds," as most popular songs do when perform
often to a note of resignation rather than to a thrilling, transcenaen ...
Even in the midst of the song, the singer seems to step away from it, singing
behind the beat and slowing down the delivery by trailing away, as in the
lingering play with her vibrato that Lee Wiley often uses for a signature
once she has completed a moment of musical thought. As James Gavin
recently put it, "She ended phrases with a lazy falling vibrato, and often
trimmed them with a 'mordent'—a little grace note—that evoked a flirty
wink."[13] This artifice has been compared to baroque ornament and is
frequently complained of as affected by those who cannot get into her
singing. I experience it as the anima singer's reflection, conveying perhaps
her resentment over the dysphoria occasioned by having to breathe and
thus break the feeling-connection that has been established with the audience
whenever a line in the lyric and a phrase in the music has come to the end
of its musical thought.

The desire of the singer is to make an emotional connection with her
audience. This is as true for Ethel Waters as for Billie Holiday and for Judy
Garland as for Lee Wiley, despite the very obvious differences between
these performers in the level of theatricality vis-à-vis an audience and their
absorption in the world of their own creation. The anima singer, far more
than an actress in a movie, breaks down the distinction between actual
woman and anima because, as a live performer with a voice of her own,
she seems to be an actual woman who will only say no to the breaking of
connection. The superbly oppositional jazz singer Anita O'Day would be
an example of an artist who regularly asserts her independence and
autonomy from the audience—she refuses to stay too connected—and for
this reason I do not see her as embodying the anima archetype.

The singer herself seems to come from somewhere else. Another way of
saying this is that she seems to be beyond the everyday social experience
of the listener. Billie Holiday does not seem to occupy the same universe
as her 1940s contemporary Jo Stafford or her 1950s contemporary Patti
Page; one can't imagine her singing in a high school production, with proud
parents and teachers predicting that she will have a great career. Nor can
one so imagine Lee Wiley or Mildred Bailey. The fact that Holiday was
black and Wiley and Bailey partly of American Indian descent does not
explain the lingering peculiarity of their vocal presences, though of course
their often-asserted differences in "race" contributed.

Nor is the uniqueness in their voices simply a disguised aspect of class
difference, the reinvention of self that attends the attempt to transcend class.
Wiley, whose willowy, ladylike voice concealed an underlying eternal orphan

toughness, was a high school dropout who ran away from home in her mid-teens to become a singer. Holiday, similarly, had worked as a prostitute before she started to sing at eighteen, and there is a constriction in her voice, too, that never quite went away, even when musical opportunities opened up her life. Both women felt themselves to be freaks and had the scars to prove it. But this, again, is only part of what we hear in their voices. Ella Fitzgerald was no less class-afflicted in her early life or class-transcending later: she had been in a home for delinquent girls in her early teens, before she parlayed her musical gifts to become what by the mid-1950s was the quintessentially American mainstream voice, its sound the echo of the nation's postwar social success. Fitzgerald's vocal persona was never controversial for middle-class music lovers.

Holiday, by contrast, was always a harder sell. In her time, she sounded, with her stringy sweet-potato voice laced with balsamic vinegar, like she came not just from the wrong side of the tracks but from the other side of the moon. She also sounded stoned. Bailey, too, whose astonishingly pure chime-like sound preceded Fitzgerald's, had a voice that was almost too eerily musical. Married for a long time to the jazz vibraphonist Red Norvo (they were billed as Mr. and Mrs. Jazz in the 1930s), she began to sound more and more like a vibraphone herself, her sound almost too shimmering to be real, despite its appealing human accent. Judy Garland, with her clarion trumpet of a voice, preternaturally robust yet broken open with vulnerability, was a dynamo and an invalid in one. Lee Wiley had an idiosyncratic accent, Oklahoma mixed with Park Avenue, that led her to pronounce almost every word a bit differently from anyone else.

Though we think of them today as quintessential 1930s singers, none of these women really belonged in the world that mainstream people in the thirties knew. That world usually stamped the voices of African American women and white women who grew up in lower- and lower-middle-class communities with an inevitable sense of their place. Though there were clues in the accents of Holiday, Wiley, Bailey, and Garland as to their origins—that is, one sensed they came from humble beginnings—a listener could not with any certainty "place" any of them. Their way was to individuate their roots, not to adopt the affectations of another, international class, as did, for instance, Bobby Short and Eartha Kitt en route to elegant cabaret careers. A forbear of all of these singers, Ethel Waters, was not above taking elocution lessons that taught her, as they did Cab Calloway, to roll her R's, but even before her efforts to improve it, her diction outclassed that of any white singer of her day. A white listener was never confused as to which word she was singing, in contrast for instance to the challenge of listening to the black drawl of Bessie Smith.

The effect of listening to the way Waters, Bailey, Holiday, Wiley, or Garland have chosen to acculturate themselves is to make you feel you are listening to someone who cannot possibly have grown up in the society we think we know and who must have emerged, full-blown, out of the head of some Columbia or Decca Records Zeus who had recognized that Tin Pan Alley was ready to receive an interpretive Athena. The command of lyrics by each of these singers may be goddess-like, but the sound, because it retains the terror of its true origins, remains earth-bound. The effect is uncanny for being produced in a recognizably homemade way, not a transcendent one. These singers offer the most natural possible access to the transcendent function of psyche, perfectly conveyed in Judy Garland's teenage reading of the lyric to "Over the Rainbow."[14]

The "other" in these songs is implied, not present. The songs of these singers are almost always about love for a man, but unless he is part of a duet with her (as in Lee Wiley's charming 1947 pairing with Bing Crosby for "I Still Suits Me"[15]), the loved man is not present to the singer, and the audience cannot visualize him. Usually he is longed for, missed, or appreciated without his knowledge and without our seeing who he is, as in Vincent Youmans's 1929 "More Than You Know," arguably the greatest love song in the repertoire of the anima singer. (Wiley, Bailey, and Holiday all sang it with especial conviction.) The man is more "seeable" when the singer is in an oppositional mood, as when an onscreen Ethel Waters singing "Birmingham Bertha"[16] (also in 1929) announces, "Now *we's* in Chicago" en route to catching up with her absconding man.

The singer demonstrates an unusual capacity to engage with life. This is one trait the voice of the anima in popular singing shares with the figure of the anima in film.[17] Judy Garland's vocal enthusiasm was infectious, and it animated her screen performances as well. Edith Piaf, her transatlantic echo, could squeeze every ounce of emotion out of a song. (There is a telling photograph of Garland, her face rapt with thrilled respect, looking at Piaf after a performance in the 1950s.) Holiday insisted on feeling everything there was to feel. Her 1937 reading of "Why Was I Born,"[18] a song about unrequited love, is instructive. She begins with a series of questions:

> Why was I born?
> Why am I living?
> What do I get?
> What am I giving?

> Why do I want for things I dare not hope for?
> What can I hope for?

And then comes Billie's answer, "I *wish* I knew." The emphasis on the word "I" followed by the accent on the word "wish," found in no other singer's reading of this song that I have heard (everyone else seems to place the accent on "knew"), is classic for the anima woman, who finds in everything, however hopeless in other ways, an occasion to imaginatively participate.

The song the singer sings is often a major comment on existence itself. It can even offer advice. In his first discovery of the anima figure during his active imaginations of 1913–1914, Jung met his anima in the form of the biblical Salome, but beside her was Elijah the prophet.[19] The linkage of anima figure as archetype of life itself with wise old man as archetype of life's meaning was therefore established. In the tradition of popular singing, this pairing incarnates as the singer and the song. This is one aspect of the American tradition that has become transatlantic, in accord with its archetypal character. The way Gertrude Lawrence sang Cole Porter's "Experiment" in the London production of Cole Porter's 1933 musical *Nymph Errant,*[20] which never reached Broadway, survives in a recording I came upon in college. It had such a powerful effect on me that I wrote down the lyrics and carried them around in my wallet for more than a year. Here is the final stanza:

> Be curious,
> Tho' interfering friends may frown,
> Get furious
> At each attempt to hold you down.
> If this advice you'll only employ
> The future will offer you infinite joy and merriment,
> EXPERIMENT
> And you'll see.

These words served me as a sort of commencement address, well in advance of my actual college graduation; the singer had convinced me that they should be my credo in life.

The singer exerts a protective effect on the listener simply by singing her song, with its feeling for life, its vitality, and its wisdom. This is not as easy to bring off as it might seem. "Summertime," for instance, invites an anima reading, but usually (even by Billie Holiday and Ethel Waters) this song is sung in too consciously wise a fashion, with too much emphasis on the ego of the singer as the protective agent, to qualify as an anima song. For a song to evoke the anima, it has to contain a mystery. Harold Arlen's

"A Sleepin' Bee," for instance recounts what purports to be a bit of Caribbean superstition to celebrate an omen betokening unbroken good fortune in love:

> When a bee lies sleepin'
> In the palm o' your hand
> You're bewitch'd and deep in
> Love's long look'd after land
> Where you'll see a sun-up sky
> With a mornin' new,
> And where the days go laughin' by
> As love comes a-callin' on you.
> Sleep on, Bee, don't waken . . .

When Lee Wiley sings this song on her final studio album she misreads the line as "Don't weaken," so far is she into the spell she is casting—and so unconscious is she of its full potential effect.[21] The anima's ability to protect is a mystery the singer can appreciate but never fully understand. Often the most moving expressions in all popular singing are expressions of incomprehension.

The singer seems to embody a wisdom that is born of experience.[22] The role of instructor of how to feel about the losses in life was one that the most celebrated cabaret singer of her time, Mabel Mercer, was able to play into her eighties, when she had lost her own voice and managed to keep on performing by developing a technique called parlando, a rhythmically accented form of rapid speech that managed to well serve the lyric-driven songs she preferred to perform. I saw her perform in her ripe late middle age at a New York club at the end of the 1950s, when her musical technique was in transition, and at the end of the 1970s, by which time all that was left of her singing voice was its parlando. On the first occasion, I heard her do "Just One of Those Things." Each time she spoke Cole Porter's title line (it is repeated often in that song), she gave it a different nuance of meaning, as if she understood every one of the things the brief but exciting affair that had just ended was one of.

The singer actually performs an anima function for her listener, by which I mean connecting the listener to the actual situation in the unconscious, a function usually reserved for our dreams, our symptoms, and our strongest feelings. I can offer a pair of personal examples, which illustrate the intensely private nature of the experience that can be constellated and its power to reorient the person who has the experience.

When I saw Mabel Mercer in the late 1970s, she was 78. I was accompanied by a companion of nearly a decade, and we were both

unaccountably moved when we heard Mercer begin to recite one of her
warhorses in her strong parlando style:

> Once upon a time a boy with moonlight in his eyes,
> Put his hand in mine
> And said he loved me so.
> But that was once upon a time
> Very long ago.[23]

My partner started crying, and it was obvious that the love that had started
our relationship was beyond recovery, though it would take time for us to
admit that to each other. There was a measure of solace, however, in our
shared, wordless appreciation of what Mercer could articulate about the
common human reality that had overtaken us. The song's lyrics are
sentimental, but Miss Mercer invests the material with healing wisdom.

Another time, the visitor to San Francisco was Blossom Dearie, and
listening to her sing, I suddenly recovered my relation to my own anima
and realized how angry I was that I had let my woman analyst take over
that function for me. I left the club in fury, restored and determined never
again to let anyone but me be the expert where my own emotions were
concerned. This helped me, in the long run, integrate my good analysis
and make it my own.

It is part of the integrity of the singer to say when she thinks a
problem in living is insoluble. One of the most moving examples of
this is Ruth Etting's reading of the 1930 Richard Rodgers-Lorenz Hart
song, "Ten Cents a Dance,"[24] which reveals the life of a dance-hall hostess
during the Great Depression:

> I'm one of those lady teachers,
> A beautiful hostess, you know,
> The kind the Palace features
> At exactly a dime a throw.

The song surveys the clientele she meets in such a joint and concludes:

> Sometimes I think
> I've found my hero,
> But it's a queer romance.
> All that you need is a ticket:
> Come on, big boy, ten cents a dance!

The understanding that integrity in admitting failures in life is a
function of the anima is something that emerged for me in the aftermath
of writing my book *Integrity in Depth,*[25] but I have no doubt that I was led

to the discovery by the examples of anima singers. Unfortunately, their efforts to be honest in this regard are often received by critics of the genre as expressions of masochism or at least self-pity, the implication being that as self-defeating love addicts they have brought their suffering on themselves in some unconscious way.

I think this view disrespects the tradition in which the singers are working. I have found it helpful to amplify the contribution of these American singers by listening to anima singers from other cultures. Three who stand out for me are Amália Rodriguez, the *fados* diva of Portugal, with her meditations on fate; Edith Piaf, the definitive vocal asserter of the authority of the French in matters of love; and Pastora Pavón, the Spanish singer who recorded her country's folk flamenco classics under the name of "La Niña de los Peines" (The Girl of the Combs). I will focus here upon Pavón, the Spanish artist, whose presence and aesthetic was referred to in a famous lecture Federico Garcia Lorca gave in Argentina in 1933, "Juego y teoria del duende" ("Play and Theory of the *Duende*"), the "*duende*" being the spirit that forces an artist to recognize the tragic limitations of life with which the flamenco musician feels called upon to contend. Christopher Maurer, editor of the standard collection of Lorca's prose and poetry on this theme, writes:

> The notion of duende (from *duen de casa*, "master of the house") came to him from popular Spanish culture, where the duende is a playful hobgoblin, a household spirit fond of hiding things, breaking plates, causing noise, and making a general nuisance of himself. But Lorca was aware of another popular usage of the term. In Andalusia people say of certain toreros and flamenco artists that they have duende—an inexplicable power of attraction, the ability, on rare occasions, to send waves of emotion through those watching and listening to them.[26]

Maurer identifies four elements in Lorca's vision of artistic *duende*: "irrationality, earthiness, a heightened awareness of death, and a dash of the diabolical." These are aspects, I believe, of the demonic side of personality, with which the anima must finally contend. According to Maurer,

> The duende is a demonic earth spirit who helps the artist see the limitations of intelligence, reminding him that [as Lorca puts it] "ants could eat him or that a great arsenic lobster could fall suddenly on his head"; who brings the artist face-to-face with death, and who helps him create and communicate memorable, spine-chilling art.[27]

William Dufty, in his notes to *The Billie Holiday Story*[28] (which collected Holiday's 1944–1950 Decca recordings), says that he played recordings by Pastora Pavón for Holiday, who immediately said upon hearing them, "Oh my god, that chick is in trouble." The "trouble" Holiday understood was not, I think, the singer's personal pain; it was the sound of her struggle with the *duende*. For rather than simply channel the demonic spirit and surrender to it, Lorca understood that the artist working in this tradition has to "battle it skillfully," as Lorca puts it, "'on the rim of the well,' in 'hand-to-hand combat.'"[29]

Assuming, as I do, that this is the tradition that ultimately informs the anima artist's integrity, what then constitutes the skillful methods of her struggle?

First, I would list something I have already referred to in Holiday's case: *fidelity to feelings*. This is something only the greatest of anima artists can bring off, and it is impossible not to recognize when it is the case. Here is a description by Will Friedwald of Lee Wiley singing "My Funny Valentine":[30]

> Wiley is nothing if not direct and believable; there's no artifice whatsoever about the woman or her singing. Few singers are able to use "Valentine" to so vividly describe someone in their life, someone whom they love, perhaps in spite of, perhaps because of, his weaknesses. . . . As with Billie Holiday or Judy Garland, when Lee Wiley sings, you can really hear the hurt.[31]

This needs a bit of correction. Wiley might be described as a bit *too* given to breathy artifices were she not so bent on delivering the essence of a song. Her style, in common with that of other anima singers, tends to reach for the sublime where emotion is concerned.

The same can be said of Pastora Pavón's extraordinary flamenco singing,[32] which I was first exposed to at the age of seven when I encountered her 78 rpm Columbia recordings[33] in my mother's record collection—perhaps the very sides that William Dufty played for Billie Holiday. You could not deny the sense of raw hurt that emanated from her, and yet you could not ignore the artistry with which it was delivered, which involved a discipline as real as that which informs a flamenco dancer. Pavón carefully considered each step of sound as she enacted a kind of bullfight with her voice.

In the greatest anima singing, there is always an *assertion of self*. Judy Garland in her great Carnegie Hall concert probably did this better than any anima singer, perhaps nowhere more definitely than in her astonishing rendition of "Come Rain or Come Shine," which has the effect of asserting her right to orgasm. What keeps this from being impossibly vulgar is that it is not an ego-utterance but an upwelling of the right to joy from the self itself. Yet Billie Holiday is asserting herself no less when she sings of her unfree relationship in "My Man,"[34] which she ends by singing, "But whatever my man is, I'm his, forever more"— the triumph of love over fate.

Another mode of the anima in popular singing is *rueful reflection,* a vein no one has mined as successfully as Mildred Bailey. Her masterpiece, "Me and the Blues,"[35] has her confess:

> I'll never know why men are so deceitful,
> They never treat you like they should.
> They love you and deceive you,
> Then they up and leave you.
> What makes them so no good?

What keeps this from being nothing but a blaming of men is the humility with which this singer admits her own lack of consciousness as to why her bad luck should be the case and a certain chagrin in the tone with which she confesses her ignorance—not just of herself, but of life as well. There are few more moving statements in popular singing.

Hope despite low self-esteem is a part of anima singing. One hears it in Ruth Etting, not just in the low status she assigns to the work she must do, but in the way she depreciates her own experience. For instance, when she sings "Easy Come, Easy Go"[36] with its line, "No remorse, no regrets, we should part exactly as we met; just easy come, easy go," one gets the sense that she doesn't expect more of her life than that she will be able to be a good sport. Jungian psychology understands that in the hierarchical typology of consciousness,[37] the anima archetype is the one associated with the inferior function, which is the part of our complement of potential intelligences that doesn't differentiate itself as brilliantly, as effectively, or as competently as any other, so it is not surprising that this part of the self is the one that isn't sure it deserves much success.

When the anima singer does find comfort and enduring love, she is appealingly self-deprecating and grateful, as when Lee Wiley sings "Oh Look at Me Now,"[38] Ethel Waters sings "Bread and Gravy,"[39] or Sylvia Syms sings "It Amazes Me."[40] Ruth Etting's immediate successor in this psychological tradition was Connee Boswell, who sang from a wheelchair. Her even, yearning voice weighs the bitter with the sweet and finds grounds for the endurance of hope just in earnestly remembered miracles of transient romantic attachment ("The Isle of May" and "Sand in My Shoes"[41]), no less sublime for being minimal in scale and fleeting

in time. Boswell was Ella Fitzgerald's inspiration in the 1930s, and
Fitzgerald's few forays into anima singing (for instance, "Miss Otis
Regrets," on her 1956 Cole Porter album[42]) echo Boswell's ability to
find staying power in the face of adversity.

Resilience based on acceptance of life is a characteristic of the anima.
Judy Garland's ability to move in the space of a single song from vulnerability
to transcendence is part of what it means to be an anima singer, someone
who has the stamina to go the course in channeling the archetype of
life. One hears the affirmation of life itself that this permits at the
beginning of Garland's Carnegie Hall concert,[43] which is not without
awareness of the manic possibilities of exuberance but nevertheless
comes squarely down on the side of loving the world just as it is and being
able to meet it in the moment.

What makes this work is the acceptance of self and life that is entailed,
heard as participation in the presence and absence of the texture that life
offers. Of all the singers I have described here, Lee Wiley's is the voice
with the most texture. Dave Garroway included this note in a 1956
compendium that contained her "Stars Fell on Alabama," in which the
embers of the cosmos that sometimes drop into a life in the midst of
lovemaking warm Wiley up:

> On everything . . . she does, there is a marvelous texture to her
> voice, something like running your hand over a piece of fine
> Harris tweed—and they both tickle.[44]

Wiley uses the complex timbre of her own voice psychologically as
well, to evoke the textures she recalls from her own lived experience in
her songs. Her version of W. C. Handy's "The Memphis Blues,"[45] often
thought to be the first blues song, one the composer used to showcase his
pioneering blues band in Memphis, becomes for Wiley an anima
celebration of the entire tradition of jazz springing from this Dixieland
root. Where Handy had written "And when the big bassoon seconds to
the trombone's croon," she sings, "And when the clarinet seconds to the
trombone's croon," and we trust that she is persuasively recalling to us the
characteristic clarinet sound of the swing era. Her swinging 1971 version
of "Back Home Again in Indiana"[46] is peculiarly effective in its ability to
induce the actual sensations that would accompany returning to a farm
one had known in youth. When I hear Wiley sing, "And the new mown
hay, in all its fragrance," I actually see and smell the hay. I believe that her
voice can have this effect because it is so closely identified with the anima
that it becomes a carrier of the archetype's ability to convince us that
experience, however fleeting or illusory, is real.

Another effect of a great anima singer, which is no less hypnotic, is to summon the experience of *the self that endures* the burden of experience. This is what Connee Boswell manages to do in her best songs of the 1930s. She likes to start a song slow to make sure the sentiment is faithfully conveyed (and at first this seems the only way to carry it) before she breaks into her true stride and strength—swing rhythm—in the second chorus, which displays her ability to integrate what she has felt into the larger ongoing narrative of her life. Along this journey of emotional self-mastery, Boswell's voice steadily rises and falls, not unlike the mysterious, hypnotic gear action that drives a train's wheels to turn around as they carry the train forward. Listening to the best of Boswell's singing is like being borne along by a capable rhythmic engine—Boswell's own indomitable musical spirit. Throughout, she is circling round the ups and downs of the words, turning over and over the meaning of the experience she is singing about. The lyric of her June 1941 release "Sand in My Shoes,"[47] for instance, uses the lingering gritty reminder of romantic interludes on a Havana beach that now can never be repeated to get us to think about the relationship that has been lost. Hearing Boswell sing it, going round and round the feelings evoked, one can imagine that a contemporary listener would have heard her as the very personification of the 78 revolutions-per-minute record itself. The technology that produced the tradition of anima singing was no more (or less) than a record turning round and round on its platter. When, however, it released Connee Boswell's voice, with its low but feminine timbre and its reassuring steadiness of rhythmic purpose, the record became a homegrown mandala, securing in the aftermath of the Great Depression an experience of the ongoing affective aliveness of the self.

The anima, as I have been suggesting throughout these reflections, is an archetype of connection. We don't have a good conceptual language for how we hold the human objects of our affections, but the voice of the anima in popular singing leads us to recognize our feelings for them as internal relations with ourselves as well, which is pretty much what the psychoanalysts since Freud have been telling us. What psychoanalysis has not been so good at limning is the magnificent authority our emotions can have. It was not until the rock era that female voices were completely free to voice the power of their outrage (Grace Slick singing "Somebody to Love"[48]) and the raw pain of experience (Janis Joplin singing "Cry Baby"[49]). After that breakthrough, the recordings of the earlier singers who had been able to deliver emotion in the anima role could be heard as anticipating the "new" articulation of actual women's experience.

The recordings Rosemary Clooney made in the last half of her career survey the landscape of the American popular song from the standpoint of someone who had heard and seen Billie Holiday, Lee Wiley, Mildred Bailey, Judy Garland, and Mabel Mercer and had connected with her own homemade voice at last. Clooney's recordings for Concord Jazz came in the feminist era, when finally an older woman singer could afford to simply sound like herself. On them, the eros in her voice fairly crackles with affection for the musical tradition in which she came of age. She loved being what she describes with anachronistic irony in the title of her autobiography (and the recording that was issued to accompany it) as a "girl singer," and in her last years she took the tradition of anima singing to the same level that her male friends and mentors—Bing Crosby, Frank Sinatra, and Tony Bennett—had achieved when crossing over from popular to jazz singing and back again. Descending from the thrilling artifice she had mastered in her youth, which might have made her an American Amália Rodriguez, she relaxed her voice into an American sound that was satisfied with its grasp of what life could offer. She was never better, nor was her tradition, than when she started to sing Dave Frishberg's "Sweet Kentucky Ham," a song that enabled her to reflect ruefully yet lustfully on a life spent on the road, always taking her away from the loves she liked to sing about.

> It's six P. M.
> Suppertime in South Bend, Indiana
> And you figure what the hell, you can eat in your motel
> So you order up room service on the phone
> And you watch the local news and eat alone
> You got to take what little pleasures you can find
> When you've got sweet Kentucky ham on your mind, on
>   your mind
> Nothing but sweet Kentucky ham on your mind.[50]

It's the lack of shame at her appetite for life that I treasure in Rosemary Clooney's voice as she sings these lines. It's one of many qualities that place her, psychologically, near the head of the class of singers I have been talking about and makes her the culminating articulator of their tradition.

NOTES

John has suggested Tracks 12 and 13 on the accompanying CD as examples of the voice of the anima. They are Connee Boswell singing "On the Isle of May" and Lee Wiley singing "The Memphis Blues."

[1] Whitney Balliett, "Profiles: Tony Bennett," *The New Yorker,* 7 January 1974, p. 34.

[2] See for instance C. G. Jung, "Concerning the Archetypes, with Special Reference to the Anima Concept," in *The Collected Words of C. G. Jung,* vol. 9i, *The Archetypes of the Collective Unconscious* (1936; repr., Princeton: Princeton University Press, 1959); James Hillman, *Anima: The Anatomy of a Personified Notion* (Dallas, TX: Spring Publications, 1985); Verena Kast, "Anima/Animus," in *The Handbook of Jungian Psychology: Theory, Practice, and Applications,* ed. Renos K. Papadopoulos (London: Routledge, 2006).

[3] This is my understanding, following Hillman, of what Jung meant in "The Archetypes of the Collective Unconscious" when he described the anima as "the archetype of life itself." See Hillman, *Anima,* pp. 66–67.

[4] Lee Wiley's "This is New," on her album *West of the Moon* (LP, RCA Victor, 1956), would be unimaginable without Lawrence's original of this song (available on *Miss Gertrude Lawrence* in The King and I, Lady in the Dark, *and* Nymph Errant, CD, Pearl, 2005), which I feel sure Wiley heard Lawrence perform on Broadway.

[5] See my essay "Understanding Consciousness through the Theory of Psychological Types," in *Analytical Psychology: Contemporary Perspectives in Jungian Analysis,* ed. Joseph Cambray and Linda Carter (New York: Brunner-Routledge, 2004), pp. 83–115.

[6] Commodore Records, #527, 1944. These sides are now available on *Billie Holiday: The Commodore Master Takes,* CD, Polygram Records, 2000.

[7] Continental Records #10006, 1946. These sides are now available on *Ethel Waters: The Complete Bluebird Sessions,* CD, Definitive Records, 1998.

[8] Majestic Records # 1101, 1946. These sides are now available on *Mildred Bailey: The Complete Majestic Savoy Sessions,* CD, Definitive Records, 1999.

[9] Available on *Lee Wiley Sings the Songs of George Gershwin & Ira Gershwin & Cole Porter: The 1939–1940 Liberty Music Shop Recordings,* LP, Audiophile, AP-1, 1985.

¹⁰ Available on *Lady Day: The Master Takes and Singles,* 4-CD Box Set, Sony, 2007.

¹¹ Also available on *Lady Day: The Master Takes and Singles.*

¹² Available on *Solitude: The Billie Holiday Story,* Vol. 2, CD, Polygram, 1993.

¹³ James Gavin, liner notes to *Lee Wiley: Live on Stage,* CD, Audiophile, ACD-39, 2007; also available online at Gavin's Web site at http://jamesgavin.com/page160/page176/page176.html.

¹⁴ Available on *Judy Garland: Her Greatest Movie Hits—Original Soundtrack Performances 1936–1963,* CD, Rhino, 1998.

¹⁵ Available on *The Legendary Lee Wiley, 1931–1955,* CD, Tono Records, 1999.

¹⁶ Available on *Ethel Waters on Stage and Screen (1925–1940),* CD, Columbia, 1995.

¹⁷ See my essay "The Anima in Film," in *The Presence of the Feminine in Film,* ed. Virginia Apperson and John Beebe (Newcastle-on-Tyne: Cambridge Scholars Publishing, 2008), pp. 187–203.

¹⁸ Available on *Lady Day: The Master Takes and Singles.* As is common in anima singing, Holiday has slightly altered the lyric to move away from language that might seem pretentious. Here, Oscar Hammerstein had written "Why do I want a thing I daren't hope for?"

¹⁹ The full account is in C. G. Jung, *The Red Book: Liber Novus,* ed. Sonu Shamdasani (New York: W. W. Norton, 2009).

²⁰ The entire song is available on the 2005 Pearl CD *Miss Gertrude Lawrence in* The King and I, Lady in the Dark, *and* Nymph Errant.

²¹ *Back Home Again,* LP, Monmouth-Evergreen, 1971, now available in CD format, Audiophile AUDP 300, 1995.

²² In "The Psychology of the Transference," Jung wrote of four stages of the anima in the acculturation of Eros: Eve, Helen, the Virgin Mary, and Sophia. Sophia is the wisdom stage, when it is truly possible to reflect psychologically on one's personal experience with attachment and loss, which of course form the warp and woof of most of the songs the anima singer sings. In *The Complete Works of C. G. Jung,* vol. 16, *The Practice of Psychotherapy* (1946; repr., Princeton, NJ: Princeton University Press, 1985), §361.

²³ "Once Upon a Time," lyrics by Lee Adams and music by Charles Strouse, is found on *Mabel Mercer: Previously Unreleased Performances,* CD, Harbinger, 2002.

[24] Available on *Ruth Etting: Ten Cents a Dance,* CD, ASV Living Era, 1994.

[25] (College Station, TX: Texas A& M University Press, 1992).

[26] Christopher Maurer, "Preface," in Federico Garcia Lorca, *In Search of Duende* (New York: New Directions, 1998), p. ix.

[27] *Ibid.*

[28] Decca 2-LP set, DXSB 7161.

[29] Maurer, "Preface," p. ix.

[30] From her 1954 LP *Lee Wiley Sings Rodgers and Hart,* Storyville 6132.

[31] Will Friedwald, *Stardust Memories: The Biography of Twelve of America's Most Popular Songs* (New York: Pantheon, 2002), p. 369.

[32] It can be heard in digitally remastered sound on *La Niña de los Peines: Cantes Gitanos,* CD, Nuevos Medios, 2005.

[33] *Cante Flamenco: La Niña de los Peines,* LP, Columbia C-59, 1941.

[34] The 1948 Decca 24638 78 rpm record (along with its matching B side, "I Love You Porgy") has been remastered on *Billie Holiday's Greatest Hits,* CD, Verve, 1995.

[35] Recorded on Savoy records in 1946, reissued as the title track of the compilation *Me and the Blues,* CD, Atlantic/Savoy, 2000.

[36] Available on *Ruth Etting: America's Sweetheart of Song,* CD, Living Era, 2001.

[37] Beebe, "Understanding Consciousness through the Theory of Psychological Types," pp. 102–103.

[38] Available on *Lee Wiley: Night in Manhattan/Sings Vincent Youmans/ Sings Irving Berlin,* CD, Collectors' Choice Music, 2001.

[39] Available on *Ethel Waters: Takin' a Chance on Love.*

[40] We have to hope that one of her live performances of this song late in her life will become available.

[41] Both of these and other classic Boswell sides can be heard on *Connee Boswell: Heart and Soul,* CD, Living Era, 1997.

[42] Available on *Ella Fitzgerald Sings Cole Porter,* CD, Polygram Records, 1997.

[43] The live concert of 23 April 1961 is preserved in a remastered fortieth anniversary edition as *Judy at Carnegie Hall,* CD, Capitol, 2001.

[44] Liner notes to *Dave Garroway Presents the Wide, Wide World of Jazz,* LP, RCA, LPM-1325, 1956.

[45] On *A Touch of the Blues,* LP, RCA, 1957, remastered as a CD on BMG #7478, 1998.

[46] On *Back Home Again,* LP, Monmouth-Evergreen, 1971, now available as Audiophile CD, AUDP 300, 1995.

[47] Decca 78, DLA 2483, available on *Connee Boswell: Heart and Soul.*

[48] On *Surrealistic Pillow,* LP, RCA, 1967, remastered on CD, RCA, 2003.

[49] On *Pearl,* LP, Columbia, 1971, remastered on CD, Sony, 2001.

[50] This is from a cut on her 2006 Concord CD *Girl Singer.*

3

The Innate Transformational Properties of Beethoven's Passion Music

HELEN ANDERSON

Let a work of art act upon us as it acted upon the artist. To grasp its meaning we must allow it to shape us as it shaped him. Then we also understand the nature of his primordial experience. He has plunged into the healing and redeeming depths of the collective psyche, where man is not lost in the isolation of consciousness and its errors and suffering, but where all men are caught in common rhythm which allows the individual to communicate his feelings and strivings to mankind as a whole.[1]

An analysand underwent a deeply transformative experience after listening to three sections of the third movement of Beethoven's *Piano Sonata No. 31 in A-Flat Major,* Op. 110. Using active imagination in an attempt to identify her powerful emotional reaction to the music, she was able to bring material to consciousness, which served a deeply valuable function within her individuation process. The experience verifies Emma Jung's statement:

For music can be understood as an objectification of the spirit; it does not express knowledge in the usual logical intellectual sense, not does it shape matter; instead it gives sensuous representation to our deepest associations and most immutable laws. In this sense music is spirit, spirit leading into obscure distances beyond the reach of consciousness; its content can

> hardly be grasped with words—but strange to say, more easily
> with numbers—although simultaneously, and before all else,
> with feeling and sensation. Apparently paradoxical facts like
> these show that music admits us to the depths where spirit and
> nature are still one—or have again become one.[2]

Beethoven, like Emma Jung, understood that the spirit and music are
inseparable.

> Music is the wine which incites us to new creation; and I am
> the Bacchus who presses this glorious wine for mankind, and
> grants them drunkenness of the spirit. When they are again
> sober, they will have fished up much which they may take with
> them onto dry land.[3]

The power of music has been vividly portrayed in many archetypal
stories. However, the most powerful example (as well as the one most apt
for this discussion) is the Greek myth of Orpheus, for it is within this
myth that we encounter the true function of music. Orpheus had the power
not only to stay the gates of death (he attempted to rescue his wife, Eurydice,
from the underworld) but also to charm all of nature. In addition, through
the celestial harmonies that sprang from his magical lyre he promoted
images of "wild chaotic rocks arising which he shaped into walls and
staircases, gates and palaces, citadels and temples."[4] With his lyre, he
mediated between the celestial god Apollo, who is the god of light, prophetic
utterance, and wisdom, and the chthonic, passionate Dionysus, god of the
underworld. In this mediating process he not only served as an apostle of
Apollo's reason and spirit but was also animated by the creative energy of
Dionysus, thereby existing within the realms of formal containment and
liberated energy.[5] It therefore became the human task of Orpheus to
reconcile these two gods and to establish a necessary harmony between
them. This is essentially the function of music—the creation of harmony
by uniting the opposites.

Just as with Orpheus, the work of any composer consists in knowing,
as accurately as possible, the symbolic relations of all sounds so as to
reproduce in us, through the magic of these sounds, the feelings, passions,
visions, and images that evolve out of these sounds.

This is particularly the case in Indian music, where each musical
scale—known as a *raga* (which, incidentally, means "that which charms")
is designed to create a specific image and emotion. Indian music, like
Arabian and Persian music, always centers on one particular emotion that
it develops, explains, and cultivates, upon which it insists, and that it exalts

until an impression is created in the listener that is almost impossible to resist. The *raga* determines a state of feeling that can also be expressed in poems or in pictures, and the musician can, if his or her skill be sufficient, lead the audience by means of the magic of sound to a depth and intensity of feeling undreamed of in other musical systems.

This does not always happen in Western music because through the creation of equal temperament,[6] we have reduced the natural evocation of the purest forms of sound. However, the ear has made some sort of adaptation to equal temperament. According to the musicologist A. Langel, "The ear became accustomed to the continual approximations of temperament only at the cost of a part of its natural sensitivity."[7] It therefore takes the genius of a Bach, a Mozart, a Beethoven, or a Chopin to reveal to us the absolute and inevitable meaning of a chord or a melodic interval.

Essentially music is a listening art, and it uses the transformative abilities of the ear to provoke the deepest emotions of the heart. This provoked emotion can be transformed into some form by the ever-present archetypal capacity of the psyche to produce images. As the mystics tell us, human nature transforms itself according to the images that the ego (as the conscious sense of self) receives. The combination of image and feeling becomes deeply valuable in the healing process. Jung, in discussing the practice of active imagination, stated, "To the extent that I managed to translate the emotions into images—that is to say, to find the images that were concealed in the emotions—I was inwardly calmed and reassured."[8] Reflection and contemplation upon these images create the possibility of a mystical encounter with our divine essence—the Self.

THE RELATIONSHIP BETWEEN MUSIC AS A LISTENING ART AND THE SELF

In Jungian psychology, the term "psyche" pertains to all mental and emotional activity that is conscious and unconscious within the individual. Central to Jungian thought is the concept of the Self. Defined as the archetype of unity and order, the Self is perceived as regulating the total psyche. Jung recognized that the properties of the Self existed within the human psyche not only as an archetype but also as the creative locus of the image of God within the psyche. The essential nature of the Self has been defined as that which is representative of "wholeness, union, the totality of opposites, the axis of the universe, the creative point where God and man meet and the point where transpersonal energies flow into personal life."[9]

Sound is defined as a form of energy that is caused by vibration, and it has long been associated with the Self. In the Gospel of St. John we read that "In the beginning was the Word, and the Word was with God and the Word was God." To the Sufis, the soul is sound before its incarnation, and in India, God, the Creator, is sound. In the Old Testament we are told that movement (vibration) preempted the emanation of light.

Consequently, archetypal accounts of spiritual realization occurring through the ear appear frequently. The Buddha is often portrayed with large ears! In the Tibetan Book of the Dead the incantation "Listen, ye of noble birth" is chanted repeatedly in an effort to order the chaos within, and in Zen, the art of refined listening to silence leads to wakefulness. Another example occurs within an ancient Christian legend, which states that Jesus was conceived through Mary's ear. The Holy Ghost as spirit was sent to Mary and inspired her with its own breath, which entered through her ear. Mary was able to absorb this spiritual infusion because she was virginal. This implies that she was uncontaminated by the usual preconceptions of society.

Other examples of the ear as an organ of subtle transformation occur within the Synoptic Gospel of Mathew as well as in the Gnostic Gospel of Thomas and in the Coptic (Egyptian) Gospel of Mary Magdalene, where Christ repeatedly challenges "Those that have ears to hear, should hear."[10] According to Jean-Yves Le Loup, who translated the Gospel of Mary Magdalene, these words are "a request to contemplate the intelligence that arises from endless wonder at all Being, a kind of feeling for the infinite open, without which the unveiling of true being is impossible."[11] For the real offers itself only to those who take the time needed to hear, those who can endure and listen fully to the silence of the fathomless before it finally begins to speak. The apparent purpose of the Gospel of Mary Magdalene (where these words of Christ appear repeatedly) is to awaken the creative imagination within the human psyche, thus giving us access to that intermediate realm between the purely sensory and the purely spiritual. Much has been written about this "intermediate realm" by Henry Corbin, who termed it the "imaginal." In the Jungian context, James Hillman writes that we are able to know the soul only through the images formed within this realm. Similarly, Jung himself commented that it is as if we did not know, or continually forget, that everything we are conscious of is an image and that image is psyche.

Images and dreams have one special quality in common—the power to convert the invisible energies of the unconscious into forms that are accessible to the conscious mind. Images are therefore a picturing of psyche's vital activities, or, as Hillman has written, "The psyche uses images to speak about its depth."[12] Jung developed the technique of active imagination as an aid in bringing to consciousness unconscious contents that could in turn be analyzed by pursuing the thought and wishes of the ego. He believed that all symbols are alive with hidden interior meaning and that we just need to fathom what this is. He described the process of active imagination as follows:

> Active imagination is a method (devised by myself) of introspection for observing the stream of interior images. One concentrates one's attention on some impressive but un-intelligible dream image, or on a spontaneous visual impression, and observes the changes taking place in it. Meanwhile of course all criticism must be suspended and the happenings observed and noted with absolute objectivity.[13]

There is, however, no record of Jung ever having used music as a stimulus for active imagination. With regard to the role of sound and or music within the psyche, Jung had this to say:

> The auditory stimulus releases a whole series of images which associate themselves with the stimulus. They will be partly acoustic images, partly visual images, and partly images of feeling. Here I use the word "image" simply in the sense of a representation. A psychic entity can be a conscious content, that is, it can be represented, only if it has the quality of an image and is thus *representable*. I therefore call all conscious contents images, since they are reflections of processes in the brain.[14]

He stated that music "represents the movement, development, and transformation of the motifs of the collective unconscious."[15] According to Aniela Jaffé, Jung became deeply distressed when listening to the Beethoven piano sonatas and the late string quartets churned him up "almost beyond endurance,"[16] but he never appeared to investigate the cause of these reactions.

The more open we are to the living symbol created by sound, the more open we will be to the transformative energy of the deep currents of our souls.

BEETHOVEN'S *PIANO SONATA NO. 31 IN A-FLAT MAJOR*, OP. 110: THE THIRD MOVEMENT

The music renders incarnate the tenuous connection between fallible human passion and infallible divine order and attains that peace which passes understanding.—Wilfrid Mellers[17]

Beethoven borrowed from the Baroque era a particular style of composition known as Passion music in the third movement of this piano sonata. This music is a portrayal in sound of the sufferings and crucifixion of Christ and consists of an interrelationship of three styles of music known as recitative, arioso, and fugue (sometimes the arioso would be replaced with an aria). Within the compositions of the Baroque composer J. S. Bach, recitative, arioso, and fugue were given special significance. The character of Jesus in the *St. John Passion,* for example, habitually sings in arioso style. In the *St. Matthew Passion,* Jesus speaks in recitative that is accompanied by a halo of strings. It is only in the final moment of his agony that the accompanied recitative is abandoned. Synonymous as it is with deprivation, suffering, and death (the crucifixion archetype), Bach appeared to have reserved this style of operatic composition for moments of particular significance. An extremely important aspect of the arioso and its specific harmonic structure is that "the structure tends towards transitions between the mundane and the divine, and in so doing brings about a transcendent experience."[18]

As mentioned earlier, for a composer to induce in us the appropriate emotional reactions, he or she needs to know as accurately as possible the symbolic relations of all sounds. In the third movement of his Sonata No. 31, Beethoven conveys the pathos and pity of the passive suffering of not only the historical Christ but also the "crucified Christ" within his own psyche and potentially within that of every human being. Structurally, he attains the acoustical image of the Passion through using the Baroque combination of recitative, arioso, and fugue. In the sonata these sections unfold in an unusual manner in that both the arioso and the fugue return. They appear as follows:[19]

> Recitative (Track 14 on the CD that accompanies this volume)
> Arioso dolente (Track 15)
> Fugue (Track 16)
> Return of the arioso (*L'istesso tempo dell'arioso*)
> Inversion of the fugue (*L'istesso tempo della fuga,*
>   *poi di nuovo vivente*)
> Homophonic conclusion[20]

A certain amount of clarification regarding these various musical styles, particularly as used by Beethoven, is necessary; without a basic understanding of their nature, the reader may be left feeling overwhelmed by unfamiliar terminology.

A recitative is defined as "a reciting, declamatory style of vocal music in imitation of speech."[21] It is therefore not purely musical. It was used to evoke the immediacy of a situation, and its particular tone induced the awareness of an intense dramatic situation about to unfold. An arioso is a melody in slow tempo with a deep expressive character that is something between a recitative and an aria (for "air," an elaborate song or melody).[22] It will become evident that an arioso that contains elements of both a recitative and an aria serves a very specific emotional function within the Baroque structure, for it usually occurred when people were "beside" or "out of" themselves. The fugue is composed within the contrapuntal style of music and will be defined more fully below.

The homophonic conclusion in the context of this composition refers to the remainder of the preceding fugue, which transforms into a lyrical hymn.

BEETHOVEN'S INTERWEAVING OF RECITATIVE, ARIOSO, AND FUGUE

Recitative

The structure of Beethoven's recitative does not imitate speech as found in the Baroque examples "but awakens instead, the whole keyboard to ghostly sonorities, and a harmonic scene which dissolves into astral mists."[23] It is obvious that deeply subjective utterances are to follow this passionate declamation. According to Rosen, the recitative is essentially representative of a cry of pain,[24] and Mellers suggests that in it Beethoven evokes a Christ-hero's physical presence and that certain tones speak "vocally" in the tongues of men and of angels.[25]

Arioso Dolente

Beethoven's instruction that the arioso be expressed in a *dolente* manner (to be played mournfully) adds greater depth to an already evocative musical composition. It is a tragic lament that conveys the pain of purgatory. In addition, in the emotional passages he employs an accompaniment of throbbing chords, thus conveying a doleful outpouring of unbearable suffering that ultimately finds solace in the fugue that follows.

The arioso is composed in a harmonic style that involves the use of chords, their constructions, and their progressions. Thus, when a piece of music is essentially a melody supported by chords, the texture is said to be harmonic. Due to the vertical structure of a harmonic chord, harmony is often said to refer to the vertical aspect of music. This vertical aspect provides the ear with musical experiences of richness and subtlety as well as the dimension of depth in music. An example of a harmonic chord appears as follows:

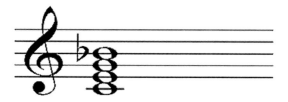

Fig. 3.1. Harmonic chord: vertical.

A fugue, on the other hand, is essentially a melody accompanied by other melodies (known as voices). This texture is referred to as contrapuntal or polyphonic and represents the horizontal aspect of music, which focuses on how independent musical lines or melodies interact. The simplest way to understand counterpoint is described by David D. Boyden in *An Introduction to Music* as follows:

> Everyone who has sung rounds like "Three Blind Mice" or "Row Your Boat" has experienced counterpoint without being aware of it. In both these pieces melody is accompanied by melody, and in a particular way. In "Three Blind Mice" one voice begins the tune, and after a short interval of time the second voice begins with the *same* tune while the first voice continues on its way. Then the third voice enters in its turn with the *same* tune that began the round, while the first and second voices continue—and so on, depending on the number of voices taking part. In simplified form the procedure is as follows:
>
> 1. Three Blind Mice, See how they run, They all run after . . .
>   2. Three Blind Mice, See how they run, . . .
>   3. Three Blind Mice, . . . [26]

This is an example of horizontal melody. However, having stated that harmony stresses the vertical aspect and counterpoint the horizontal aspect, it is important to note that the individual parts that make up harmony contain various degrees of melodic interest and, similarly, that counterpoint contains vertical or harmonic aspects at any given point.

In music, the opposites (in this case vertical and horizontal) are not discreet but rather form a continuum in relation to each other. As stated above, each contains an element of the other, and it is this aspect that ultimately draws the opposites together resulting in a unification that enables transformation to occur. The spiritual implication of the cross as symbolized for instance, in the Christian religion, indicates a conversion from an earthly life of living in the tension of the opposites into the spiritual world. Music at all times serves as a transcendent function, for by its very natural structure it is always mediating between the opposites and resolving them into a state of harmony. The power of this attribute of music will become evident in the case presentation that follows.

In the Passion music of Beethoven's Passion, the portrayal of the arioso-fugue relationship therefore takes on the overall symbolic shape of the cross through its distinguishing harmonic (vertical) and polyphonic (horizontal) textures. This is demonstrated graphically in Fig. 3.2.

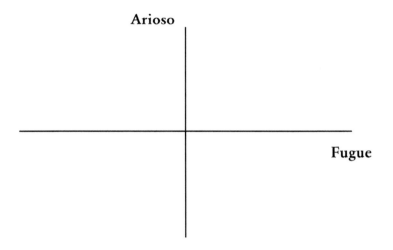

Fig. 3.2. Vertical (Arioso) and Horizontal (Fugue) Textures in Beethoven's *Piano Sonata No. 31 in A-Flat Major.*

Fugue

The fugues in this particular composition are described by Rosen as being representative of the stirring of new life. He states that Beethoven achieves this

> through the driest and most academic of counterpoint that all young musicians were forced to learn as soon as they finished going through their species exercises: these are the inversion of the *fugue* theme, the augmentation (playing it slower) and the diminution (playing it faster). Contrapuntal ingenuity consists of combining these various devices together, and it is usually a

purely academic exercise. For the first time in the history of
music, however, these hackneyed devices have become the
elements of a dramatic scenario.[27]

After the doleful outpouring of the arioso, the three-voice fugue serves
to create a serene flow within the ear of the listener. The deep sorrow of
the arioso is therefore quietly contained by the rhythmic and melodic
discipline of the fugue. The fugue resolves the harmonic pain and becomes
a linear act of prayer that emanates from the depth of the psyche. The
different voices, which resolve within the fugue, are brought back into
relationship with something fundamental. The fugue therefore illustrates
that although the three voices could represent disparate parts, there is yet
a semblance of deeper unity, for there is the constant "scent" of the
fundamental within the listener's ear. The various voices, which are relating
and engaging but not necessarily resolving (not until the end of the
composition, that is), can be held in the music until such time as a harmonic
resolution occurs. The fugue serves to hold together all parts that emanate
from the whole. Essentially, fugues imply reconciliation and wholeness,
for they attain a multiplicity in unity.

In discussing the relationship between Beethoven's ariosi and the fugues
in this sonata, pianist Alfred Brendel has the following to say:

> The first part of the *fugue* attempts to counteract the "lamenting
> song"—which, it has been noted, bears a resemblance to the
> *aria* "It is finished" from Bach's St. Johns Passion.[28]

Mellers speaks of the theological truth in musical terms, which is what the
fugue represents, and suggests that in this structure resides the affirmation
that paradoxically owes its sense of liberation to discipline.[29]

It is important in the context of this chapter to note that Beethoven's
use of these powerful Baroque themes became particularly evident in his
late-period instrumental music when he was personally experiencing his
own form of psychological crucifixion. According to Mellers, "His late
music is the creation of a man who has returned through penance and
purification, to the pure fountain."[30] In the piano sonata under discussion,
Beethoven's use of the recitative and arioso portrays the struggle involved
in attaining rebirth after the dark night of the soul. Beethoven differs from
Bach in that Bach was concerned with the historical Christ, whereas
Beethoven seems more concerned with the crucified Christ within his own
psyche. "It is in this sense that it is legitimate to speak of Beethoven's late
music as the artistic equivalent of "religious meditation on a symbol no
more complex than a circle, cross or triangle."[31]

The arioso, which is composed in harmonic style, represents the pain and suffering the hero encounters when being crucified. What is required is a surrender to and defeat by the tension of the opposites (the cross symbolizing the bringing together of all opposites within the psyche) in order to dissolve into a transcendent place. This state can provoke deep feelings of hopelessness and desperate despair in the listener. The fugue provides the spiritual discipline required to deal with that pain. As stated, the structure of these two pieces, the arioso in harmonic, vertical style and the fugue, in contrapuntal, horizontal style, form the universal archetype of the cross which, in turn, symbolizes the sacred center of creation. The vertical axis represents the spine or pole of the universe. This is the pathway that unites the world—that is, heaven and earth. In the Gnostic Acts of John, the true cross—the Cross of Light—is a celestial principle. The cross represents "wisdom in harmony" and "harmony as wisdom." The cross "has separated off what is transitory and inferior," yet by the same token it "has united all things."[32]

THE SPIRITUAL BEETHOVEN

We have a notion of Beethoven's deep spiritual search from entries he made within his *Tagebuch,* the intimate diary he kept from 1812 to 1818, to which he confided his innermost thoughts. He was deeply interested in Homer, Schiller, Kant, and Herder among the ancient classical writers and modern romantics and in Brahman and Masonic texts. Solomon states:

> The *Tagebuch* revealed Beethoven's surprising familiarity and espousal of remote and ancient religious conceptions documenting his interest in esoteric, ritual practices of the religions of the East and the Antique, and his fascinations with amorphous descriptions of the attributes of a supreme being. . . . These seem to add up to an ecumenical Deistic view of the sacred that opens up the spectrum of feelings that accompany ideas of initiation into ever higher states of being or of entry into sacrosanct states—usually identified with mystical and ecstatic varieties of religious experience.[33]

In his last decade Beethoven particularly alluded to what "the Eternal Spirit has infused into my soul and bids me complete." He said, "My kingdom is in the air. . . .As the wind often does, so do harmonies whirl around me, and so too do things often whirl about in my soul."[34] Solomon says that "it is noteworthy—and not without implications for his music— that these remarks are characterized by the use of spatial metaphors, and especially imagery of height and depth to represent value and judgement."[35]

He saw the conflict between the celestial and the earthly as a dialectic in which art attempts to escape from the world even as it is implicated in it. Psychologically, these metaphors resonate with Jung's two archetypal domains—the infrared (which represents instinct and therefore the physiological aspects) and the ultraviolet (which represents the spirit, dreams, conceptions, images, and fantasies). Beethoven's reference to his dominion being in the air conveys his deep connection to and understanding of the relationship between music and the spirit.

> We do not know what it is that grants us knowledge. The grain of seed, tightly sealed as it is, needs the damp, electric warm soil in order to sprout, to think, to express itself. Music is the electric soil in which the spirit thinks, lives and invents. Philosophy is a striking of music's electric spirit; its indigence, which desires to found everything upon a single principle, is relieved by music. Although the spirit has no power over that which it creates through music, it is yet joyful in the act of creation. Thus every genuine product of art is the divine when achieved, connected with men only in as much as it relates the spirit to harmony. An isolated thought yet feels related to all things that are of the mind: likewise every thought in music is intimately, indivisibly related to the whole of harmony which is oneness. All that is electrical stimulates the mind to flowing, surging, musical creation. I am electrical by nature.[36]

As this was written long before electricity as we know it was discovered, "electric" here presumably means something like "spirited" (as in imbued with spirit), "thrilling," "dynamic," or "charged."

The composer Bettina Brentano quoted Beethoven in a letter to Goethe in 1810:

> Music is a higher revelation than all wisdom and philosophy. It is the only incorporeal entry into a higher world of knowledge, which surrounds one, but which one cannot grasp. . . . Just as thousands marry for love's sake, without love once being revealed in these thousands, though they all carry on the business of love, so thousands have dealings with music, but no revelation of it. . . . The more the soul creates its sensible nourishment out of the spirit, the more the spirit ripens toward a blissful accord with it.[37]

It is evident from the above that Beethoven sought consistently and vigorously for his soul to be nourished by the spirit, and, like that he sought to convey this union of spirit and soul to all those who listened to his masterworks. Moreover, he understood, perhaps far more than any of his predecessors, the importance of integrating the chthonic realm of life (the dark instinctual elements within the psyche) with the spiritual aspects, thereby creating a transcendent experience through sound.

The universal image of the spirit is that which is synonymous with the breath or the wind, *pneuma* in Greek and *ruach* in Hebrew. The word *spiritus* is connected with *spirare* (to breathe), which is also the root of the word "inspiration." Yet the spirit is not easily defined or contained. In a parable, Jesus said that "the wind bloweth where it listeth, and thou hearest the sound thereof, but knowest not whence it cometh, and whither it goeth."[38] Making a connection between "the wind" and spirit, he went on to say, "That which is born of the flesh is flesh, and that which is born of the Spirit is spirit."[39] Although unseen, the spirit is believed to vivify everything everywhere and is the immediate cause of all generation and motion. This represents a kind of universal principle of life energy. Jung claimed that spirit is always active, winged, swift, and moving and that its purpose is to infuse us with energy, to inspire and stimulate. In relation to the soul, the alchemist Gerhard Dorn considered spirit to be a sort of window into eternity. The soul is an organ of the spirit and the body an instrument of the soul.[40]

The soul, being the personalized aspect of the spirit, has to do with individuality. It is perceived universally as having its home in a particular individual or object in matter and therefore takes on a particular shape. Regarded as the emotional seat of the individual, it is related to a person's capacity to feel expressions such as of depth, value, relatedness, heart, and personal substance. The soul animates the body just as it is believed to be animated by the spirit. According to the Dalai Lama, "The creative soul craves spirit[,] therefore the soulful divinity needs to be mated with the spirit."[41] In other words, a fusion between spirit and soul is continually being sought within the psyche.

In what manner does music express spirit? The spirit that "bloweth where it listeth" is given shape through sound and tone. That part of sound that we call "musical," which is distilled from noise, is thus created. The transforming power of the spirit requires fusion with the soul in order for anything new to be created. Once fusion has occurred, soul becomes expressive of tone. As all musical tones create motion, this, through the evocative nature of tones, transforms into emotion within the psyche. It is this added attribute of the soul (tone) that serves the psyche so powerfully when images created out of sound are used.

In his last years Beethoven's music underwent a transformation "which forever enlarged the sphere of human experience accessible to the creative imagination."[42] It is believed that in this final phase of his life, Beethoven created music that plumbed deeper and soared higher than the music of any composer who preceded him. In fact, there are those who argue that this interplay between deep chthonic forces and the upward striving toward the eternal spirit that, he believed, infused his soul is the quintessence of all his music. Through the tumultuous interplay between these opposing forces he ultimately arrived at transformational experiences.

As his descent into total deafness, his awareness of his increasing vulnerability to ageing, his own mortality and his extreme isolation and introversion increased, there appeared to be a sweeping re-alignment of his understanding of nature, divinity, and human purpose. It would appear that he had allowed the fabric of his ordinary life to disintegrate and in so doing had completely opened himself up to the spiritual world in which he so firmly believed and from which he received his strength. This allowed him to build an ever deeper connection with all parts of himself, which, in turn, led to deeper resonances within his music.

His Passion music served as an expression of the crucifixion of the Christ within, and he portrayed this as a fundamental situation in life. In the third movement of Op. 110, he demonstrated that after unbearable suffering we may again be restored to unity.

The following discussion demonstrates the similarity between the suffering of Beethoven and the suffering of an analysand in that each had their own experience of profound pain that could be imaged as a crucifixion. The Passion music Beethoven created, being so close to her own nature, ignited something in the analysand.

CASE MATERIAL

The analysand, whom I call Anne, was born to a mother with borderline personality disorder who had found the baby "so ugly at birth that all who saw her vomited!" Anne was subjected to severe "annihilatory" experiences during infancy, which included her mother pricking her fingers with needles each time she cried. Doctors who saw her noted physical evidence that her vagina had been harmed. The father, who was extremely protective, "doctored" her and took her to hospital following these traumatic attacks by the mother. This resulted in a very firm, loving bond between father and daughter. However, "psychological incest" developed that put Anne at further risk of attack by her mother.

Due to these traumas Anne developed a fragile ego that resulted in her having no inner container for positive growth. This fragility was manifest in episodes of loss of consciousness that were initially suspected to be epileptic in origin. It also manifested in an inability to express herself. For example, although she was musically very talented, she was not able to give recitals due to a paralysis that resulted in her being bedridden. She also experienced extreme anxiety about death, always imagining that any physical complaint was a malignant disease, and had recurring nightmares that featured her watching her hands being chopped off, her scream filtering into the blackness of the entire universe. As a result her ego had not been able to form a relationship with her true Self.

She began therapy with me fifteen years ago, having been originally referred by a neurologist. From the beginning she was completely committed to her therapy and personified Jung's requirements of "insight, endurance and action."[43] Gradually she has been able to tolerate positive regressive states; this has resulted in an emerging awareness of the Self.

Anne is an accomplished musician who used music both defensively and as a transformative agent during her analysis. However, she was not familiar with the Beethoven piece under discussion or with the history of the piece. (She had, in fact, avoided playing Beethoven compositions due to her fear of the persistent chthonic expressions within his music.) It was while she was part of a listening group that she encountered this work for the first time. Upon hearing the arioso she found herself experiencing unbearable emotional pain—a pain that she could not consciously connect with anything specific within her psyche. She therefore decided to bring the music to therapy and I requested that she apply active imagination while listening to the music.

What follows is a description of the images that emerged during the musically induced active imagination.

THE RECITATIVE

As the recitative unfolded, she listened to the music in a contemplative manner. This appeared to encourage a receptive attitude to what was to follow. With the added dynamic of repeated notes came a sense of instructive focus. The image of a small bird on a windowsill pecking persistently at the window came to her mind. She felt as if this little bird was insisting on imparting some information to her. (Track 14.)

THE ARIOSO

As the repeated single notes developed into harmonic chords Anne felt these chords embrace her as if to form a connection with her and, in so doing, prepare her for some form of ritual. Once the melody was introduced, and especially as it entered into a descending progression, she felt as if it had come to meet her. The compassion, sympathy, and gentleness the melody contained created an emotional fusion between Anne and the melody that simultaneously appeared to represent some guiding principle.

The melody beckoned Anne to follow her up a flight of stone stairs. During the ascent Anne once again became overwhelmed by emotional pain and began to sob. She realized that she needed to climb the stone staircase steadfastly. The ascending harmonic progression in the music was acute in its continually changing tone color, and this added to the intensity of the emotional experience. The music seemed to reach a subtle, quiet plateau, prompting an image of a stone platform where, to Anne's surprise, her therapist stood. Imaginally she stepped onto the platform and the therapist clasped Anne's right hand. With this a sense of stability seemed to descend on Anne. She then became aware of a bright light shining upon

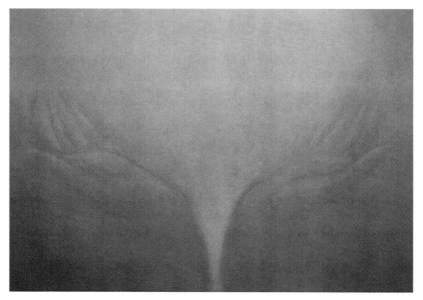

Fig. 3.3: Receiving the Light. Gillian Mathew. Used by permission of the artist and the owners of the work, Michael Oak School.

her from above. Spontaneously she turned her arms toward the light (as in the image on the preceding page) and opened her palms as if to infuse them with the healing spirit of the light. She remained in this position until the arioso came to an end. (Track 15.)

THE FUGUE

As the various voices of the fugue were introduced, Anne realized that their opening intervals emulated the ascending passages of the arioso. Consequently she knew that the arioso process was not yet complete. As she focused on the tranquillity of the music, she became aware that her hands felt the warmth of new life. A spontaneous feeling continued to fill her with this warmth, and she realized that something had been released within herself. Because she felt contained by the fugue, she was able to tolerate the power of the chthonic voices as they made their entrance. Paradoxically, although fugue means "a flight" or "to flee," Anne felt that the structure of the fugue had helped her to internalize the experience. (Track 16.)

RESTORATION OF THE EGO-SELF AXIS

The Self, according to Jung, is a structure of the psyche whose function is to further the development of the individual, a willing matrix that is both purpose and container. The paradox is that we need an other to release this potential into expression (at least at the beginning of life). The role of the parent (the first other) is twofold—to facilitate the Self's potential into real life as well as to establish stable ego structures. This creates the foundation for a viable ego-Self axis. Should the early environment fail to establish a viable ego-Self axis, and particularly if the failure occurs at a very early stage of development, then both components of this axis are damaged, if not entirely ruptured. It would appear that this is what happened to Anne in her formative years. The unreliability in her infant care process constituted a trauma, and each trauma resulted in an interruption of her "going-on-being"[44] and a rupture of her developing ego-Self axis. Essentially Anne was denied a connection with that magical other (the Self) that not only transforms us but is the locus from which self-expression occurs. Hillman in *Re-Visioning Psychology* has written of symptoms as being evidence of, and reminders of, our estrangement from the Self.

After her many years of therapy Anne is able to view the trauma from a unitary place. Initially in her therapy she had to avoid this primal space due to the fragility of her ego. It would appear that the combination of listening to the recitative, arioso, and fugue and the practice of active imagination aided the strengthening of Anne's relationship to the Self. The music seemed to have brought her into a transcendent space. The symbols of the ascent, the stone staircase and platform, and the light are all powerful evocations of an encounter with the Self. Sound is believed to be a primordial expression of the Self ("In the beginning was the Word"), and the melody that beckoned her served also as a vehicle of the Self. She was very gently embraced by this melodic-Self presence, and it was at this point that the music (the melody and the supporting chords) began the ascension toward a transcendent space where her spirit and soul could be reunited. The stone staircase she ascends is an archetypal image of absolute and indestructible reality—and therefore points to this quality existent within the Self as well as to a new wholeness and solidity within herself.

With the most subtle change in a single harmonic chord she finds herself in the company of her therapist who has clasped her hand. The opening of her arms to expose her palms to the light emanating from above indicates a receptivity to the blessing and divine grace that comes from that light. Shining upon her, this light points to the archetypal aspects of Apollo, the sun god of music and light. In addition, Christ as an image of the Self is "the light of the world," and this light refers to the revelation of Christ's love and the penetration of that love into darkness.[45] Importantly, in Gnostic thought the "Light" in the Gospel of St. John refers to "light in its psychic function, as the inner process of illumination and as the psychic content of illumination."[46] This light not only serves as a path, in the sense that the Tao is a path, "but gives insight, inner sight and is an illumination and wisdom in the Gnostic sense. This illumination, in which the illumined one himself illumines, *is a process and not a static image.*"[47] It is within this process that Anne will continue to experience the soul's illumination.

THE ASCENSION THAT RESULTED IN PAIN

Upon reflection, Anne realized that she was grieving the early severance of her soul from the Self. The arioso had moved her to feel not just the beauty of the Self but also the agony of the loss of a true connection to it. She made an association with Rumi's poem "Love Dogs," which had always appealed to her but now conveyed a truly meaningful explanation of "this longing."

> This longing you express is the return message.
> The grief you cry out from draws you toward union.

> Your pure sadness that wants help is the secret cup.
> Listen to the moan of a dog for its master.
> That whining is the connection.[48]

Through the harmonic structure of the arioso her soul remembered the primal connection to the Self. In the remembering, the soul recognized that union. The deep pain had forced her to appreciate her unconsciousness of having stayed in the struggle. She now knew that she had to relinquish this part in order to attain the whole.

In my mind it was the aspect of the cross formed by the relationship between the arioso and the fugue that brought the realization that she had lived her life in a linear mode—clinging, holding, and grasping. This had now been intercepted by the height and depth (the arioso) that is outside of time. The incarnation the music expresses brings consciousness, which brings both pain and joy.

Anne experienced the hand of the analyst holding her hand as a moment of transformation that ushered in the beginnings of a different way of being. I think that she was fully experiencing herself in the mystery of the Self. *This was a moment of Self meeting Self.* Although we may live in the linear mode we are being intercepted by the vertical and are often not feeling it.

As Anne continued to surrender to the mystery of the Self, she was filled with a quiet, melancholic joy for she had opened her heart! This was followed by an awareness of a sadness at leaving behind her previous life but also of an inherent acceptance by the Self that soothed her pain. Gradually she experienced not only joy in this spirit of acceptance but also joy in the defeat of the ego—this being the paradoxical nature of the ego-Self relationship!

The encounter with the Self's energies felt to Anne as an act of grace. Her previous ego orientation had encountered something profound, resulting in the humbling of her ego. To be touched by grace is to feel a life process that is not of you. In essence, she had been touched by God! "I am known by God," she quietly stated and with this gentle acceptance she felt more at peace, for her extreme death anxiety appeared to have abated. Finally, she brought the following poem to her next session for she felt that it poignantly expressed what the music of Beethoven had revealed to her.

> Then dawns the invisible; the Unseen its truth reveals
> My outward sense is gone, my inward essence feels:
> Its wings are almost free—its home, its harbour found,
> Measuring the gulf, it stoops and dares the final bound.[49]

NOTES

¹ C. G. Jung, *The Spirit in Man, Art, and Literature* (Princeton, NJ: Princeton University Press, 1972), p. 105.

² Emma Jung, *Anima and Animus* (Woodstock, CT: Spring Publications, 1957), p. 36.

³ Jeremy Siepmann, *Beethoven: His Life & Music* (Welwyn, UK: Naxos Books, 2005), p. 2.

⁴ Heinrich Zimmer, "The Significance of Tantric Yoga," in *Spiritual Disciplines: Papers from the Eranos Notebook,* ed. Joseph Campbell and Rudolf Bernoulli (Princeton, NJ: Princeton University Press, 1985), p. 22.

⁵ Wilfrid Mellers, *Bach and the Dance of God* (London: Faber & Faber Ltd., 1980), p. 120.

⁶ In equal temperament, no interval other than the octave is acoustically correct or pure. An interval is the distance in pitch between two tones. An octave incorporates eight tones and is the most perfect of all the intervals.

⁷ Quoted in Alain Daniélou, *Music and the Power of Sound: The Influence of Tuning and Interval on Consciousness* (Rochester: Inner Traditions, 1943), p. 132.

⁸ C. G. Jung, *Memories, Dreams, and Reflections* (London: Routledge, 1966), p. 177.

⁹ Edward F. Edinger, *Ego and Archetype: Individual and the Religious Function of the Psyche* (London: Shambhala Publications Inc., 1972), p. 4.

¹⁰ Jean-Yves Leloup, *The Gospel of Mary Magdalene* (Rochester: Inner Traditions, 2002), p. 25.

¹¹ *Ibid.,* p. 47.

¹² James Hillman, *Re-Visioning Psychology* (New York: Harper and Row Publishers, 1975), p. xi.

¹³ C. G. Jung, *Collected Works of C. G. Jung,* vol. 9ii, *Aion: Researches into the Phenomenology of the Self* (Princeton: University Press, 1959), p. 190.

¹⁴ C. G. Jung, *The Structure and Dynamics of the Psyche* (Princeton University Press, 1991), p. 322.

¹⁵ Quoted in Mary Butterton, *Listening to Music in Psychotherapy* (Oxford: Radcliffe Publishing, 2008), p. 102.

¹⁶ Aniela Jaffé, *From the Life and Work of C. G. Jung* (Einsiedeln, Switzerland: Daimon Verlag, 1989), p. 132.

¹⁷ Wilfrid Mellers, *Beethoven and the Voice of God* (London: Travis & Emery, 2007), p. 253.

[18] Mellers, *Bach and the Dance of God,* p. 90.

[19] Only sections 1, 2, and 3 of the third movement are discussed here, as these are the sections used by the analysand. Sections 1 ("Recitative"), 2 ("Arioso"), and 3 ("Fugue") can be heard on the accompanying CD. These excerpts are from *Piotr Anderszewski Plays Bach: English Suite BWV 811/ Beethoven: Piano Sonata Op. 110/Webern: Variations Op. 27,* EMI Classics B000239ABU. Used by permission of EMI/Virgin Music, Canada.

[20] I have not discussed sections 4, 5, and 6 of this work. After the second arioso, Beethoven does, however, achieve a glorious ecstatic "return to life," which Rosen considers to be a most brilliant and triumphant finale to this great piano sonata. In the second arioso he creates a movement choked with despair as he includes an accompaniment of throbbing chords that give the impression of an act of deep sobbing. The return to the final fugue, which is marked *poi a poi de nuovo vivente* (little by little coming back to life), differs from the initial fugue in that the ascending voices are now inverted and descend. This technique therefore mirrors the first fugue, which emulates the words of Christ in Gustav Holst's *The Hymn of Jesus,* where Christ says before his crucifixion, "I am a mirror to thee who understandest me." The homophonic conclusion of the fugue, which transforms into a lyrical hymn, achieves complete unity. This too echoes what occurs within *The Hymn of Jesus.* See G. R. S. Mead, *The Hymn of Jesus* (London: The Theosophical Publishing Society, 1907).

[21] Donald Jay Grout, *A History of Western Music* (New York: W. W. Norton & Co., 1973), pp. 345–347.

[22] Mellers, *Bach and the Dance of God,* p. 90.

[23] Denis Arnold, *The Beethoven Companion* (London: Faber & Faber, 1976), p. 178.

[24] Charles Rosen, *Beethoven's Piano Sonatas: A Short Companion* (New Haven, CT: Yale University Press, 2002), p. 240.

[25] Mellers, *Beethoven and the Voice of God,* p. 230.

[26] David D. Boyden, *An Introduction to Music* (New York: Alfred A. Knopf, 1970). p. 43.

[27] Charles Rosen, *Beethoven's Piano Sonatas: A Short Companion* (New Haven, CT: Yale University Press, 2002), p. 240.

[28] Alfred Brendel, *Music Sounded Out: Essays, Lectures, Interviews, Afterthoughts* (London: Robson Books, 1990), p. 70. "It is finished" were the final words of Jesus on the cross; see John 19:30. This and all other biblical references are from the King James Version.

[29] Mellers, *Beethoven and the Voice of God,* p. 234.

[30] *Ibid.,* p. 27.

[31] *Ibid.*

[32] David Fideler, *Jesus Christ, Sun of God: Ancient Cosmology and Early Christian Symbolism* (Wheaton, IL: Theosophical Publishing House, 1993), p. 280.

[33] Maynard Solomon, *Late Beethoven: Music, Thought and Imagination* (Berkeley: University of California Press, 2003), pp. 8–9.

[34] Mellers, *Beethoven and the Voice of God,* pp. 23–29.

[35] Solomon, *Late Beethoven,* p. 94.

[36] Mellers, *Beethoven and the Voice of God,* p. 23.

[37] Beethoven, quoted by Bettina Brentano in a letter to Goethe, [28 May] 1810, quoted in Hans Erhard Lauer, "The Evolution of Music Through Changes in Tone-System," in *Cosmic Music: Musical Keys to the Interpretation of Reality: Essays,* ed. Joscelyn Godwin (Rochester, VT: Inner Traditions, 1989), p. 168.

[38] John 3:8.

[39] John 3:6.

[40] John P. Dourley, *The Psyche as Sacrament* (Toronto: Inner City Books, 1981), p. 84.

[41] James Hillman, *Puer Papers* (Irving, TX: Spring Publications Inc., 1987), p. 59.

[42] Solomon, *Late Beethoven,* p. 1.

[43] James Hollis, *Swamplands of the Soul: New Life in Distant Places* (Toronto: Inner City Books, 1996), p. 16.

[44] D. W. Winnicott, *The Maturational Processes and the Facilitating Environment: Studies in the Theory of Emotional Development* (London: Karnac Books, 1965), p. 60.

[45] J. D. Douglas et al., *New Bible Dictionary* (Leicester, England: Inter-Varsity Press, 1992).

[46] Max Pulver, "The Experience of Light in the Gospel of St. John," in *Spiritual Disciplines: Papers from the Eranos Notebook,* ed. Joseph Campbell and Rudolf Bernoulli (Princeton, NJ: Princeton University Press, 1985), pp. 249–258.

[47] *Ibid.*

[48] Coleman Barks, *The Essential Rumi* (London: Penguin Books, 1995), p. 156.

[49] Emily Brontë, "The Prisoner," in *The Poems of Emily Brontë,* ed. Derek Proper and Edward Chitham (New York: Oxford University Press, 1995), p. 179.

4

An E-Mail Interview with Mario Jacoby

CONDUCTED BY PAUL W. ASHTON

Mario Jacoby, Ph.D., is a lecturer and a supervising and training analyst at the International School of Analytical Psychology (ISAP) in Zürich, Switzerland. For many years (until 1997) he was a member of the Curatorium (Board of Directors) at the C. G. Jung Institute in Zurich. He is also a guest lecturer at the Alfred Adler Institute and at the Burghölzi, the psychiatric clinic of the University of Zurich. He has been invited on lecture tours and training courses in major cities all over the world. He has a private analytical practice in Zurich. His first interest was in music, and at a young age he studied under Georges Enesco at the Ecole Normale in Paris and under Max Rostal at the Guildhall School of Music and Drama in London. He became a professional violinist, touring with the Zurich Chamber Orchestra to the United States and Canada.

Mario Jacoby has published several books on analytical psychology, including *The Analytic Encounter* (1984), *Individuation and Narcissism* (1990), *Shame and the Origins of Self-Esteem* (1994), and *Jungian Psychotherapy and Contemporary Infant Research* (1999). He has also published more than fifty articles on analytical psychology in various psychological journals.

Realizing that Paul's interview with Mario attempted to address various ideas about music and the psyche and did not give a picture of Mario the man, we decided to add some material from an interview conducted by R. Henderson that was published by Spring Journal and Books. This is used by kind permission of Spring and gives fascinating glimpses into the earlier days of Jungian psychology and some of its characters.[1]

This is Mario Jacoby speaking:

> Dora [Kalff] was a member of the Psychological Club, and the Club wanted to arrange a program to entertain Jung at their Christmas dinner.
>
> Dora told them that she wanted to play for Jung on the piano, but she only could do it together with me, on the violin. This seemed to be a serious problem for the Club, as I was at that time just a student and could not be invited to sit next to the initiated ones. But they somehow still wanted us to play. And I also wanted to play for Jung, of course, but not at all costs. After much back-and-forth with the president of the Club, I offered to play after they had had their dinner. That was OK, but then she telephoned again to say that it would be better to play before dinner, just when Jung came in, to be sure that he would hear it. They were afraid that after dinner he possibly might just say good-bye and not stay on to hear the music. I refused, feeling that it would not be the right moment, because when Jung comes in, everybody, first of all, wants to talk to him, and it would not be appropriate to play music then. I said that I would rather risk that Jung would leave and miss the "great occasion" of hearing Dora and me. Thus we agreed, after all, that I would come after dinner.
>
> I lived not too far away from the place where the Club had this dinner; I stayed home to practice, to warm up my fingers. . . . The telephone rang. It was someone from the Club committee with a very agitated voice saying: "Please come at once, Jung is ready for his dessert and he may leave any minute." So I went there, and Jung was still sitting at his table. Dora and I had planned to play La Follia by Corelli and a lovely sonata by Tartini. These are works composed between the late 17th and the early 18th centuries in Baroque style. I had also received the warning that I should not play anything in the Romantic style, and no Beethoven, because that would be emotionally too moving for Jung. During our playing I saw Jung listening very attentively, and

after we had finished he stood up and came to shake my hand, saying that he liked it. But after that, he left immediately.

Next morning, I had my analytic session with Jolande Jacobi. She had not been invited to the Club dinner. She was very disliked by the Club members for many reasons, but especially for her outspoken bluntness. The first thing she said was: "I heard bitter complaints about Dora Kalff from Club members. They said that Dora had managed to attract Jung's attention for 20 minutes, just for her, and nobody else could speak with him. And after that he left immediately, and apparently he could not sleep after that music. Nobody complained about you." Of course, being just a student, I was no real rival to the Club ladies. I thought to myself that analysis and the individuation process did not seem to liberate people from envy.[2]

And now, in our attempt to understand how Music and Psyche interact, we move from the very personal to the theoretical.

Paul W. Ashton: Can you say anything about music and typology? Can one guess what typology a person may have from the music s/he listens to? Or the other way round: Can one guess what music a person might like to listen to from his/her typology?

Mario Jacoby: This is a difficult question to answer. As music speaks mainly to our emotional realm it means that music mainly affects us via the unconscious, yet the psychological types are mainly concerned with the conscious attitudes—apart from the fourth function, which Jung named the "inferior" function. The inferior function seems to be closest to the unconscious, and if it happens to be the sensation function, it would usually be pragmatic and down to earth in contrast to the feeling-intuitive side. Thus the whole typology seems to be something very complicated. We rather imagine that music lovers belong more to the intuitive-feeling side. We have the impression that we have to "feel" the beauty of music; it is also the feeling function that judges whether a music is beautiful or touching or boring and without much substance.

Now, while staying with my theme and writing about it, I notice that I have to strain some of my reflective thinking in doing so. And probably it is the thinking function that is the furthest away from what we understand by music. Yet there were some people especially gifted in mathematics who were also famous musicians. Rhythm is mathematically based. And wherever there is a conductor it is his main task to keep the rhythm by beats. I personally played some years in different orchestras, and once there was on the program *Le Sacre du Printemps* (*The Rite of Spring*) by Stravinsky. The music sounds wild and archaic—according to Stravinsky's intention. At its first performance in Paris at the beginning of the twentieth century it provoked a scandal. Much later, in Zurich, I used to play in the symphony orchestra when this Stravinsky piece was performed. The score is written in the most complex way, mathematically worked out, and you had to keep on sweating because you had to count the most complex beats. That meant concentration of the thinking function all along. Yet the music had to come out intensely emotional and passionate.

That is an example for me to show that in music all the four functions are needed in varying degrees. Good music speaks to the whole person. Thus the question of the relation of typology to whatever kind of music is not easy to answer. What music actually needs, is, of course, a differentiated sensitivity and an openness toward the "life of the unconscious" while being as conscious and alert as possible.

P.A.: Related to that but more toward the pathological, do you think one can imagine what music would be tolerated/loved or not tolerated/hated by the diagnosis or level of psychological development of an individual?

M.J.: This question brings to mind a pianist I met who gave a lecture at the Psychological Club in Zurich. She specialized in music therapy and worked in a psychiatric hospital. She said that for depressive people it is intolerable when they have to listen to lively, gay, and cheerful music. They get moved by music that is sad, slow, and heavy, as that is in accord with their own state. They cannot be cheered up by a Viennese waltz, for example, or by some jazz.

P.A.: Your comments in your interview with Henderson about Jung and his concern about being too moved emotionally, for example by Beethoven, suggest that perhaps Jung's lack of exploration of music was more to do with his fear of its effects on him rather than that he found it irrelevant. ("What I heard from Aniela Jaffé and Jolande Jacobi was that Jung avoided listening much to music, because this stirred up his emotions too much; he seemed to be oversensitive to the effects of music."[3]) Could you comment further on that idea?

M.J.: I think that music was not irrelevant to Jung. Perhaps in his old age, after Emma had died, he may have been too easily touched by the effects of music. Yet his main interests were to do with the meaning of texts—be they Gnostic, alchemical, mythological, religious, etc. He was a master of the interpretation of symbolic texts but also of symbolic images. Dreams were most important to him. Of course you can hear or play music in your dreams. I remember myself having had dreams in which music played its part. But such dreams are rare and are usually accompanied by some sort of action. Music itself needs to be interpreted. In other words, the written score needs to *be performed* and brought to life by singing or various kinds of musical instruments. If somebody performs, for example, the *Kunst der Fuge* (*The Art of the Fugue*) by Bach with instruments, I personally feel it as an experience of *wholeness in time* (in contrast to a mandala's expression of wholeness in space) and can visualize it, even experience it, as a special type of mandala.

P.A.: Would you expect different music to touch one in different moods? Or would you expect the same music to touch one in different moods but to touch one differently?

M.J.: Yes, I am pretty sure that there is a relation between the mood we are in and the way we get touched by the "mood" expressed in a piece of music. If we are sad, for instance in a process of mourning, we usually cannot stand, we even find it disturbing and "sacrilegious," to get swamped by yodeling or a Viennese waltz. I used to get engaged to play my violin in the church at funeral services. The music I chose to play had to be carefully adapted to the general mood of the people attending the funeral service. I often chose a slow movement by Handel or Haydn, sometimes also by Mozart. The chosen music should not have been too heavily "depressive" but at the same time it should have been deeply consoling and have a hopeful atmosphere.

P.A.: Can you relate the phrase "affective resonance," which you use, to both music and psychotherapy?

M.J.: Daniel Stern writes about "affective attunement," which is similar to how I use the phrase "affective resonance." Psychotherapy converses mainly with words while music communicates via tones. Words need mainly intellectual understanding or verbal correspondence. Yet the spoken word also contains some kind of music and it may invite musical composers to compose songs (e.g., Schubert) or even whole operas. We notice that in speaking there is not only a content but also a tone of voice, which, voluntarily or involuntarily, betrays the emotion within the content of the speech, much like with body language. There is a French proverb: *C'est le ton qui fait la musique* (It's the tone that makes the music), meaning that there are affects that are usually contained in the sounds of the speech.

To your question whether I can relate what is called "affective resonance" to both music and psychotherapy, I would say, according to my experience, the following: Winnicott used a highly descriptive term for a fruitful patient-analyst relationship. He said that it needs a "facilitating environment." The task of the analyst has mainly to do with his capability in providing the "space" in which the "facilitating environment" may operate. As an analyst I may have to prepare for being a kind of instrument and as such being available to the patient's process.

The metaphor that the analyst serves a kind of instrumental function seems to me appropriate, or at least useful, because it promotes a certain way of engagement that may be optimal. Of course, if I talk of being instrumental in order to be available for the psyche of the patient—Winnicott called it to be of use or useful for the development of the patient—I am again referring to the Self in the Jungian sense, in its organizing, enfolding, and also compensatory function, which may have an effect on both patient and analyst. We do have to differentiate this relationship from all kinds of misuse, like egotistic wishes and manipulations by the patients and maybe even by the analyst's own weaknesses. To become aware of any conscious or unconscious misuse and to respond adequately is often quite difficult, yet this belongs to the craft and art of the analyst's work.

I feel that for an analyst the metaphor of being an instrument may be helpful in finding an adequate approach to our difficult task. I imagine such an instrument above all as a sounding board. For an analyst to really convey "resonance" he or she must have a keen ear for the vibration of those strings (*cordes*) that are touching him or herself. To find resonance is an extremely crucial human experience. Without it, we are basically not certain whether we exist at all.

Next to Descartes' famous dictum "I think, therefore I am" we would have to add "I experience resonance to my being, and therefore I am." Thus it is essential for an analyst to have a sensitive ear to perceive how the specific "music" of each person sounds. Analysts may ask themselves: What are the feelings, ideas, tensions, fears and so forth that are coming up in ourselves in the presence of this particular patient? What are we called on to do; how should we respond? To feel the resonance that is evoked in the analyst by the patient is of great importance, whether the therapist expresses that in words or otherwise or not at all.

P.A.: Your comment in your interview with Henderson about Jung's presence that "filled the room" being a hindrance "to his analysands in finding their own inner space" intrigued us. Do you think that there are some composers who "fill the room" in such a way that they inhibit listeners from "finding their own inner space" while others leave a lot of space for their listeners to fill? How would you see various composers in that regard, for example Bach, Vivaldi, Mozart, Beethoven, and Pärt?

M.J.: I do not think that this comment can be applied to musicians versus listeners. But what I want to say in the context of Jung is that his genius and presence may have had the effect of wiping out the analysand's thoughts, feelings, or opinions to a certain extent. For instance, the patient may have come to feel: "What I had, or would have, to bring is just too small and ridiculous to bother such a genius like Jung with. It is not worth bringing up, even ridiculous to bring up, and he would find me totally uninteresting. Rather I want to listen to what his genius has to say."

I mean that such an idealization may wipe out the subjective point of view, even to a certain extent the feelings of self-worth of the patient. It was also said that Jung got bored with simple everyday stuff. And who wants to be boring in front of the genius? It is better to keep quiet and listen to what the great man has to say.

There is also the problem of too much idealization, by which I mean the identification with the great master as an ideal. Jung himself warned against such identification. "I only hope and wish that no one becomes a 'Jungian,'" he said:

> I do not stand for a doctrine, but I describe facts and propose
> certain views which I consider worthy of discussion. I proclaim
> no cut-and-dried doctrine and I abhor "blind adherents." I leave
> everyone free to deal with the facts in his own way, since I also
> claim this freedom for myself.[4]

P.A.: Do you differentiate "complex" from "simple" music with regard to its effects?

M.J.: What do we understand by this distinction? There is music that touches your heart that may be simple operetta, or folk songs. With complex music—I understand rather modern twelve-tone compositions that may be very interesting, but I usually have to say: "I prefer Mozart." Mozart is of course never "simple." Even when he wrote a kind of folk song in *The Magic Flute* or in *Figaro,* that song expresses authentic emotion. Complex music may be "interesting," often just speaking to the head. But Schoenberg's oratorio *Moses and Aaron,* for instance, is very "complex" and at the same time also extremely moving. But not for those who do not have enough musical context.

P.A.: Can you give examples of the "musical ear" at work in psychotherapy?

M.J.: The "musical ear" just has to do with a sensitivity to the nuances of the tone in the voice of patients. This may express their inner emotional state, which may be in quite a contrast to the overt content that they are expressing.

P.A.: Please comment on the possible role of music in training a person for psychotherapy as well as its role in training him/her for life. We would be interested in the idea of playing solo as well as playing in an orchestra and also whether you think that singing, again solo or in a choir, is different in any way from playing an instrument.

M.J.: I think that music can have a great effect on the level of emotional sensitivity. Of course I find it very important to develop "affective resonance." The rhythm of speech and breathing also needs to be discerned as sensitively as possible. Daniel Stern speaks of "vitality affects," which he observed in the mother-infant dialogue. "Vitality affects" manifest themselves as well in the dimension of time—that is, vitality expresses itself in terms of speed; for example, *allegro molto*—and it also suggests timing. If there is an *accelerato* wanted by the composer, the performer would respond accordingly. In the mother-child interaction, this "dialogue" happens mostly nonverbally, whereas in the analyst-analysand relationship this "dance" occurs both verbally and nonverbally.

I think that in training psychotherapists, all we can do is try to awaken the awareness of the students to these important matters.

What is the difference in playing solo or playing in an orchestra? If you have the task of playing or singing as a soloist, then certain real psychological problems may arise. I am thinking mainly of what we call "*trac*" or "stage fright." Of course there is the problem of exhibiting yourself, drawing the attention of the public to your own performance. This needs a certain amount of self-assurance (but not inflation). Stage fright is quite a well-known psychological problem, and many clients come to an analyst for help with this symptom. I wrote my thesis for the diploma of the Jung Institute in Zurich on this particular issue.

When I was a performing musician, we played and practiced a number of string quartets. That meant that each player had to listen sensitively and adapt to the rhythm and the phrasing of the whole quartet. Each of us had to have a very sensitive feeling of the others. Yet there were also places for one to take the lead whenever the music gave a leading role to a particular instrument. Such sensitive flexibility, I think, was good training for having an ear for the emotional nuances in analytical practice and for making sensitive responses.

P.A.: You state in the interview with Henderson that "attempts by psychologists [to translate music into psychological terms] have never been convincing"⁵ to you. Yet one can write about both psychology (and psychotherapy) and music in a reflective way. The puzzle is how to write about them, even explain them, and yet keep them alive. Can you comment on that?

M.J.: You are right, of course, it all depends on *how* it is written about. My statement is very subjective. There are, for instance, beautiful passages on music in the novel *Mozart on His Journey to Prague* by the German poet Eduard Mörike. In *Doctor Faustus* by Thomas Mann there is much interesting writing about music theories in connection to the ideas of Adorno. There are also Schoenberg's ideas of twelve-tone theory. But neither Adorno nor Schoenberg translate "contents" of music into psychological terms. They stay within the boundaries of music, yet in a very intellectual way. What I had in mind were mainly examples of some Jungians, who use "anima/animus problems," for example, to "explain" certain passages in a sonata. Yet I am aware that where the Self is concerned I used this idea myself, just a while ago, in connection to Bach's *Kunst der Fuge,* when I tried to talk about the "mandala" as an expression of a totality expressed over time.

There is music in great poems (Goethe, for example), even in works of prose. There is of course a significant connection between what we perceive by means of hearing (music) or seeing (visual arts) and what we conceive of through reflection (e.g., in literature). The "Muses" did, and do, belong together in their totality.

P.A.: This last question may not have much relation to music except in the way that silence is an integral part of music. We notice that "void" is not referenced in Jung's writings at all. "Voidness" is used three times but only in relation to the *Tibetan Book of the Dead,* and yet "chaos" is used more than fifty times. Have you any ideas about why this might be?

M.J.: Silence is an integral part of music. Something usually comes to a halt. Within music it usually is left to the performer how long this pause (musically known as *fermata*) shall last. It is left to the feeling-judgement of the performing artist. Very often it occurs at a place with the highest tension (where everything comes to a halt) or where the theme cannot be expressed better than by a silence full of tension.

Then the thread is taken up again with the same or, perhaps, with an opposite intensity. It is a temporary void, but usually a preparation for a continuation. It usually does not express "emptiness" or "voidness," yet it may also do that. I think that in any meditation, voidness is practiced in order to receive something new, unexpected. It makes room for the new.

When asked by Henderson what pieces of music touched him most deeply, Mario responded as follows.

> There is, of course, Bach, especially his *Passion of St. Matthew.* Mozart, the G-minor String Quartet, the late piano concertos, the opera *Don Giovanni.* Schubert, of course, is a favorite of mine, mainly the String Quintet with Two Cellos; the A-minor String Quartet; *Death and the Maiden,* and, of course the late Piano Sonata in B-flat Minor. Not to forget the series of songs: *Schöne Müllerin* and *Winterreise.* Also Brahms: all four symphonies, the violin concerto, the two piano concertos.[6]

NOTES

[1] Mario Jacoby, "Where My Soul Begins to Move Me Deeply: Mario Jacoby at 84," in *Living with Jung,* vol. 2, *"Enterviews" with Jungian Analysts,* ed. Robert and Janis Henderson (New Orleans, LA: Spring Journal, Inc., 2008).

[2] *Ibid.,* pp. 11–12.

[3] *Ibid.,* pp. 18–19.

[4] Carl Jung to J. H. Van der Hoop, 14 January 1946, in C. G. Jung, *Letters,* vol. 1, *1901–1950,* ed. Gerhard Adler and Aniela Jaffé, trans. R. F. C. Hull (Princeton, NJ: Princeton University Press, 1973), p. 404.

[5] Jacoby, "Where My Soul Begins to Move Me Deeply," p. 19.

[6] *Ibid.,* pp. 17–18.

5

The Matrix of Music and Analysis

PATRICIA SKAR

"**D**o you think I'll be a pianist?" reads my mother's caption beneath a photo of me taken when I was just six days old. She and I are intently gazing at each other; my fingers seem almost poised to touch a keyboard. As my mother surrounded me with her singing and piano playing, at three I was pleading for piano lessons and by seven also learning the violin. Just as natural as my perfect pitch, becoming a musician grew out of my maternal matrix like a dream entering the real world in active imagination.

Later on this dream became more complex: that is one reason I am now a Jungian analyst as well as a musician. When I first entered analysis, I had been earning my living primarily as a piano teacher. Most of my students were adults in midlife; although they were ostensibly there to learn the piano, psychologically it appeared to be more about looking for something they had lost, or never found in the first place. In many cases, it became clear that learning the piano was a disguised attempt at working on some other, deeper aspect of themselves.

The timing of beginning lessons was often significant. For example, "Jane" arrived at her first lesson immediately after quitting her job. We were able to see together, as her emotions emerged while struggling with a piece, that the decision to return to the piano was an unconscious affirmation, synchronous with leaving a job where her skills were greatly undervalued.

Most of my students had studied the piano as children and therefore came to me with a rich history of bodily and emotional experiences at the instrument. I saw repeatedly that the actual physical process of playing the piano could be a potent catalyst for facing long-repressed feelings from childhood. All too often, early music-making experiences had been severely contaminated by technical and performance demands imposed by parents and teachers. Some of my students were surprised that I initially asked them what *they* wanted to play, rather than placing them in the Procrustean bed of a "method." Once they realized they had a say in what we would work on together, they usually started to get on with the real reason they were there. I often found that an attraction to certain types of music could indicate what was lying dormant in the unconscious, or what aspects of the personality were in need of balance.

For example, "Ann" had studied piano throughout her childhood and was quite an advanced pianist. What I noticed immediately in her playing was a lack of flow and a dryness and rigidity of sound; I could see that playing the piano was a rather limited, somewhat painful experience for her. So I asked Ann what she would *really* like to do at the piano. Ann replied without a moment's hesitation that she would love to be able to improvise on an idea of her own, or play popular or jazz music. She had never ventured into this type of playing before, and was visibly excited at the prospect of being allowed to explore these clearly unlived areas of her musical development.

We decided together to approach the instrument as if she were a beginner, learning to let the energy for the sound production come from the center of her body. Then we started working without a score, learning simple harmonic patterns over which she could create her own melodies. Within a few weeks she was coming to her lessons nearly ecstatic, saying that she had never dreamed this was possible—playing without being "bound to the notes" and actually creating music on her own! But Ann soon realized that it would be a long process to build the repertoire of musical patterns she needed to give free rein to her ideas, and she became somewhat discouraged.

It was clear that Ann needed something more concrete to serve as a bridge between her former and new ways of playing. I suggested some transcribed jazz tunes. One that she particularly liked was Vince Guaraldi's "Cast Your Fate to the Wind."[1] The title itself gives a good indication of the character of this piece, which was immensely freeing for Ann. The expansive quality of the melody seemed to create space for her, and she began to move in a much rounder, more feminine way as she played.

This piece also gave Ann the opportunity to confront a particularly difficult rhythmic problem for her: a triplet figure in the right-hand melody against a four-beat division in the left-hand part. This "three-against-four" pattern is difficult for everyone to master at first—it somehow feels like the struggle between the masculine and the feminine. In this piece, the triplet figure has a round, lyrical feel that propels one forward, while the quadruple grouping has a more square solidarity. When the two rhythms are combined, three-against-four produces a tension of opposites that heightens the expression of the musical theme.

Since Ann's dominant function was thinking, in tackling the three-against-four measure, she diligently worked out mathematically where the notes should fall. Although she was able to play the measure slowly by itself, she could not fit it into the context of the surrounding music without the rhythm falling apart. Her intellectual approach, which had the effect of isolating this particular bar of music from its context, had to be sacrificed in order to bring the measure back into a feeling mode with the rest of the music around it. We did this by playing each hand separately, connecting the problem measure to what came before and after, feeling the flow of each part. Gradually she was able to put hands together and link up this section with the rest of the piece. It was a joy to see the abandon Ann developed as she "cast her fate to the wind." As we worked together, Ann continued to learn other blues and jazz transcriptions, happily exploring sides of herself that were quite remote from her conscious personality.

The psychological process Ann experienced through her piano lessons was in many ways similar to what occurs in analysis. First, there was an evaluation of her history at the piano, which had formed the "personality" of her playing of today. We could say that she had developed a faulty relationship with the instrument; it was necessary to go back to the beginning and start over, finding a new approach to the piano. The contrast of the freedom of the new way with the rigidity of the old patterns initially produced an "inflation." But this soon disappeared, as she realized the amount of hard work necessary to achieve her goals. Likewise in analysis, the analysand's positive or idealizing transference will often produce a honeymoon effect in the relationship. However, as the analyst inevitably fails to fulfil all expectations, more realistic inner parameters slowly begin to emerge.

Through Ann's struggle with the rhythmic problems in "Cast Your Fate to the Wind," she learned that her dominant thinking function needed to cooperate with her inferior feeling in order to integrate the three-against-four passage into the piece. This is similar to the analytic task of coming to terms with one's typology and understanding how it affects the way life problems are approached. Additionally, after establishing that her lessons with me were a "safe container," Ann worked through persona issues (connected with performance fears), identified and integrated elements of her shadow (expressed through the jazz tunes), and confronted aspects of her negative animus. This appeared in the form of a critical inner judge, who always entered the scene when she was not making "good enough" progress. By facing these repressed aspects of herself, Ann became more whole musically and as a person. She was also able to free blocked areas of emotional expression in her body and gain access to new states of feeling. As in analysis, a dialogue opened between the unconscious and conscious parts of her psyche, furthering her individuation process.

As I experienced my own first analysis while continuing to teach the piano, it became increasingly obvious to me that the symbolic relationship constellated between music teacher and student has many aspects in common with the analytic relationship. Of course, music teachers are not analysts in the traditional sense—they are generally not thinking about transference, or indeed their students' personal histories, except in terms of their musical backgrounds. However, because of the one-to-one nature of the teacher-student relationship, music teachers often receive huge transferences, as well as the full brunt of their students' complexes.

One of my own piano teachers opened our first lesson with the remark: "I must tell you that I do not do therapy; I am a *piano* teacher and it is my responsibility to give you some insights into the *music* during your lesson." This kind, warm-hearted man had probably received many idealizing transferences; perhaps he was also reminding himself to stick to the business of teaching rather than become emotionally involved with his students. But even though he kept his word and we concentrated on the music during my lessons, being in the atmosphere of his warmth and acceptance had a tremendously therapeutic effect on me. An important aspect of this was that he mentioned—but did not concentrate on—my mistakes. Rather, he helped me develop an overall feeling for the expressive possibilities inherent in a piece. Moreover, if he suggested something musically, he invariably backed this up by playing it. This showed me the *sense* of his conception and, more importantly, that *he could do it*: he had "lived through it." This is similar to Jung's suggestion that "the analyst is successful with his treatment just so far as he has succeeded in his own moral development."[2] Struggling with a musical passage is not the same as "moral development," but any performer will readily tell you that learning a challenging piece of music develops character. At the very least, it requires the ability to stay with the physical process of learning the work until the musical goals are met.

While musical goals and physical processes may seem like two separate things, they are of course completely intertwined. Even scales and arpeggios can have musical goals, but sadly, the mechanics of piano playing is often taught as something completely separate from making music. Sometimes I encountered students who seemed to be completely unaware of their bodies, concentrating only on their fingers as they played; the sounds that emerged were correspondingly cut off from depth and tone quality. One of my own teachers referred to this type of playing as "little soldiers marching on the keys." In this context, I remember the words of another teacher, who said that we are born with all the finger technique that we need; the secret is learning to relax and "let it go." This man had an incredible facility at the keyboard, and I thought he had probably worked for it: at the time, I found his statement too simplistic. What I now realize he meant was that the key to good technique is in the coordination of the whole body—the fingers are only the endpoint of the process. Since the entire body is part of the "musical instrument" that produces the sound, it needs to be an unhindered channel for the flow of that sound. One sees this union of body and instrument in all great performers: although each individual is different, they are all somehow "one" with the *intention* (in the archaic sense of "meaning") in the music.

I am reminded here of Charles Cooke's story about two pianists famous for their technique—Leopold Godowsky (1870–1938) and Josef Hofmann (1876–1957):

> Godowsky, it seems, was at a party at which, among others, Josef Hofmann and a large, outspoken lady were present. The lady, an ardent amateur pianist, was excited at being in the company of these titans of the keyboard. She shook hands with Hofmann and exclaimed, "What small hands you have, Dr. Hofmann!" Then, "And yours, too, Mr. Godowsky! How in the world, gentlemen, can you great artists play the piano so magnificently with such small hands?" Godowsky replied: "Where in the world, madam, did you get the idea that we play the piano with our hands?"[3]

Of course, getting to the stage where we are no longer playing the piano with our hands can be a long process. A common problem I encountered with my students was their eagerness to play a piece at the final (fast) tempo, long before they could manage the difficult passages even at a slow speed. When one is just beginning a new work, the melodic and harmonic configurations have not yet formed automatic patterns linked to muscular responses. The mind is occupied with the mechanics of note production, hindering a connection to what we might call music's more "archetypal" elements. In order to get beyond this stage, it is necessary to play slowly enough to keep all elements of the music intact, as one gradually increases the tempo. Finally, a more complete gestalt begins to emerge, and eventually, when we have lived with the music long enough, the piece starts to become part of who we are. The problem is that almost everyone is impatient, wanting to get as quickly as possible to this goal.

Similarly, many people entering analysis think they should be able to sort themselves out quickly once they have been able to identify their main issues; they are dismayed to discover they may be only at the beginning of a long journey. However, as they stay with the process, they may discover that, as Jung put it, "the goal is important only as an idea; the essential thing is the *opus* which leads to the goal: *that* is the goal of a lifetime."[4]

Jung used the term "individuation process" for this "goal of a lifetime." As Jung says, the idea of a specific goal may be useful as a target, but individuation lies in the process, not the endpoint itself. In working on a great piece of music, we continually discover new dimensions in the music and in ourselves. A piece learned in childhood and revisited throughout the years will also reflect changes in our personalities that come with life experience. I remember Artur Rubinstein saying (in a documentary filmed late in his life) that he had been playing a certain Chopin etude for fifty years and was now just beginning to understand it—to "play all the notes." In other words, as he had changed and matured, so had his relationship to this work of Chopin.

Reflecting on this lifelong connection to a piece of music, Glenn Gould's recordings of Bach's *Goldberg Variations* come to mind. Gould recorded the *Goldberg* first in 1955, when he was only twenty-two years old, and again in 1981, near the end of this life. During the intervening years, his conception of the piece changed considerably. In a 1982 interview with music critic Tim Page,[5] Gould confesses that he was happy to have the opportunity to record the work again, since he no longer identified with "the spirit of the person" who made the earlier recording. Listening to the opening theme of both performances, we note immediately that the tempo of the later version is much slower—about two-thirds the speed of the first. Overall, the 1981 recording seems more sober and introspective. Gould admits: "As I've grown older, I find many performances, certainly the great majority of my own early performances, just too fast for comfort." However, it turns out that the speed of the variations is not the critical conceptual difference between the two recordings. Gould explains that he has "come to feel over the years that a musical work, however long it may be, ought to have basically . . . one pulse rate, one constant rhythmic reference point." It was just this sense of overall rhythmic continuity that he felt was lacking in his 1955 interpretation. By contrast, in the 1981 version, each variation's "subsidiary pulse" is based on a multiplication or division of an unchanging but flexible "basic pulse" running throughout the work. Gould describes how this system creates a subliminal rhythmic coherence to the thirty variations, linking their wide variety of moods and textures. We could compare this musical process to Jung's idea of the self as an archetypal ordering principle underlying the many variations of human emotion and behavior. This is related to Jung's concept of individuation, which can be seen as the process of making a coherent whole out of the disparate parts of our personalities. Whether we prefer Gould's 1955 or 1981 recording of the *Goldberg*, the progression from the early to the late interpretation could be viewed as a musical composition undergoing a unique process of individuation in the mind of a performer.

In my own experience as a pianist, the commitment to the long process of learning a work like the *Goldberg Variations* mirrors the kind of development Jung had in mind when he described the ego-self relationship throughout the stages of life. In musical terms, we first battle with the notes, just as a baby struggles to walk and learn independent skills. As we reach adolescence and young adulthood, we are playing most of the "notes," but it isn't until much later that we begin making sense of the whole. As we stay with the "opus," both musically and in our lives, a "center" begins to emerge that is more than the sum of the parts.

In describing the individuation process in a person, Jung comes very close to this idea:

> If we can live in such a way that conscious and unconscious demands are taken into account as far as possible, then the centre of gravity of the total personality shifts its position. It is then no longer in the ego, which is merely the centre of consciousness, but in the hypothetical point between conscious and unconscious. This new centre might be called the self.[6]

Jung describes the self variously throughout his *Collected Works,* sometimes referring to it as a defined mental structure that organizes the personality, and at other times simply as the totality of the psyche. But in the quotation above, Jung is describing an *emergent* view of the self—not an entity that is fixed or pre-existent in the unconscious, but one that evolves jointly through our lived experiences in the world and our openness to unconscious processes.

Emergence is a word we encounter in many different contexts these days. In science, it can refer to the way complex systems and patterns, such as those that form a hurricane, arise out of many relatively simple interactions: something new evolves that is more than the sum of its parts. From an emergent perspective, human intelligence develops from dynamic connections between neurons, not from individual neurons themselves. Anyone who has tried to learn a musical instrument experiences emergence in a real, physical way. For example, in playing the piano, we start with basic five-finger positions, gradually moving toward passing the thumb under groups of three and four fingers as we learn scales and arpeggios. Applying these patterns to pieces, our brains are constantly reorganizing themselves, forming new neural networks that contain pathways representing the most-used formulations. These networks are being changed every time we play a piece, just as all the experiences we have in life are constantly affecting who we become.

In learning a particular piece of music, most of us expect our playing to improve with regular practice. But this does not take into account what is happening when we are *not* working on the piece. I first discovered this when one of my piano teachers told me that the best way to prepare for a recital was to learn all the music very well about six months in advance, and then not play it again until about two weeks before the recital. At that point, he assured me, all the mistakes and difficult places will have "ironed themselves out."

At first I thought this idea was madness, but decided to test his theory: I found to my amazement that it actually worked. What I did not know then was that he was talking about a kind of holistic ordering that occurs in the brain. When I stopped practicing my recital pieces for six months, the main structural features of the music I had learned remained and strengthened, while the activated "complexes" around the difficult passages were able to calm down and fall away.

Of course, learning a piece of music where all the notes are written down is different from improvising on a theme, as any classical musician who has tried to learn jazz will know. In jazz we are typically given only a melody and underlying chord progression; our ability to improvise around the tune is built up through a gradual assimilation of jazz patterns, rhythms, and harmonies. An interesting account of this process can be found in David Sudnow's book *Ways of the Hand.*[7] Sudnow describes the long journey of turning his classically trained hands into "jazz-making hands." He details his frustrations along the way, as his attempts to improvise continually fail him when he goes on stage. But somehow, after years of practice, finally his hands reach another level—they now know what to do and where to go. There is "a new being, *my body,* and it is this being . . . that sings."[8]

Sudnow's story reminds me of Jung's idea of the "transcendent function,"

> "function" being here understood not as a basic function but as a complex function made up of other functions, and "transcendent" not as denoting a metaphysical quality but merely the fact that this function facilitates a transition from one attitude to another.[9]

Jung describes this process as arising from the tension between consciousness and the unconscious. According to Jung, the transcendent function seems to have more chance of appearing if we stay actively *with* a process, holding the opposites rather than retreating from the problem or looking for a quick solution. The patience required to stay with learning a musical instrument is a good analogy.

As I lived with my own process—moving from teaching piano to training as a Jungian analyst—I wondered how my experiences of playing and teaching music could contribute to my analytic work. I initially looked for what Jung had to say about music, and found disappointingly little. Interestingly, though, I discovered that Jung had met, late in life, with the concert pianist and music therapist Margaret Tilly. She had previously published an article entitled "The Psychoanalytical Approach to the Masculine and Feminine Principles in Music"[10] and was for many years head music therapist at the Langley Porter Clinic in San Francisco. While in Switzerland to give a concert in 1956, Tilly sent some of her case histories to Jung, and he immediately invited her to his home to discuss her work. As Tilly describes their meeting,[11] Jung told her that he had always thought music therapy was "sentimental and superficial," but her papers were "entirely different." He asked Tilly to treat him exactly as if he were one of her own patients, inviting her to play his grand piano while he sat behind her. Jung "fired question after question" at her but warned: "Don't just tell me, *show* me." As they worked together, Jung became more and more deeply moved, finally saying:

> This opens up whole new avenues of research I'd never even dreamed of. Because of what you've shown me this afternoon—not just what you've said, but what I have actually felt and experienced—I feel that from now on music should be an essential part of every analysis. This reaches the deep archetypal material that we can only sometimes reach in our analytical work with patients. This is most remarkable.[12]

If Tilly isn't exaggerating Jung's response, she must have made him very aware of music's possibilities to act as a catalyst to opening up unconscious material. Perhaps if Jung had been exposed to Tilly's work earlier in his life, he would have experimented with the possibilities of using music in analysis in the same way that he encouraged patients to draw and paint their fantasies.

Today, over fifty years since Tilly visited Jung, very few analysts have as yet explored the potential for using music improvisation within analysis. There are diverse reasons for this, including the need for the analyst to have training in music therapy techniques and to acquire the requisite instruments. It remains an open question whether analytic training programs in the future will move toward incorporating some form of training in music improvisation within analysis, in the way that sandplay and analyzing "pictures from the unconscious" have long been a part of many Jungian training programs.

Even though there were no established models for the use of music improvisation in analysis, I was motivated to explore different schools of music therapy during my analytic training. Eventually, I discovered an approach that, for me, came the closest to a practical model for the use of music in analysis: Analytical Music Therapy (AMT), which was conceived and developed in England in the early 1970s. I subsequently decided to train privately with Mary Priestley, one of the founders of the method.[13] Later, I adapted some aspects of AMT into my own analytic practice.

I have explored this in detail elsewhere,[14] but basically, I keep a range of simple percussion instruments (drums, xylophones, shakers, etc.) in an open bookshelf at the side of my consulting room. While not in the patient's constant view, they are available at any time to be used, just like the drawing materials I also keep in the room. Generally I do not mention why the instruments are there unless I am asked. If there is interest in trying them, we might set aside a session to do so. This can be quite a process of discovery: the analysand may feel an emotional connection to one instrument in particular or a sound may constellate a memory, much like a dream can open up unconscious content.

After the initial exploration, I usually invite the person to feel free to return to the instruments, should the right moment in a session arise. Some analysands seem to intuitively choose instruments that enable them to enact a repressed aspect of themselves. If it seems appropriate and they agree, I might play another instrument in dialogue with them; this can be very positive in terms of establishing a feeling of "empathic resonance." While improvising together, there is the opportunity for the analyst to intuitively reflect and contribute to the ongoing sound expressions of the patient. A "sound-world" may be created that is similar to positive attunement between mother and child. At other times, when more conflictual patterns emerge, the analysand may connect to painful memories that can then be discussed and worked through together. I have found the instruments quite useful in acting out situations from a dream, especially when the patient is split off from the emotional side of the material or from parts of the psyche inherent in the dream characters. The act of playing together allows the analysand to feel heard or mirrored in a new way. As Mendelssohn put it:

> People usually complain that music is so ambiguous; that they are doubtful as to what they should think when they hear it, whereas everyone understands words. For me it is just the reverse. . . . The word remains ambiguous; but in music we would understand one another rightly.[15]

Sometimes it is possible to hear a thought or emotion being expressed in an analysand's music that has never been accessible through words. Playing together also seems to clear the way for verbal discussion. After a patient feels met on a musical level through the dialogue with the instruments, feelings often flow more easily into words.

I have not used recorded music in my practice, although my analysands often speak about music they have heard outside the hour. Sometimes they will ask me if I know a particular piece, and if I do, this provides a symbolic link to further associations. Of course, it is not the piece of music itself, but the feelings that arise from it that can lead to new insights and transformation.

One of the most vivid accounts I have encountered of the transformational effects of music comes from neurologist Oliver Sacks.[16] After a bad fall on a mountain, Sacks needed an operation to reconnect a torn tendon in his leg. After the operation, he discovered that he had no feeling in his leg. In fact, "it looked and felt uncannily alien—a lifeless replica attached to my body."[17] Sacks describes his slow process of relearning to walk, but his leg remained "a peculiarly clumsy, and unstable, robotic contraption, an absolutely ludicrous artificial leg."[18] Then one day, he imagines the music he's been listening to (the Mendelssohn Violin Concerto) and "suddenly, with no warning, no transition whatever, the leg felt alive, and real, and mine, its moment of actualization precisely consonant with the spontaneous quickening, walking and music."[19]

Sacks asks:

> What was it, then, that came suddenly back—embodied in
> music. . . . It was the triumphal return of the quintessential
> living "I," . . . not the ghostly, cogitating, solipsistic "I" of
> Descartes, which never feels, never acts, *is* not, and *does*
> nothing . . . . What came, what announced itself, so palpably,
> so gloriously, was a full-bodied vital feeling and action,
> originating from an aboriginal, commanding, willing, "I." . . .
> What appeared with the music was organization and center, and
> the organization and center of all action was an agency, an "I."
> What appeared in this moment transcended the physical, but
> instantly organized and reorganized it into a seamless perfect
> Whole. This new, hyper-physical principle was Grace. . . .
> Grace entered . . . at the very center of things, at its hidden
> innermost inaccessible center, and instantly coordinated,
> subordinated, all phenomena to itself. It made the next move
> obvious, certain, natural.[20]

This idea of Grace reminds me of Jung's description of the self as the "God
within us."[21] Sacks's ego-strength had already failed to move his leg: it took
this particular music to lift his consciousness out of the *control* of the ego
and into the realm of the self (the "aboriginal, commanding, willing 'I'"),
where his connection to vital feeling and action was restored.

Conclusion

The connection to vital feeling is at the heart of the matrix of music
and analysis I have been exploring in this chapter. "Matrix" was originally
a Latin word and has now become a part of many languages; it is derived
from *mater* (mother) and, among its many definitions, can mean "a
substance, situation or environment in which something has its origin,
takes form, or is enclosed."[22]

I began with an image of my maternal matrix, which led to music
becoming an integral part of my being. Later, as I experienced my first
analysis while teaching piano, a new matrix began, in which the exploration
of the two fields of music and analysis continues to form a path of
discovery. There is much more to be said concerning the use of music in
analysis, but on another level, the practice of analysis *itself* could be
considered a musical improvisation. I am reminded here of Mario Jacoby,
who is interviewed in this collection. Jacoby was a professional violinist
before becoming a Jungian analyst, so it is no surprise to find him describing
the analytic relationship in musical terms:

> Certainly it is important first and foremost to tune into the "melody" of the analysand, because only in this way is it possible to truly listen for and detect noticeable dissonances. The therapist undoubtedly brings his own "melody" and "rhythm" into the field as well; and soon enough, discrepancies between the two individuals may develop. Yet when two people "make music" together, a consistent and mutual listening to one another, along with mutual adjustments, is essential. Of course, it is primarily the therapist who must consciously adjust himself to the emotional state of the patient, without at the same time losing himself in the emotional world of the person sitting across from him.[23]

This process of attunement—to others and ourselves—is something we can develop through both music and analysis. One of the important tasks of analysis is to further a dialogue between consciousness and the unconscious, so that a new wholeness is facilitated. Jung was aware of music's importance in connecting us to the transformative power of the unconscious. As he wrote late in life:

> Music expresses, in some way, the movement of the feelings (or emotional values) that cling to the unconscious processes. . . . Music expresses in sounds what fantasies and visions express in visual images. . . . I can only draw your attention to the fact that music represents the movement, development, and transformation of the motifs of the collective unconscious.[24]

Jung's idea of the collective unconscious links us to the common developmental patterns we share with all other human beings. How a piece of music gradually works through a set of opposing themes or dynamics, tonally and rhythmically coming to terms with them to create a dynamic whole, seems very similar to processes that we find in living organisms, as in this description by biologist Mae-Wan Ho:

> An intuitive way to think about it is in terms of a symphony orchestra or a grand ballet, or better yet, a jazz band where every individual is doing his or her own thing, but is yet in tune or in step with the whole. This is precisely the biochemical picture we now have of the living system.[25]

Probably one of the reasons music affects us so deeply is that we identify with its sound-structuring process, and this in turn promotes a reordering process within our minds. Music seems to mirror the movement and gestural qualities of *both* our physical and psychic processes. It literally imbues time with the experience of change and transformation. We could say that music "tunes" our minds and bodies with its ordered sound-expression of our myriad states of being, mirroring the consciousness we can achieve of our emotional and physical experiences as we move through life. Learning a musical instrument provides a rich ground for individuation. As we stay with the instrument, we realize that the music we are drawn to often contains dynamic qualities that connect to undiscovered sides of ourselves. Working on this music brings into consciousness not only rejected parts of our personalities, but also sides of ourselves that have never been in consciousness.

When we return to a piece of music we have not played for many years, it is sometimes uncanny how our fingers know what to do. The shadow side of this familiarity is that a traumatic memory associated with the piece might return as well—perhaps in a difficult passage bungled in performance, or in a part that through lack of careful practice has remained broken off from the whole. This is similar to the discovery of old wounds and the reenactment of painful complexes in analysis. Just as with an emotional complex, in returning to these difficult passages, we discover that they cannot be forced into submission or instantly "fixed." Rather, we must patiently work through the mixed messages that have become embedded in the body-mind connection.

In both music and analysis, active engagement is the key, creating the ground for the "emergent properties" of meaning, spirit, and soul to appear. As Jung suggests, "If we understand and feel that here in this life we already have a link with the infinite, desires and attitudes change."[26] The right music (playing or listening) for each one of us could be this link to the infinite, or at least a pathway to the coherence of the self. As Jung's wife Emma eloquently put it, music "gives sensuous representation to our deepest associations and most immutable laws" and "admits us to the depths where spirit and nature are still one—or have again become one."[27]

NOTES

Some material from this chapter was previously published in Patricia Skar, "Music and Analysis: Contrapuntal Reflections," in *Zurich 95: Open Questions in Analytical Psychology,* ed. Mary Ann Mattoon (Einsiedeln, Switzerland: Daimon Verlag, 1997), pp. 389–403; and Patricia Skar, "The Goal as Process: Music and the Search for the Self," *The Journal of Analytical Psychology* 74, no. 4 (2002): 629–638.

[1] This piano arrangement of "Cast Your Fate to the Wind" (copyright 1962, 1963 by Atzal Music, Inc., New York) appears in *47 Modern & Jazz Piano Pieces,* arranged by John Brimhall, Hal Peterson, and Jim Progris (Miami Beach, FL: Hansen House, 1982), pp. 24–26. Free listening access to the Vince Guaraldi Trio performance (from the CD *Jazz Impressions of Black Orpheus*) can be found at http://www.last.fm/music/Vince+Guaraldi+Trio/Cast+Your+Fate+To+The+Wind:+Jazz+Impressions+Of+Black+Orpheus.

[2] *The Collected Works of C. G. Jung,* vol. 4, *Freud and Psychoanalysis,* trans. R. F. C. Hull (Princeton, NJ: Princeton University Press, 1970), para. 587. All future references to Jung's *Collected Works*, abbreviated as *CW,* are followed by volume number, volume title, and paragraph numbers.

[3] Charles Cooke, *Playing the Piano for Pleasure,* rev. ed. (New York: Simon & Schuster, 1960), pp. 16–17. Cooke attributes the story about Hofmann and Godowsky to Moriz Rosenthal.

[4] Jung, *CW* 16, *The Practice of Psychotherapy,* para. 400.

[5] All quotations from Glenn Gould in this paragraph are taken from his interview with Tim Page that was recorded on 22 August 1982 in Toronto, Canada, and is included in the three-CD set: Glenn Gould, *A State of Wonder: The Complete Goldberg Variations (1955 & 1981),* Sony Classical Legacy SM3K 87703 (2002).

[6] Jung, *CW* 13, *Alchemical Studies,* para. 67.

[7] David Sudnow, *Ways of the Hand: A Rewritten Account,* with a foreword by Hubert L. Dreyfus (Cambridge, MA: MIT Press, 2001). The first version, *Ways of the Hand. The Organization of Improvised Conduct,* was published by MIT Press in 1978.

[8] Ibid., p. 130.

[9] Jung, *CW* 6, *Psychological Types,* para. 828.

[10] Margaret Tilly, "The Psychoanalytical Approach to the Masculine and Feminine Principles in Music," *The American Journal of Psychiatry* 103, no. 4 (January 1947): 477–483.

[11] Margaret Tilly, "The Therapy of Music," in *C. G. Jung Speaking: Interviews and Encounters,* ed. William McGuire and R. F. C. Hull (Princeton, NJ: Princeton University Press, 1977), pp. 273-275.

[12] Ibid., p. 275.

[13] See, for example: Mary Priestley, *Music Therapy in Action,* rev. ed. (St. Louis: Magnamusic-Baton, 1985); and Mary Priestley, *Essays on Analytical Music Therapy* (Phoenixville, PA: Barcelona Publishers, 1994).

[14] See, for example: Patricia Skar, "Music and Analysis: Contrapuntal Reflections," in *Zurich 95: Open Questions in Analytical Psychology,* ed. Mary Ann Mattoon (Einsiedeln, Switzerland: Daimon Verlag, 1997), pp. 389–403; Patricia Skar, "The Goal as Process: Music and the Search for the Self," *The Journal of Analytical Psychology* 74, no. 4 (2002): 629–638; and Patricia Skar, "Sound and Psyche: The Common Rhythm in Mind and Matter," in *Cambridge 2001: Proceedings of the Fifteenth International Congress of Analytical Psychology* (Einsiedeln, Switzerland: Daimon Verlag, 2003), pp. 533–541.

[15] Heinrich Jacob, *Felix Mendelssohn and His Times,* trans. Richard and Clara Winston (London: Barrie & Rockliff, 1963), pp. 185–186.

[16] Oliver Sacks, *A Leg to Stand On* (New York: Harper & Row Perennial Library, 1987).

[17] Ibid., p. 125.

[18] Ibid., p. 144.

[19] Ibid.

[20] Ibid., pp. 149–150.

[21] Jung, *CW 7, Two Essays on Analytical Psychology,* para. 399.

[22] *Collins Dictionary of the English Language,* 2nd ed., ed. Patrick Hanks (London & Glasgow: Collins, 1986), p. 951.

[23] Mario Jacoby, *Jungian Psychotherapy and Contemporary Infant Research* (London: Routledge, 1999), p. 161.

[24] C. G. Jung, *Letters,* vol. 1 (Princeton, NJ: Princeton University Press, 1973), p. 542.

[25] Mae-Wan Ho, *The Rainbow and the Worm: The Physics of Organisms* (Singapore: World Scientific Publishing Co., 1993), p. 151.

[26] C. G. Jung, *Memories, Dreams, Reflections,* rev. ed., ed. Aniela Jaffé, trans. Richard and Clara Winston (New York: Vintage Books, 1989), p. 325.

[27] Emma Jung, "On the Nature of the Animus," trans. Cary F. Baynes, in *Animus and Anima: Two Essays by Emma Jung* (Dallas, Texas: Spring Publications, Inc., 1985), p. 36.

6

Creative Torment or Tormented Creativity: Robert Schumann and Nineteenth-Century German Romanticism

Laurel Morris

This chapter is about creativity, about creativity in psychic process, in artistic expression, and in the patternings common between them. I use the device of examining selected aspects of the life and work of a prodigiously creative man in the context of his historical milieu. The man is Robert Schumann; the context, romanticism in the early nineteenth century. One of the core concepts of German romanticism is *Witz*, meaning a linking and, to varying degrees, an amalgamating of opposites. *Witz* is a mode of thinking and expressing. It is mercurial, creative, and poetic, but it can also be unsettling. It demands and invites a vital imaginal involvement on the part of the listener or reader. Some connections strike like lightning; some seep in subtly, almost unnoticed; while others fall back into the unreceived. My subject invites expression through a "Witzian" mode; that is, through creatively linking elements of Schumann's life and work (particularly his music) and Jungian theory (particularly aspects of the alchemical and gnostic work) within the context of a fiery transformative period in history.

When I began to work on this topic, I was not prepared for the staggering degree of resonance between the images and patternings of early German romanticism and Schumann on one hand and those of analytical psychology on the other. These include, for example: duality, dialectical process, the mercurial element, the principle of correspondence, the use of historical patterns as an informing lens, multiple centers within an encompassing whole, the faculty of the imagination, the role of reminiscence, creative linking, and even the alchemical monstrum.[1] I have chosen to focus primarily on the theme of duality and related dynamics, and, in the music section, more specifically on imagination, creative linking, and reminiscence.

This historical period was a time of nuclear transformation in ways of thinking and feeling. In the thinking of Isaiah Berlin, German Romanticism is one of three "turning points" in the history of Western thought. Here, a turning point is "a radical change in the entire conceptual framework . . . new ideas, new words, new relationships in terms of which . . . the agonising problems and doubts of the past seem . . . [to] belong to a world which has gone."[2] The paradigm shift was from absolute to relative, objective to subjective, determined to self-directed. This revolutionary cultural shift of the early eighteenth century impacts us, our psyches, and the way we work as clinicians today. We often see this kind of turning point within individual psychic processes as well.

The classical sonata form prevailed in German music just prior to romanticism. It is a dramatic overarching form—a struggle between the tonic and the dominant that requires resolution and that, typically, has a cohesive movement that drives from beginning to end. This too shifted radically. As in the change away from reason as the ultimate authority that was embedded in the philosophy of Kant, likewise in music, new transformative energies appeared in isolated but radical departures from classical form. A primary example of this is Beethoven's song cycle *An die ferne Geliebte,* to which I will return shortly.

Analogous theoretical patternings are expressed in the alchemical paradigm of an ongoing suffering of the relation of opposites. This process of differentiation and integration—dissolving and coagulating, volatilizing and fixing—is creative, but it is not simply the making of something new. It is the paradox of making something new, which is, at the same time, that which it was all along, the *lapis exilis* at the beginning, the *lapis philosophorum* at the end.

Creative change consists of the process of movement out of preconscious wholeness. There is a stone that is no stone, a nonexistent god, a predifferentiated psychic content, an unlived aspect of the unique, individual but paradoxically universal ground plan. Then, as Jung quotes from Eckhart, "Only the Father, the God 'welling' out of the godhead, 'notices himself,' becomes 'beknown to himself' and 'confronts himself' as a Person."[3] This is a shift from one-sided perfection toward the inclusion of the "other." In discussing the god-image, Jung writes that it is "not something *invented*, it is an *experience*."[4] In other words, it happens to us, it wells up in us from deep within. If we don't "notice it," if it does not become "beknown" to us, it will sink or rise out of potential grasp and confrontation, out of linking and making. The welling up is not an action, but it is creative, the creativity of the unconscious. But the first stage of the created's creativity is the effectively generative act of "noticing himself."

This corresponds to the relation of the ego to the unconscious. The movement is out of unconsciousness, out of the state of the nonexistent god where the implicit capacity for "secondness" is not yet lived. The shift is away from the "suprareal"[5] into the real, into the territory of twoness, of process: separation, conflict, reconciliation, relatedness, coalescence, the coming into real being of that which already is and is not. This is the territory I define as the creative.

Although I am looking at the creative products of an individual of great musical genius, the greater interest in terms of psychic process (and analytic work) is that these patternings of creativity are reflective of the processes that allow us to become more truly ourselves. As the great Austrian pianist Artur Schnabel once said of great music, of music that attracted and engaged him, it is "better than it can be performed."[6] And we, in our "world-creating significance" are better than we can become. On the other hand, unplayed music, like the nonexistent god, doesn't exist until played —that is, until it is noticed, confronted, lived. Likewise, the potential for us, to a degree, is to "break the compulsion of the stars," to not just unconsciously, for good or ill, unfold according to plan, but to become creative participants in fulfilling the individual aspect of the godhead that each of us carries. It is my hope that within the limited scope of this chapter, I can communicate to you some of these aspects of creative striving in Schumann's life and work as well as a sense of their resonance with the creativity of the work that we are privy to and participate in everyday as clinicians.

The historical period of German romanticism was a time when the old ruling patterns could no longer express the life energy of the collective. At such points of radical change, the "fiery center"[7] (as Jung, citing Picinellus, puts it) with all of its dual propensities for creativity or destruction, breaks loose.

At this point in time, on 8 June 1810, Robert Schumann was born in the village of Zwickau in the eastern reaches of Germany. The quest of German romanticism for authenticity—for harmony with deep roots— was expressed in ideals of aesthetics and form. Typical gothic elements such

as gloomy moonlit nights, old ruins, lonely wanderers, and dual realities
were emphasized as well. There was a belief in the coexistence of natural
and supernatural realms, and obsession with ideas of the doppelganger,
inner division, intra-relatedness, creative madness, and even suicide as the
ideal of lived creative authenticity was pervasive. This dynamic juxtaposition
of the celestial and the infernal, the positive and the poisonous residing
side by side, is historically expressive of the image in *Aion* of "the fiery
centre in us from which creative or destructive influences come."[8] There
was (and is in psyche) a constant and perilous potential for the destructive
side of creative energies, the infernal aspect of compulsion—whether
coming from the shadow or from the anthropos to run amok.

Schumann was highly sensitive and, in a way, both typical of and more
extreme than his times. Unlike the tendency of the Zeitgeist, though, he
did not idealize creative madness. He feared madness profoundly. He was
drawn inexorably to reflection on and relationship to his inner voices out
of the necessity of his being. An extreme price was exacted. The insane
and the creative are both close to the reality of the inner other, to the god
level, and to the interplay between the opposites. The insane and the highly
creative, somewhat like the smiths of old (those who handled the fiery
infernal transformative powers), were honored or despised. In eighteenth-
century Germany, madness and creativity were seen to be linked and were
often revered. The romantic era replaced the priest with the artist as the
one who suffered the relation to the outer reaches, upper and lower. In
this sense, Schumann was fortunate, for though he was reviled and dismissed
in some quarters, he was beloved and recognized in others.

Schumann's personal life from the age of three on was a disturbing
mix of abandonment, family illness, and exposure to war with its
attendant horrors. He also experienced a classical education, wonderful
extraverted play with his brothers, and opportunity, though unguided,
to express himself creatively. Early on Schumann evidenced a dual nature,
a kind of personality number one and number two. One side was poetic,
pensive, shy, serious, and disciplined; the other, outgoing, energetic,
chaotic, and indulgent of both himself and others, particularly those close
to him.

Between his fifteenth and sixteenth years, Schumann's beloved sister
committed suicide and his revered father died suddenly. His fear of death
and disease became a morbid preoccupation. At seventeen, while still
mourning, Robert began to keep a diary. He describes writing to "fight
the painful hours [from] eating up memories of happier times."[9] His natural
introversion was developing into profound reflection and the pattern of

his life became increasingly characterized by a struggle between opposites so extreme as to be intolerable.

Fast forward to the spring of 1831, a time when the dance between opposite extremes in Schumann's life became manifest. He had not returned home for two years, and he had just contracted what seems to have been syphilis. Though he had been enrolled in university study, he had continued his frenzied path of self-education and self-expression, researching and beginning a play on Heloise and Abelard, working on a novel called *The Philistines and the Beggar King,* writing poems in the manner of Petrarch and Schiller, and completing and publishing his Opus 1, the Abegg Variations. The Abegg Variations give musical expression to a kind of cabalistic system of correspondences in which the musical notes correspond to letters of the alphabet. The combination of these note-letters in different permutations points to names and places, and the interlacing of themes is a hidden communication, similar to what would later be expressed in his *Carnaval.* The layering of correspondent meanings, the simultaneity of the manifest and the occult and the distant and the near as well as the interweaving of the concrete, the imaginal, and that which cannot even be imagined are dominant here.

In the midst of these myriad threatening and exhilarating energies, Schumann was immersed in reading and re-reading Jean Paul's *Adolescent Years.* He was taken with the idea of twin brothers who have diametrically opposed and complementary personalities. One brother— dutiful, shy, and poetic—stays home and studies, while the other— adventurous, satirical, and aggressive—leaves home and lives as a traveling musician. The two correspond to the two extremes of Schumann's personality. Notice here the themes of the double and, in the plot, rounds of separation and conjunction.

On Schumann's twenty-first birthday, he awoke feeling as though just born, sensing that "objective humanity wants to separate itself completely from the subjective, as if I'm standing between my existence and my appearance, between form and shadow."[10] Despairingly, he challenges his own spirit: "My genius, are you going to abandon me?"[11] Whereupon Florestan, mirroring the character of the extraverted brother in *Adolescent Years,* is "born."[12] A personification of one of the multiple centers of the personality had imaginally sprung forth, full blown.

Within the month, a second part-self was born, whom he called "Eusebius."[13] Eusebius, quite the opposite of Florestan, is rather like the introverted tender brother of Jean Paul's book. Schumann imaginally engaged these "personalities" to contend with the tension of his own inner division and to coalesce himself. He reengaged in disciplined study and work and made his first pass at writing music criticism, his famous "Hats off, gentlemen, a genius!" review of Chopin.[14] Structurally, he used the device of a conversation between Florestan and Eusebius. This review introduced Schumann the critic to the outer world with all of the originality and idiosyncrasy that was to mark his critical style.

Die Allgemeine Musikalische Zeitung, the conservative journal that published this review, had been ambivalent about it, but wishing to include youthful perspectives, did print it. However, no further opportunities to publish criticism were forthcoming from them to Schumann. In 1834, he began publishing his own music journal, *Die Neue Zeitschrift für Musik,* which was to become the most influential radical instrument of review of the time. He ran it nearly single-handedly for ten years. Much of his music criticism would be articulated by Florestan and Eusebius. Schumann's productivity attests to a level of functioning in the world that one would assume to be impossible given his depression and anxiety.

As great a contribution as his critical writings were, they are dwarfed by his compositions. The spectrum of resonances between concepts of analytical psychology and Schumann's life and times also applies, astonishingly, to his music as well. I will give three musical examples: first, of the faculty of the imagination and its role in the paradoxical making-real of the nonexistent; second, of creative linking and its relationship to fragmentation; and third, of the role of reminiscence. I am indebted here to the work of many fine theorists and musicologists, but most especially to Charles Rosen, John Daverio, and Bernhard Appel.

The faculty of the imagination is preeminent in both analytical psychology and German romanticism. The *Rosarium philosophorum* directs that the opus be performed *"per veram imaginationem et non phantasticam."*[15] Jung renders this as "with the true and not with the fantastic imagination,"[16] and elsewhere he distinguishes imagination from fantasy. Jung writes "a fantasy is your own invention and remains on the surface of personal things and conscious expectations. But . . . images have a life of their own. . . . All the time we are dependent upon the things that literally fall into our consciousness. . . . In German we call them *Einfälle.*"[17] This is the falling in, so to speak, of an idea. True imagining is the voice of the non-ego psyche expressed through images. It is expressive of the inner other or others and as such may be ego-distant or ego-near, dystonic or syntonic, destructive or creative. It is the territory of telos, of the expansion into oneself.

Schumann himself was a master of fluidity and linking in his creative process. On an ego level he was profoundly open and respectful of non-ego energies. His process of composing was, until his late twenties, largely through improvising for hours on end at the piano and working with the intuitive ideas, the *Einfälle,* of his improvisations. Thereafter he began to compose entirely in his head. For most of his life, he was also subject to hearing music—terrible music, heavenly music, eternal music. Descriptions of Schumann, particularly his self-observations, suggest an intensive inward turning of his attention toward these inner musical expressions. This hearing of the music was both receptive and creative. It came to him and he engaged it, bringing it from the "suprareal" to the "real."

Both analytical psychology and the music of Schumann emphasize the labor of true imagination: analytical psychology, through working with psyche's symbol-forming capacity; Schumann, through composing in a way that demands that the listener hear, actually hear, through imagining that which is not there on a concrete level. In both cases the nonconcrete "real" is brought into the realm of real experience through the function of the imagination.

This is analogous, in the language of the Gnostics, to the nonexistent god emerging from the realm of the suprareal into the real. The faculty of true imagination has latent within it the attracting substance, magnet that resonates to the preexistent. This is the agency of the hearing of the "absent melody," of humanity's capacity to find and make the music that is there but is hovering outside concrete reality.

For example, in Schumann's *Humoreske,* we see the designation "*innere Stimme*" (inner voice). Charles Rosen parses this beautifully on a musical level. In the written music we see three staves: the uppermost for the right hand, the lowest for the left, and in the middle the melody that is never played. (See Fig. 6.1; you can hear a recording on Track 17 of the CD that accompanies this book.)[18] The melody is to be imagined. It is, as Rosen says, "embodied in the upper and lower parts as a kind of after-resonance—out of phase, delicate, and shadowy. What one hears is the echo of an unperformed melody. . . . The middle part . . . the *innere Stimme* . . . is both interior and inward . . . an inner voice that is never exteriorized. It has its being within the mind and its existence only through its echo."[19] We see/hear out of the interplay of opposites as expressed by the notes of the left and the right hands together the emergence of a third that is of both and yet neither.

Creative linking, the second of my musical illustrations, paradoxically figures strongly in Schumann's work with the musical fragment, a form particular to the German romantic movement. Franz Brendel, in an 1845

Fig. 6.1

review of Schumann, contrasts his work with that of the classical composers. He describes the latter as being characterized by a "comprehensive whole[ness]."[20] It is as though the achieved coagulation/fixation, the achieved wholeness of the classical period, had to give way to the next round of coming apart, being dismembered to accommodate the unfolding and making of musical history. Schumann was the primary promulgator of the musical fragment. For him it was a consciously cultivated reflection of the necessity of foregoing the completeness of the "untroubled whole,"[21] a conscious choosing to work with fragments and fragmenting energies and simultaneously suffering and celebrating the product as an expression of creative process, something underway, not completed. This form is exemplified by pieces such as *Carnaval,* which consists of a series of independent pieces that are made into a whole in surprising new ways. The disparate parts are sharply juxtaposed. Though there are unifying elements, there is also a quality of the monstrous. It is a musical expression resonant with the figure of Mercurius in his/her monstrous aspect. Mercurius is fluid. He/she is the "begotten of the hermaphroditic seed of the Macrocosm"[22] and is "a paradoxical double."[23] In Arabic alchemy the mercurial element is depicted as a composite beast that holds the key to renewal and transformation.

Carnaval simultaneously expresses fragmentation and the press toward wholeness. Two transition points between subsections of *Carnaval* illustrate this. The first is between subsections expressing "Eusebius" and then "Florestan." And then between "Florestan" (Track 18) and "Coquette" (Track 19). (See Fig. 6.2 and Fig. 6.3.) Analogously, at points of development when the ruling principle (the "untroubled whole") gives way, the psyche is thrown into the suffering of new and various part-selves whose relationship to the ego may be difficult. The potential is for the emergence of a richer, more flexible, co-creative existence to emerge. This process, as a rule, involves varying degrees of pain.

In the dynamics of Schumann's music, as in those of the psyche, the agent of the connecting of opposite or disparate elements is of central importance. This is our mercurial element in its myriad forms. As noted above, for the German romantics, this was called *Witz.* Etymologically *Witz* goes back to the old Swedish, meaning wisdom or knowledge.[24] It came to mean cleverness, quick wittedness, and now means joke. For the romantics, it meant that which links and to varying degrees amalgamates disparate elements. Jean Paul describes it as a "lightning flash,"[25] the agency behind the discovery of "relationships between incommensurable magnitudes, likeness between the physical and spiritual worlds."[26] Schlegel says it is "the synthesis of dichotomies."[27]

This is akin to and derives from the same spirit underlying and pressing the Zeitgeist of the time as expressed in Hegelian dialectic. Webster's Dictionary defines Hegelian dialectic as "the process by which a concept or the realization of a concept passes over into and is preserved and fulfilled by its opposite."[28] This is a "witty" (that is, a creative) act that resonates to the fact of the coincidence of opposites and is able to find and make

Fig 6.2

likenesses out of opposites. *Witz,* the psychic transformation through the agency of our Mercurius, and Hegelian dialectics all function through an intuitive creative linking. They all draw on the fact of the reality of the coincidence of opposites. In order to link, the bridging agency must have something (however slight or great) in common with each of the opposing

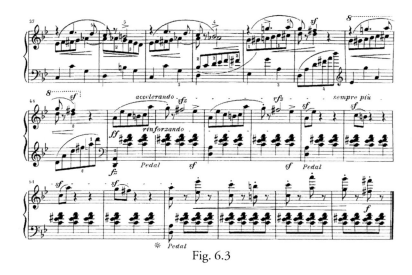

Fig. 6.3

elements. By virtue of its flashing recognition of likeness, however distant, it reaches across. This is a core creative function in our work. Fluidly resonating to the whole field of *materia* in a way that allows slight or distant degrees of likeness to reverberate enhances the constellation of these renewing energies. The mercurial, like *Witz*, tends to function as a kind of intuitive *Einfall*, which requires the mating labor of sensation, thinking, and feeling.

In Schumann's music, *Witz* plays a central role. In the *Novelletten*, it supports the simultaneous preserving of the self-conscious quality of fragmentation and the passing of the fragmentary elements over into their opposite, a unity. Daverio parses an example of *Witz* thusly: "The F-major idea at measure 17, a chromatically enriched descending pentachord, points in two directions."[29] Viewed through the lens afforded us by the eighteenth-century sense of *Witz*, we hear here a musical element that, by virtue of reaching out in opposing directions, finds and makes of itself a unifying element) (Fig. 6.4, Track 20). He continues, "It is at once the source for the rising chromatic tetrachord of measures 25-32 [Fig. 6.5; Track 21] and the descending diatonic tetrachord of measures 73-76 [Fig. 6.6; Track 22] which in turn generates, upon reappearing in the coda, a fully chromatic descent through the octave from C# to C#" (Fig. 6.7; Track 23). We hear an almost magical simultaneity of movement in opposite directions.

Fig. 6.4

Fig. 6.5

Fig. 6.6

Fig. 6.7

Creative linking of opposing images and energies is a central aspect of analytic work, just as creative linking of disparate musical elements is central to the creation of a piece such as the *Novelletten*. In either case, the mercurial energy or the romantic *Witz* supports a press toward the amalgamation and differentiated elaboration of a new wholeness. Creative linking also takes place imaginally in both Schumann's music and analytic practice through reminiscence. This is expressible by the form of mercurial energies that Jung alludes to in *Aion* as "leading to the other shore," his translation of the Indian *para-da*.[30]

I will now reach back into Schumann's musical past to open the issue of musical quotation, of reminiscence, as a creative linking function. Schumann's much-revered Beethoven, though preeminently a classical composer, forecasts the romantic style in his song cycle, *An die ferne Geliebte* (To the Distant Beloved). It opens with a hopeless seeking into the mists of the past (Fig. 6.8; Track 24). While Beethoven, with this

Fig. 6.8

reminiscence, reaches back longingly to "that which will never be," he is, at the same time, reaching forward. By virtue of the fulfillment of his capacity to feel and to express, he becomes more fully himself. That fullness is also concretely realized in the product, the song. In this sense, the reminiscence looks back but fulfills the present. Finally in the last verse we come to the fulfillment of the theme (Fig. 6.9; Track 25).

In holding the duality of the reminiscence, the efficacy of the memory as mercurial gets activated. The medicine is made through the relation of the opposites, whether through sharp juxtaposition as in the monstrum

Fig. 6.9

or through any of the forms the linking takes as the process unfolds. Jung's perspective on regression is germane here. He writes of "reminiscences . . . [as] . . . staging . . . an ostensible etiology" for the current conflict.[31] There are, throughout the opus, throughout individual process, expressions of what one has always been and will (while potentially being utterly transformed) remain. Reminiscences express the past, the current, and the emergent. Held in this way, reminiscences become an aspect of the mercurial agency par excellence.

Schumann's *Fantasie,* opus 17, is partially organized around reminiscence and exemplifies its transformative aspect. This musical quote from *An die ferne Geliebte,* this memory of Beethoven's longing and his paradoxical unfulfilled fulfillment, is part of Schumann's personal history as well as part of the collective history of German music. On a personal level he resonated strongly with Beethoven's frustration and longing. He and Clara had declared their affection for each other at the end of 1835, but Clara's father forbade them from communicating in any way. Opus 17 was completely sketched four months later. They were to be separated for eighteen months. Schumann worked steadfastly and productively all the while, yearning for his Clara and not knowing if they would ever be united, at times not even having a sense of surety in her commitment to him. Finally Clara overcame her submissiveness, and they became engaged in August 1837. He completed Opus 17 in March 1838. In a letter to Clara, he said: "The first movement is surely the most passionate work I ever did, a deep lament about you."[32]

At the beginning of Opus 17 Schumann quotes this motto from Friedrich Schlegel: *"Durch alle Toene toenet / Im bunten Erdentraum / Ein leiser Toen gezogen / Fuer den der heimlisch lauschet"* (Through all the tones that sound in Earth's colored dreams, One quiet tone comes forth for him who secretly listens.).[33] In the *Fantasie,* we are invited and forewarned. There is something inherently dramatic in the opening. Its violence could not have happened in classical music. On the page the left hand looks quite orderly, but in your ear you hear a wild shape-shifting blur foretelling the shape of the *An die ferne Geliebte,* laying the pathway to its fulfillment (Fig. 6.10; Track 26). This theme is felt throughout the *Fantasie* as it mercurially blends into the background, pops in unexpectedly, asserts itself, and sacrifices itself to its unfolding.

Fig. 6.10

   This passage is a reminiscence that has a life of its own. It shifts and is elaborated in the retelling. It reaches back to a memory and to the correspondent underlying capacity for desire and fulfillment. It expresses the current situation as well. Schumann is longing for union and fulfillment with Clara. He is longing for unity and fulfillment within himself. Though the home key of the piece is C Major, the key remains ambiguous throughout the body of the whole movement. It is never clearly established, which gives a sense of searching and remaining unfulfilled (Fig. 6.11; Track

27). Only at this moment is the root-position C major chord clearly present. We hear a simultaneity of nearness, the known, and the ever-so-distant, echoing even that part of the self that will never be made manifest.

Fig. 6.11

The agency of the creative function lies in the dynamic field of the self in its twoness. The path of these creative and destructive energies is expressible in what Jung calls the *longissima via*: the way full of "fateful detours and wrong turnings . . . not straight but snakelike, a path that unites the opposites . . . whose labyrinthine twists and turns are not lacking in terrors. [This is where] . . . we meet with those experiences which are said to be 'inaccessible.'"[34] This path is what Schumann was compelled to by his own fiery center.

This brings us to the tragic last part of Schumann's life. Although he had experienced cycles of depression and creative furor as well as three periods of breakdown, the diminishment he suffered during the last year and a half have a radically different quality. His symptom picture conforms to that of tertiary syphilis. Late in 1853, Schumann was again struggling with overwhelming bouts of depression and withdrawal. By carnival time in February, he was under careful watch at home.

One morning he slipped out in his pajamas, walked to the footbridge over the Rhine, and offered his handkerchief as payment for the toll. This odd behavior would normally have alerted passersby to his duress, but, because of the revelry and costumes of carnival, it went unnoticed. He walked to the middle of the bridge and plunged into the icy waters. After being rescued, perhaps unfortunately, he was besieged by fears of hurting

Clara and asked to be hospitalized. Schumann was committed to Endenich, a small progressive asylum near Bonn.

It is not possible to piece together with surety what the effect of the treatment was. However, from the perspective of contemporary standards, it was misguided—heartless really. Particularly after the first brief period, Schumann was largely calm and lucid, but he did continue to have terrible episodes of raving, of loss of control and lucidity, as well as a plethora of physical symptoms. To me the most heart-wrenching aspect of the treatment stemmed from the doctors' conviction that it would be too upsetting for him to see those closest to him, particularly Clara.

Schumann was allowed very few visitors, possibly as few as a dozen from March 1854 until his death in July 1856. In a letter written by a friend after Schumann's death, he says of his last visit with him: "When I was preparing to go, he took me aside mysteriously in a corner of the room (although we were not observed) and told me that he was longing to leave there; he had to leave Endenich, for the people there had no idea at all what he meant and wanted."[35]

This picture of Schumann, this creative giant, so painfully reduced at the end of his life, is unbearable and humbling. Perhaps it is due to the destructive aspect of the "fiery centre" taken out of the daily round where it carries the potential for renewal. In any case, it is a phenomenon we are all faced with in large and small ways both daily and at the conclusion of our lives, for good or for ill.

An attitude of humanity, respect, and humility toward this kind of suffering and loss is expressed in a letter Schumann wrote as a young man of twenty-four. He had had several recent encounters with an old composer, Johann Ludwig Boehner. He describes him as a nonconformist, an original, one who is self-sabotaging, prickly, and "as famous as Beethoven." Schumann says: "The day before yesterday [Boehner] fantasized for several hours with me at my house. Here and there the old lightning showed. Otherwise all is dark and desolate." And he likens him to "the old lion with a splinter in his paw."[36] His words ironically but touchingly describe a condition of fallen grandeur and diminished creative power, remarkably similar to Schumann's own just shy of twenty-two years later.

However, it would be one-sided to leave Schumann this way. So I call upon Goethe to celebrate the inspiring Robert Schumann: his creative energy, his ferocity and tenderness, his levity and seriousness: "By Apollo! It must have been a serious thing to dance such a pipe."[37]

───────────

NOTES

A prior version of this paper was first published in *Cambridge 2001: Proceedings of the Fifteenth International Congress for Analytical Psychology* (Daimon Verlag, 2003) and is used here by permission of Daimon Verlag.

Most of my sources were untranslated at the time of writing this chapter. Where other sources are not cited, the translations are mine, made with the guidance and participation of Ursula Meyer, a teacher of German and a specialist in early-nineteenth-century German, without whose help I could not have dealt with the translations.

[1] "Monstrum" is an alchemical term that refers to the stage of pairing opposites into one in a not-yet-integrated and hence monstrous conjunction of opposites.

[2] Isaiah Berlin, *The Sense of Reality: Studies in Ideas and Their History* (New York: Farrar, Strauss and Giroux, 1996), p. 168.

[3] Jung, "Gnostic Symbols of the Self," in *The Collected Works of C. G. Jung*, vol. 9ii, *Aion: Researches into the Phenomenology of the Self*, trans. R. F. C. Hull (Princeton, NJ: Princeton University Press, 1978), §301. (Hereafter *CW* 9ii.).

[4] *Ibid.*, §303.

[5] *Ibid.*, §301.

[6] Artur Schnabel, *My Life and Music* (1961; repr., New York: Dover, 1988), p. xiv.

[7] Jung, "The Fish in Alchemy," in *CW* 9ii, §212.

[8] *Ibid.*

[9] R. Schumann, *Robert Schumann Tagebücher*, vol. 1, *1827–1836*, ed. Gerd Nauhaus (Frankfurt a/Main: Stroemfeld/Roter Stern, 1987), p. 21.

[10] R. Schumann, *Robert Schumann Tagebücher*, vol. 2, *1837–1847*, ed. Gerd Nauhaus (Frankfurt a/Main: Stroemfeld/Roter Stern, 1987), p. 339.

[11] *Ibid.*

[12] *Ibid.*, p. 344.

[13] *Ibid.*

[14] K. [*sic*] Schumann, "Ein Opus II," *Allgemeine Musikalische Zeitung* 33 (7 December 1831), columns 805–808.

[15] Quoted in Jung, "The Psychic Nature of the Alchemical Work," in *The Collected Works of C. G. Jung*, vol. 12, *Psychology and Alchemy*, trans. R. F. C. Hull (Princeton, NJ: Princeton University Press, 1968), p. 257n36. (Hereafter *CW* 12.)

[16] *Ibid.*

[17] Jung, "The Tavistock Lectures, Lecture 5," in *The Collected Works of C. G. Jung,* vol. 18, *The Symbolic Life. Miscellaneous Writings,* trans. R. F. C. Hull (Princeton, NJ: Princeton University Press, 1976), §396.

[18] I am grateful to Steven Masi for his generosity and musicality in providing these recorded passages.

[19] Charles Rosen, *The Romantic Generation* (Cambridge, MA: Harvard University, 1995), p. 829.

[20] F. Brendel, "Robert Schumann mit Rücksicht auf Mendelssohn-Bartholdy und die Entwicklung der modernen Tonkunst überhaupt," *Neue Zeitschrift für Musik* 22 (1845), p. 82.

[21] John Daverio, *Nineteenth-Century German Music and the German Romantic Ideology* (New York: Schirmer Books, 1993), p. 87.

[22] Jung, "The Spirit Mercurius," subsection "The Dual Nature of Mercurius," in *The Collected Works of C. G. Jung,* vol. 13, *Alchemical Studies,* trans. R. F. C. Hull (Princeton, NJ: Princeton University Press, 1967), §268.

[23] Jung, "Alchemical Symbolism in the History of Religion," subsection "The Unconscious as the Matrix of Symbol," in *CW* 12, §517.

[24] *Herkunftswoerterbuch der Deutschen Sprache,* ed. G. Drosdowski (Mannheim: Duden, 1997), p. 818.

[25] Jean Paul [Richter], *Sämtliche Werke,* 5 vols. (Munich: C. Hanser, 1959–1963), 1:197–199.

[26] *Ibid.,* 1:172.

[27] F. Schlegel, *Kritische Friedrich Schlegel Ausgabe,* ed. Ernst Behler, Jean-Jacque Anstett, and Hans Eichner, 35 vols. (Munich, Paderborn, Wien: Schoeningh, 1958), 18:262.

[28] *Webster's Ninth New Collegiate Dictionary* (Springfield, MA: Merriam-Webster, 1983).

[29] J. Daverio, *Nineteenth-Century German Music and the German Romantic Ideology,* p. 85.

[30] Jung, "The Fish and Alchemy," §237.

[31] Jung, "The Theory of Psychoanalysis," subsection "The Regression of Libido," in *The Collected Works of C. G. Jung,* vol. 4, *Freud and Psychoanalysis,* trans. R. F. C. Hull (Princeton, NJ: Princeton University Press, 1985), §365.

[32] J. W. Wasielewski, *Robert Schumann: Eine Biographie,* 4th ed. (Leipzig: Breitkopf und Härtel, 1906), p. 171.

[33] Schumann, *Fantasy Pieces op. 73 for Piano and Clarinet* (Munich: G. Henle Verlag), p. 1.

³⁴ Jung, "Introduction: The Religious and Psychological Problems of Alchemy," in *CW* 12, §6.

³⁵ E. Hanslick, "Robert Schumann in Endenich [1899]," reprinted in *Schumann and His World*, ed. Larry Todd (Princeton: Princeton University Press, 1994), p. 278.

³⁶ Robert Schumann, *Jugendbriefe von Robert Schumann: Nach den originalen mitgetheilt,* ed. C. Schumann, 2nd ed. (Leipzig: Breitkopf und Härtel, 1886), p. 254.

³⁷ Quotation attributed to Goethe.

7

"I wrote what I heard": Late Thoughts on *The Rite of Spring*

KEVIN O'CONNELL

*T*he Rite of Spring is a piece of iconoclasm that has become an icon. In the culture of the twentieth century, it is perhaps the only musical work that has achieved this status. Schoenberg's *Pierrot Lunaire*, which premiered within a few months of *The Rite*, has exerted a comparable (if not greater) influence upon composers. But Schoenberg's masterpiece has remained something of a trade secret among musicians. We hear *Pierrot* at second hand in Berg's *Wozzeck* and in many Hollywood film scores. There is poetic justice in Schoenberg spending his last years in Hollywood, a fate that was by no means the only thing he shared with his greatest compositional rival. Curiously, *The Rite of Spring* owed something of its iconic status to Hollywood also. Walt Disney used the score in *Fantasia*, bringing it to the mass cinema audience. Stravinsky sued Disney over the mutilation of his score. He had failed to realize that when high art enters the commercial arena it is the arena that dictates the terms.

The Rite has been so much analyzed that people are running out of things to say about it. The piece has been the subject of extraordinarily detailed analyses by Olivier Messiaen, Pierre Boulez, George Perle, and Allen Forte, to name a few. These analyses by musicians who bring their personal creative biases to the task are a fascinating subject in themselves. Everyone re-creates *The Rite* in his own image. This is another aspect of the work's iconographic status. We no longer hear *The Rite* simply by itself; we hear others' ways of hearing it.

Here I introduce a controversial point. When a work becomes iconic, it may tell us as much about its limitations as about its strengths. Indeed, some works win iconic status by the very fact of their limitations. Satie's *Gymnopédies* are the classic instance of this: three slow dances, all in the same meter and tempo, which not only make no attempt to introduce variation or development but scorn those ideas as excrescences. This may explain why the dances become progressively boring. By this I do not mean a criticism of these pieces. It is part of Satie's originality to be deeply interested in boredom. His objection to Wagnerian musical drama and late romanticism generally was that it was too interesting. To avoid boredom, Satie would have to intervene with the technical means known to every composer—the development of themes and motifs, modulation, the introduction of contrasting material—to maintain interest. With a resolve that becomes the main fascination of the work, Satie stays his hand, and listening becomes an experience similar to that of listening to a clock tick.

But in this context I mean "limitation" also in the more everyday sense of things the composer did not (and perhaps could not) do. So let us try rephrasing our argument more argumentatively. Why are iconic works often not the best works? The reasons are many. Iconic works often present an argument in simplified form: complication is avoided; gestures are confined to the easily graspable; they distill rather than elaborate. Such works embody an aspect of what John Keats called "negative capability." As I will come back to this concept several times in the course of this discussion, I want to first explain it and then adapt it.

By "negative capability" Keats meant an artist's ability to live easily with contradictory ideas without invoking the agency of reason to decide between them. The artist that he thought quintessentially embodied this characteristic was William Shakespeare. I want to use Keats's beautiful expression in a slightly different sense, but one that I hope does not violate the spirit of what he meant by it. By "negative capability" I mean the artist's emptying the work of all or most of the traditional aspects, what we might term its content—in the case of music, melodies, motifs, development, and form—without feeling the need to give the listener any immediate and satisfying alternatives. Here I am getting close to the often-expressed objection to new works, that it is not what the artist has put in that has caused offense but what he has left out. Where is the melody, where the logical harmony, where the form?

At the premiere of the *Rite* in 1913, by the time the orchestra had reached the bottom of the first page of the score, the elderly Camille Saint-Saëns had already left the theatre. People are surprised to learn that the composer of *Carnival of the Animals* was still alive in 1913, let alone that he attended the premiere of *The Rite of Spring*. What did he object to? The opening of the work is Stravinsky's version of a Lithuanian folk song scored for bassoon. But the sound is extraordinary. In the first place, the bassoon is playing more than a full octave above its customary range, producing an unpleasantly nasal sound. Why could Stravinsky not have given the melody to another wind instrument in whose range it naturally lies, such as the flute or oboe? In the second place, the tune itself can hardly be parsed as a real tune in the traditional sense, with a satisfying arc-shape, balanced phrases, and so on. In fact, Stravinsky's tune, with its insistence on returning to the opening C, seems to be all beginning without any real continuation, a fact you can quickly verify by singing it and trying to get beyond the first phrase with accuracy. The tune is like auditory snakes and ladders where a snake keeps bringing you back to the first note.

Having defined melody as a tuneless tune, Stravinsky proceeds in the first dance of *The Rite*, "The Dance of the Young Girls," to define harmonic progression as progressionless harmony. This dance is based entirely on one chord. What musicians call a chord progression requires a minimum of two chords so that you can move from one to the other, thus establishing contrast and tension between them. In fact, the Stravinsky chord is really two chords stated simultaneously rather than successively. One could say that it is a chord progression of one. With no other chord to move to, Stravinsky is forced to repeat, the most primitive of all the means of musical extension.

To this catalogue of negatives we must add a third, that of rhythmically undifferentiated rhythm. "The Dance of the Young Girls" is entirely in two-four time, making it the longest stretch of metrically regular music in the ballet. The chord thuds along at a regular four quavers to the bar played by the strings. Against this the horns try to introduce some rhythmic tension by hitting the occasional off-beat quaver. (Disney in his film illustrates these horn chords with popping volcanoes.) But this syncopation only serves to emphasize the underlying mechanical repetition and monotony. The bassoons try to introduce an element of contrast, but they do so merely by arpeggiating the notes of the chord. Meanwhile, the remorseless quavers pulse on.

The ballet is well launched. But in a sense, nothing has yet happened. Not only are the elements that I have described strange, they do not convey any sense of an articulate musical form. I have said that the opening theme is all beginning without any sense of continuation. This may be said of the ballet as a whole. In all the short sections of which *The Rite* is made up, the music seems to consist of beginnings with little in the way of further argument or extrapolation. I believe it is this lack that many listeners felt in Paris in 1913. Their need for discourse was denied.

In summary, it is easy to describe all the things *The Rite* not only does not do but resolutely avoids doing. Avoidance was not invented by Stravinsky. The avoidance of expectations is a staple ploy of classical music; for example, the development section of a sonata form is predicated on the avoidance of the tonic key, with the proviso that the expectation is fulfilled in the recapitulation. But in *The Rite,* Stravinsky seems hell bent on not only avoiding but denying the listener's expectations. The listener wants A, and Stravinsky is happy to oblige by giving him B.

I want to suggest that the pressure of response with which listeners invest *The Rite* says something negative about it. It will I hope be clear that I am not using the word "negative" exclusively in its pejorative sense, though I am not wholly avoiding it either. The truth is, it seems to me, that *The Rite* is in some ways a vacuous masterpiece. I use the epithet vacuous with the literal implication of a space that has been vacated. In *The Rite,* much of the furniture of traditional musical discourse—melodies, harmonic progressions, modulations, organic structures—has been unceremoniously shunted out the door. But strikingly, Stravinsky has avoided what might have been the overwhelming urge to replace it with something that would compensate the listener for its loss. With a certain perversity, this absence is precisely what we have most come to value in the work. We have grown accustomed to the space. I routinely receive essays from students stating or implying that *The Rite* is basically the only piece of twentieth-century music that matters. It is as if negative capability has become the only capability.

This quality of vacuity is evident in another and more damaging sense. I challenge any listener who has heard *The Rite* twenty times to say that he still finds new things in it. By this I am not referring to the arcane structural aspects that have made the score a rich hunting ground for composers and analysts. I mean the ordinary qualities—emotional, spiritual—that we find in any piece of music. The perennial definition of a masterpiece is that you can discover new things in it no matter how often you hear it. I think we romanticize this notion too much. There are passages in Beethoven's symphonies that I used to thrill to and that now bore me because I have heard them too often. That said, we can concede the general point. In a masterpiece, even the familiar can come as a wonderful surprise.

There is a moment in the first movement of Brahms's D minor piano concerto where Brahms with absolute deliberation sets up the return of the opening theme. And the theme duly returns, but harmonized "wrongly" with an inverted dominant seventh chord instead of the expected tonic chord. As often as I hear this work, this moment makes the hair on the back of my neck stand up. I doubt if this is the kind of revelation that listeners get from *The Rite of Spring*. As it is a music of beginnings, so its wonders are the immediately obvious ones. The sense of the conventional musical landscape being dynamited is in fact a large part of the aesthetic pleasure the work has to offer. To put it another way, *The Rite*'s constructiveness remains compelling precisely because of the amount of destructiveness it incorporates.

Yet a major qualification arises when we discuss *The Rite* as an act of destruction, for we are in danger of portraying the work as a piece of naive anarchy. Soon after *The Rite,* the world was to become acquainted with this kind of anarchy in the shape of Dada. *The Rite* seems very far removed from the spirit of Dada. The work is a negative statement that resolutely refuses the final embrace of negativism. How is this so?

Stravinsky's explanations of the creation of *The Rite* are themselves interesting. He famously described himself as "the vessel through which *The Rite* passed." This is an almost mystical (and for Stravinsky oddly passive) idea of the creative role. He seems to say that *The Rite of Spring* had to happen and that God used him as the agent of its happening. Much has been made of Stravinsky's belligerent feelings toward the Austro-German tradition in music, feelings that were particularly strong at the time of *The Rite*. But musicology has since uncovered a similarly reckless approach to his native Russian folk traditions. The six or seven traditional melodies that have so far been detected in the work are treated with nothing like the scholarly respect that Bartok accorded Hungarian folk material. On the contrary, Stravinsky's brutal adaptations of some of his folk songs suggest that he does not even like them very much: the Lithuanian tune at the start of the work is a good example. Stravinsky is not interested in the individual identity of the tunes. He does not care if we "spot the melody." The melodies are merely one more raw material. Essentially, *The Rite* is a furnace in which all the sources, melodic and rhythmic, are melted down into a new alloy.

Whatever the explosive quality of the inspiration, *The Rite* is also one of the most consciously constructed works of the twentieth century. Stravinsky was still tampering with it in the 1940s. Another of Stravinsky's remarks about the work, made much later, is interesting: "I heard, and I wrote what I heard." Again, this suggests a preexistent work, which Stravinsky had then only to transcribe to paper. We know that he was able to play the most metrically dizzy part of the whole score, the concluding "Sacrificial Dance" before he found out how to write it down. His final notation of it is a miracle of logic, but the difference between hearing and writing down what he had heard suggests the opening of a gap between the rhythmically palpable and the visually communicable that for composers has been getting wider ever since. The composer's inner demon is at war with the outwardly communicable. When the outwardly communicable loses that war, the result is Dada and the autistic appeal to the integrity of the inner demon: "I say (or scream) it is so, therefore it is so." Stravinsky was deeply suspicious of that kind of plea. He always believed that even the most fugitive invention must and could submit to the demands of being communicated, which for a composer means in the first instance the demands of the notated musical score. It is no surprise that writing down *The Rite* was in many respects a more demanding task than the actual invention of the music.

Why then is *The Rite* considered a "primitive" work? As I have already said, the work depends heavily on the most primitive form of musical extension, repetition of the idea. This technique indicates yet another absence, which Schoenberg (who disliked the work) must surely have felt. This is the lack of development of the motif, which, since Bach, had been the mainstay—the conversational coinage, so to speak—of musical discourse. In fact, Stravinsky's modus operandi in *The Rite* can seem precariously like that of many an amateur composer. Harmonies move in parallel with one another, ignoring the basic law of contrary motion between soprano and bass. Long stretches of the work are based on one harmony (the "Dance of the Young Girls" is only the most extreme example of this), with very little modulation. Melodies circle around the same few pitches. Coming back to Saint-Saëns, one senses that from his perspective, Stravinsky was a composer who could not write real music. In the tight circle of professional music there are few charges that inspire more fear than that of plain technical incompetence. It was part of Stravinsky's daring to risk precisely this charge.

If I have stressed the negative in these comments, I want to conclude by drawing a boundary around it. Against the anarchistic, Stravinsky continues to emphasize the idea of *poesis,* or making. The artist makes things. The attraction of *The Rite of Spring* for us is that it remains on the near side of the divide between *poesis* and anarchy while including more from the far side of the divide than perhaps any other musical work has managed to do.

NOTES

This paper was first read at the Carl Gustav Jung Conference in the Swiss Federal Institute of Technology, Zurich, in July 2008.

8

Music, Mind, and Psyche

Paul W. Ashton

In my imagination, the mind, which I think of as the seat of reason, thinking, and intellect, resides in the brain and is dependent on brain functioning for its existence. Psyche implies something much broader—the word encompasses ideas of spirit and soul as well as intellect— and psyche extends outside of the body and brain. Anything that comes to consciousness does so through the brain; an emotion felt, an intuition experienced, a sensation sensed, a memory evoked, even a movement performed is done so through brain activity. But there are synchronistic events that occur outside of the individual, for example when a complex has been activated, and the only way for these to be stopped is for the complex to be resolved or brought to consciousness. This seems to prove the extension of psyche outside of soma.

Music affects us psychologically, not only through its "structural" effect on the mind/brain, but also through less easily defined areas such as mood and meaning. In addition, music can work transpersonally and affect spirit too.

Music also works between people, so that when individuals listen to music "in concert," an enhancement of the effects of music occurs. There are two words, "harmony" and "unison," that describe this being-together musically. "Harmony" allows for differences in individuals who can nevertheless come together with each other in a congruent and acceptable way. "Unison," on the other hand, implies sameness; individuality is lost and the group members sing or sound identical notes, or the octave of those notes, together. Martial music, national anthems, and the "war cries" before sporting clashes tend to encourage union through unison, through the obliteration of difference. (There are a variety of sayings that express this idea: "United we stand, divided we fall"; "In unity is strength"; "All for one and one for all." But, as Doug Floyd reminds us, "You don't get harmony when everybody sings the same note."[1])

An art teacher of mine gave us an exercise in which she set out about six sheets of blank paper. A different person started off each sheet with whatever mark they felt inclined to make and after a few minutes we moved to the next sheet and drew or painted on that. Slowly the sheets were filled by "co-constructed" works and we ended with six absolutely different paintings where each person's input had its significance. In a similar vein, the film *As It Is in Heaven* portrayed a village choir that was taken over by a retired orchestra conductor.[2] His aim was to teach each person to sing with his or her "true" voice, and the resultant production soared to the heavens. It was a vision of "all-together-ness" not through unison but through mutually valued difference.

Music can be thought of as "sounds made meaningful" (some would say "sounds made pleasant"), and it is that meaningfulness or pleasantness that differentiates music from "noise." But that meaningfulness is something learned, not absolute, and at each stage in musical history any composer with new ideas has been denigrated. It is scarcely believable that in their own times neither Bach nor Mozart were considered to be "the greatest" and revered as they are today. And this is attributable to the fact that part of their "greatness" resided in their abilities to move music on, to break the rules and move us out of a rut. Changing the rules of harmony meant that at first their music did not sound so "good," but the changes they wrought have long since become an established norm. Now it is more modern composers such as Stravinsky, Prokofiev, or Schoenberg who sound "wrong" at first hearing.

There are those who think of all creation as a product of sound vibration,[3] and the South African artist Lyn Smuts has found a way of making sound visible. She sets a metal plate vibrating by bowing it with a double bass bow, letting sand on its horizontal surface dance until it creates a new pattern. Lyn then embeds that sand pattern in a sheet of fine clay, which she fires. Thus she fixes the sound, giving it a permanent shape.

Music is indeed a fount of creativity. This is suggested by the very word "music," which had its origin in the nine Muses of classical Greece, the inspiring powers of the liberal arts. Polyhymnia presided over the music of sacred songs, including both harmony and singing, and Terpsichore was the goddess of dance and music.

Music is both a thinking and a feeling art. Those who have studied music tend to approach it with their left brains, analyzing and criticizing it, whereas those with little formal training tend to be engaged by music's capacity to evoke feeling; for them, undirected music listening is a right-brain activity. And yet, in both groups, when a particular aspect of music is concentrated on, for example, melody, harmony, or rhythm, similar areas of the brain "light up" on functional brain imaging. According to Oliver Sacks, music is the one art form whose effects can be detected on an MRI scan of the brain. Musicians have a thicker corpus callosum than do non-musicians. The corpus callosum carries the fibers that link the left and right cerebral hemispheres, and its thickness in musicians attests to the fact that music stimulates both left and right sides of the brain and not just in those sections that connect the left and right motor areas.[4]

The left brain is thought to be concerned with abstract thought, logic, and reasoning and the right brain with pattern recognition, feeling, and the sense of awe. In other words, apart from the sensory and motor areas that are more or less mirror images of each other, each side of the brain has well-defined functions. The religious sense is one of those functions experienced through the right side of the brain. Allan Schore, the renowned neuropsychologist, goes so far as to suggest that while the left cerebral cortex is the seat of consciousness, the right brain is "the biological substrate of the human unconscious."[5] So perhaps one could extrapolate and suggest that because becoming proficient in playing or listening to music results in a greater connectedness between left and right sides of the brain, that proficiency enhances the link between consciousness and the unconscious, or between humanity and God, or the ego and the Self.

The classical analytical psychology enterprise is aimed at making the unconscious conscious, and we use our egos (in our left brains where consciousness resides) to engage with the unconscious in order to effect these changes in consciousness. This is despite the warning from Jung that every gain for the self involves a "death" of the ego. For this "individuation" to occur requires regular "ego-cide"; how we have known ourselves dies away as the greater awareness of who we are comes to life. It is miraculous that we allow any change to happen, and we need every bit of help we can get for this process. Music, which is both ego enhancing and Self enhancing, is an ideal medium to give us that help.

Probably different types of music are involved here. That which is well known to us or has a strong rhythmic structure or well-defined form contains, or is supportive of, the ego. This need not necessarily be pop-type music; I think that even music by great composers such as Mozart or Bach can be used in this way. The music follows particular laws that have become implicitly known, even to non-musicians. When those laws are followed, the ego feels "all is right with the world as I know it."

Then there is a different sort of music by some of the minimalist composers, and clearly "spiritual" music, such as Gregorian chant or traditional religious songs as sung by Nóirín Ní Riain or as composed by Hildegard von Bingen. This music is spacious, does not foreclose, and permits the flow of psychic energy down new channels. It evokes an experience of the ultimately unknowable as opposed to expressing only the known. In this way it allows for an expansion of the personality.

Music "occupies more areas of our brain than language does,"[6] and deficits in one or other part of the brain may affect different aspects of musicality. Memories of music tend to be faithful to the original in terms of tune and feeling but also with regard to pitch, tempo, and rhythm.[7] Realizing this, Galileo used to time experiments using tunes that he hummed to himself, noting how many beats had passed for a particular event to be achieved.[8] (At school we were told that he had used his pulse-beat to time experiments and we wondered, with some amusement, what happened when he got excited at the results!)

Zadie Smith, writing in memory of the American author David Foster Wallace, states: "Complexity like Dave's is a gift. His recursive labyrinthine sentences demand second readings. . . . Their resistance 'breaks the rhythm that excludes thinking.'"[9] For her, thinking autonomously, thinking our own thoughts, is a gift that modern culture has taken away from us, and she uses the phrase "the rhythm of thoughtlessness" to highlight the idea that the loss of that gift is somehow cozy or comfortable. This thought reminded me that while rhythm is containing it can also be limiting. In an early stage of ego consciousness a firmly articulated rhythm and simple melodic structure holds one, in a cradle of thoughtlessness perhaps, whereas in a later stage that same music, by restricting free thought and feeling through imposing its structure on an expanding consciousness, may feel invasive and restrictive.

Free-associative "unconscious thinking," called "primary process thinking," spurns the sort of structure that consciousness imposes but allows connections to occur transmodally. (I am thinking here of the later-life return to associative thinking, the natural thinking pattern of the preverbal child who, with later ego development and the attainment of language, submits to rationality.)

An expanded consciousness, which may be precipitated by the awareness of looming death or simply by maturation, seems to require space within music. And that spaciousness may be evoked through the judicious use of silence, as in the music that has been called "holy minimalism": the music of Tavener, Pärt, and Gōrecki. Martha Ainsworth has written about this in a lovely article titled "Be Still and Know that I am God."[10] This is different from the spaciousness that Sacks writes about when he points out that to experience spaciousness in music we need two intact auditory systems, both left and right. With one ear only we hear monaurally and what we hear sounds flat and one-dimensional. But with two functioning ears we get three-dimensional sound.

We each spend so much of our lives constructing an ego, a tool for consciously engaging with the world, that it is usually very difficult to disengage from that consciousness and allow ourselves to enter the timeless zone from our time-bound present.[11] The music of "holy minimalism" helps in that process, as may meditation of one sort or another or one of the depth-psychological approaches where engagement with the unconscious is sought. For the unconscious is not much different from "the timeless zone" or from what Kathryn Madden terms "unitary reality"[12] and Wilfred Bion called "O," suggesting "ultimately unknowable reality," and from what others have called God, or the Great Mother (E. Neumann), the Self (C. G. Jung), the Real (J. Lacan), the Void, or, as a recent movie suggested, great silence.[13] (Was that title, *Into Great Silence,* inspired by the deafening silence that indicates the presence of God or by the still more deafening silence of God's absence?)

Ainsworth points out that these composers, these "Holy Minimalists," "reject complexity in favour of simplicity" and in this way they "open a window, allowing the listener to connect with the holy."[14] The power of their music lies in that simplicity; they compose as if they are articulating a truth that needs no embellishment. Percy Scholes, in his introduction to his explanation of harmony writes: "Harmony may be described as the clothing of melody."[15] He suggests that melody is not enough on its own; it requires embellishment. Perhaps this puts harmony in the same category as the persona in Jungian psychology. However beautiful it is, it is still exterior, still a covering of the true; as Ken Wilber would describe it, it is still "surface."[16] In order to get to depth or the true or the whole, one must get below the surface, to where the opposites are just tangible (or audible), especially the opposites of emptiness and fullness, beauty and ugliness, or, as Helen Anderson writes about Beethoven in this volume, the spiritual and the chthonic. This deeper world is the world of paradox.

Opposites are usually experienced sequentially, as an either/or dichotomy, but because the appreciation of music relies on the listener's capacity to remember what has gone before, to be aware of what is happening in the present, and to guess what will or "should" happen in the future, it is the ideal medium in which to create a "both/and" unitary reality.[17] This is very like what Jung called "the pleroma."[18] Some of the modern composers invite us to listen, without memory or expectation (or desire), to the sound of God's own Self.

The "holy minimalists" are the modern-day version of the seekers after a spiritual connection, but they are certainly not the first of those seekers. Many early peoples found a way through by means of psychoactive substances, music, dance, or extreme states of one sort or another. The trance-dances of the San people of southern Africa are probably precursors of the raves and trance parties of the present day, where serotonin, released during the dancing together or through the use of substances such as Ecstasy, gives the participants the feeling of togetherness. Gregorian chant, which echoes through the high space within a cathedral, often above the monotonous sound of a drone, seems to reach out toward God while staying rooted in humanity. Abbess Hildegard of Bingen, who described herself as "a feather on the breath of God," wrote and composed in the twelfth century. Her music likewise rises toward God. Did she explore music and poetry through spirituality or vice versa? It is hard to say.[19]

Nóirín Ní Riain is a modern Irish singer of ancient songs who also has a Ph.D. in theology. Her friend, the poet John O'Donohue, describes her music thus: "[It] climbs some kind of celestial staircase and makes you aware of doors high up in the silence where the tenderness of the divine awaits you." It has been said that "her voice has a brittle quality almost like blue egg-shells. It seems to come directly from the Spirit."[20] (Personally I would use the word "fragile" or "delicate" rather than "brittle," although at times her voice is so strong that those words are inappropriate too.)

The "holy minimalists" enable one to reach to a deeper level of one's own psyche by creating space, through their use of silence, in which one can experience more than the surface of things. They do not (controllingly) fill the space with beauty of their own making but allow psyche to speak. And we will hear psyche if we but listen, listen to the sounds of silence, listen to what Nóirín Ní Riain calls "Theosony," the sound of God. Nóirín states that music represents a vibrational conduit to the divine. I think that one can contrast this sort of music to that of Palestrina, whose beautiful harmonies clothed in exquisite fashion the melodies of many hymns. His sounds are beautiful, in and of themselves. They are offerings to God but do not necessarily lead to an experience of God.

GOD IS NOT WHERE WE KNOW GOD IS

The apophatic way of describing God can be contrasted to the kataphatic. The kataphatic way describes God by describing God's attributes, "God is good, God is immortal, God is all-seeing." But apophatics would say that such descriptions limit God—whatever God is, God is not only that—and thus they describe God in negatives, they confront the unknowable, the darkness, they obliterate the organ of conscious knowing, the ego. Apophatic spirituality leads to a supraconceptual void, a unitary reality that contains all while seeming to consist of nothing; and musically that nothing is silence.

John Cage composed a piece simply called *4'33"* which was 4 minutes and 33 seconds long without any note being played on the piano. Despite the fact that no notes were played, Cage stated: "There is no such thing as silence. Something is always happening that makes a sound." Thus every performance of *4'33"* is different. Cage himself refers to it as his "silent piece" and writes:

> I have spent many pleasant hours in the woods conducting performances of my silent piece . . . for an audience of myself, since they were much longer than the popular length which I have published. At one performance . . . the second movement was extremely dramatic, beginning with the sounds of a buck and a doe leaping up to within ten feet of my rocky podium.[21]

Ainsworth has another take on silence, suggesting that, at least with Pärt, Tavener, and Gōrecki, the notes are there to surround and contain the silence.

But it seems that silence is not enough in itself and listening is not enough, either. Silence is necessary in order to "hear," but to hear what? Describing activity in another modality, Grotstein quotes Bion's description of a beam of intense blackness that will illuminate things that normally have but a feeble luminosity. Perhaps silence works in a similar way; that which is usually inaudible may become audible when immersed in a world of silence. I have noted that we often speak of "silence" when we mean the absence of usual noise. When we are in the wild, it seems silent until we becomes aware of the shrill tinnitus-like buzz of cicadas, the call and

response of frogs, and the tumble of water in a stream. Even in a sand
desert the gentlest of breezes prevents one from hearing nothing-at-all, and
when that and other live, environmental noises cease, one becomes aware
of one's own breathing or the flow and ebb of sound as one's heart beats.

SOME EFFECTS

A physiotherapist, Frances le Roux, has written a thesis on music's
effectiveness as an analgesic. According to her, music can function as
an audio-analgesic or an audio-anxiolytic and also give rise to audio-
relaxation. Some sorts of music significantly reduce a patient's
perception of pain,[22] and listening to music, again of some sorts, is
associated with reduced heart rate, lower blood pressure, and
improvements in the oxygen saturation of the blood. Music reduces
levels of cortisol, the "stress hormone," in the blood as well as levels of
epinephrine and norepinephrine, the "fight or flight" hormones, and thus
can be useful for people undergoing medical or dental procedures. In other
words, music acts directly on our neurophysiology.

The type of music is significant. Stimulating music tends to increase
pain perception. Sensory overload caused by listening too long to music
that is too loud and fast can also aggravate pain perception. But soothing
music reduces it. The most effective "therapeutic" music in this setting or
for this purpose "should be non-lyrical, consisting of low tones, comprising
mostly strings with minimal brass or percussion and have a maximum
volume of 60dB."[23] Music with a slow regular tempo of 55–60 beats per
minute—that is, with a *largo* tempo—is best.[24] In general, better results
are obtained when individuals make their own choices and their mood is
matched by the music, but when patients are unable to make choices
because they are semiconscious or confused, Gregorian chant or baroque
music seems to work well. Discussing Gregorian chant, le Roux writes:
"It removes earthly stress and awakens peace and [a sense of] timeless
space," but at the same time it creates a strengthening structure.[25]

Music can produce a sense of predictability and thus security, but
also—and this is one of its most alluring attributes—it is ceaselessly
changing. A bit like the way waves roll in to a beach, each wave is different,
but each arises from the same oceanic source and despite its difference is
still a wave. I become increasingly agitated when being forced to listen to
the canned music that is supplied by some business or other that is too
busy to talk to you. This agitation is especially aggravated when I do not
like the music, when there is a lot of brass or percussion and when it is
(falsely) cheerful. The other day I was in this "forced" position when music

from Vivaldi's *Four Seasons* was being played. Initially I felt calm, and then the familiar agitation began. What was happening, I realized, was that the music was being played in a loop that lasted thirty seconds. So it did not go anywhere; an eternity of a few bars of Vivaldi that was blocked from its usual unfolding. This episode underscored for me the importance of some meaning in the music, even if that meaning is not immediately consciously known. It is not just about beautiful sounds being played in the range of the human voice!

According to le Roux, "music and pain share some of the same psycho-neurological processing areas." These include the thalamus (the sensory gateway to the cerebral cortex), where endogenous opiates act. These opiates are released when we listen to certain music. Presumably, this is what gives rise to some of the analgesia that music produces, although being called on to focus on something other than one's pain and the relaxing effects of listening to something that one likes may also play a part.

A few examples of music that demonstrates analgesic effects and relaxation are here listed by composer. The list was drawn up by le Roux.

Handel
> "Largo" from *Serse*
> "Largo" from *Alexander's Feast*
> "Largo" from *Concerto Grosso* in D major, Opus 6, no. 5
> "Largo" and "Piano" from *Concerto Grosso* in A minor,
>   Opus 6, no. 4
> "Largo" from *Concerto Grosso* in B minor, Opus 6, no. 12

Corelli
> "Largo" from *Concerto Grosso* in D major, Opus 6, no. 1

J. S. Bach
> "Largo" from *Piano Concerto in F minor,* BWV 1056
> "Largo ma non tanto" from *Double Concerto in D Minor,*
>   BWV 1043

Vivaldi
> "Largo" from *Violin Concerto in C Major*

Telemann
> "Largo" from *Concerto for Three Violins in F Major*
> "Largo" from *Viola Concerto in G Minor*

Also Gregorian chant, music from the Trappist Monks' Choir, and chants from Assisi.[26]

VOICES

Paul Newham differentiates vocalization from verbalization, voice from words, and suggests that often it is the tone of the voice rather than the words articulated that is most important.[27] One can think of yelling, screaming, cooing, or laughing as examples. The content is not as significant as the tone. He thinks that in psychoanalysis it is not so much the words used but the tone and timbre of the voice that we should listen to. To ignore the voice but listen to the words spoken is to miss important communication about underlying emotional dynamics.[28] Astrid Berg, who works with Xhosa mothers and children in a Cape Town township community, described how she will give "feedback" to a preverbal Xhosa child in English, and the child appears to understand. Clearly she is communicating "extra-verbally."[29] Similar ideas are articulated by Johan Norman.[30]

It is known that by restricting or inhibiting respiration one can keep instincts repressed, but the contrary is also true, that by pursuing respiratory and vocal exercises, one can experience a heightened emotional response. Newham makes the point that the "verbal articulation of affect distances the emotional experience from its expression. Words are a substitute; language signifies a lack." In fact, in order to actually learn a language a child must "bring his feelings and instincts, moods and affects . . . under the jurisdiction of words."[31]

Newham quotes Patricia Moroney as having observed that the analytic process is like the interface between silence and song.[32] He also quotes Albert Wolfson, a pioneer of voice work, who felt that he could turn dream images into sound by making the archetypal motifs audible through the human voice. For Wolfson, "'the range, strength and timbre of the voice' are determined 'solely by emotional factors.'"[33] (The idea of silence into song is the auditory equivalent of nothingness into something beautiful or meaningful. I think that that is emblematic of at least part of the analytic endeavor, which asks how we can make something individually meaningful out of the chaos of our emotions.)

Newham also writes that "singing . . . gives a musical voice to neurosis," and this hints that it can then lead to healing of the neurosis. If there is no means of expressing a neurosis, it remains unreachable.[34] This does not mean that we should all take singing lessons but that as therapists we must listen to the music in which the words are embedded as well as the words themselves.

On Music and Dying

The Chalice of Repose is the name for the so-called College of Thanatology whose members play polyphonic music on harps, usually one on either side of a terminally ill patient. When asked "why the harp?" Theresa Schroeder-Sheker, the founder of the organization, indicates that it is because "the harp is always dissolving." Or, more simply: "Because it is so beautiful." The way it is played is never intrusive. The practitioners start in silence, move through synchronization (an in-tune-ment with the patient's breathing) to entrainment, which I understand to indicate that they feel they can lead patients to where they feel the patients should go. They help patients approach death with more equanimity than they might otherwise have done.

The theory behind their work arises from the work of Ernst Chladni and Hans Jenny, who proved conclusively that sound is an organizing force, and Alexander Lauterwasser, who made photographs of the way water surfaces were affected by music. Since music creates particular patterns in liquids and solids alike, it is no surprise that it can also profoundly influence human beings. The sort of music played by these "thanatologists" to those in pain leads to marked pain relief, as evidenced by stabilized breathing patterns, deep restorative sleep, and emotional, mental, or spiritual release.[35] Therese Schroeder-Sheker states that there is a direct relationship between the melodic content of music and its neurological effects, between its harmonic content and the respiratory and circulatory systems, and between rhythm and metabolism.[36] Different aspects of music affect different aspects of physiological functioning.

At our local hospice in a suburb of Cape Town, music is played to individuals in distress from pain or because of their realization of impending death. What seems important is that music can, without words, enable one to enter "the silence" and be completely in the moment with another person. This is a form of unitary reality and is in the territory of forever-ness. For Jane Theron, a professional harpist who is sometimes called to the hospice when a patient is in extremis, music simply calms the person down. She may improvise or play something peaceful and *legato,* something with beautiful harmonies. She plays, for example, baroque music, the *Romance* by the sixteenth-century Spanish composer Cabezón, or Debussy's *Arabesque No. 1.* For her, harmony creates the mood, and she tries to end a piece with a major chord, as that imparts a feeling of hope. The music should be flowing and melodious, not dissonant or clashing, and she attempts to ensure that the pieces she plays fit together. "Music builds bridges in a language nobody understands," she says.[37]

MUSIC AND THE BRAIN

The following section is pieced together from a variety of sources.[38] The evidence for neuro-anatomical correlates of music performance or appreciation is at times contradictory. It is based on two main sources, the mapping of neurological deficits following brain injury or discrete disease such as a tumor, and the mapping of areas in normal brains through functional imaging of one sort or another. Some musical task is given and the way the brain "lights up" in response to that task is charted. A problem with the former method is that sometimes the functional pathology that is noted after trauma or disease is not due to a direct effect of the injury or disease process but to a release of inhibition that had suppressed another area of the brain. For example it has occurred that an individual with a lesion in the left speech area may suddenly develop a musicality that was not present before the lesion. This is thought to be due to "normal" inhibition, emanating from the left speech area and exerted on the equivalent area on the right side of the brain, being stopped.

Of tremendous importance to educators is the finding that sequential musical instruction is associated with increased proficiency in language capability, reading, mathematics, and cognition. In other words, music education not only enhances musical ability but many aspects of cognitive development as well. Exposure to music (probably the increased volume of the corpus callosum is implicated here) also leads to an increase in inter-hemispheric activity and range coherence (on EEG) as well as enhanced left hemispheric coherence.

Alpha waves are waves seen on the EEG that signify an alert but relaxed state. They have a frequency of 8–12 Hz, which decreases with the subject's concentration on some action. In looking at EEGs of individuals one may see irregularity in the wave patterns (a lack of coherence) or a dominance or deficiency in one or another wave type. In depression, anxiety, and stress, for example, alpha waves are decreased and beta waves increased. The sort of music listed by le Roux leads to enhancement of alpha waves.

Pitch is mainly processed by the right prefrontal area, but the maintenance of pitch while playing or singing requires the interaction of the right frontal and right temporal areas. The right prefrontal area and the auditory cortex are involved in the assessment of harmony, melody, and rhythm. Actually, rhythm is widely represented in the left frontal and parietal cortices too, as well as the right side of the cerebellum, which is particularly concerned with smoothly executed, well-coordinated muscular activity. On EEG recordings there is evidence for a sort of internal metronome in the form of induced alpha-wave activity. Once this "induced alpha-wave activity" is established, missed beats in the music do not register. This is in contrast to "evoked alpha-wave activity" where the alpha wave is in response to each beat in the music and a missed beat will result in a missed wave.

The musical experience involves many different aspects: for example, auditory, which includes hearing pitch, harmony, timbre, interval, and contour; visual, which involves reading from a score and includes both meaningful signs (i.e., the notes themselves and the staves, letters, and numerals that indicate different parameters)—and verbal instructions; motor skills (e.g., performance and dance); memory; and emotion. The elusive quality of "musicality" involves a combination of all these different aspects. As Sacks points out, it is possible to have perfect pitch and yet be non-musical if one or other of the musical skills are missing.[39] Brust notes: "The multimodal components of musical processing cannot be sharply localised to one part of the brain or even to one cerebral hemisphere. The psychological whole that emerges from their interaction is even more widely distributed."[40] The words "the psychological whole" suggest something much more complex than an ego function.

EMOTION AND MEANING

There is a link between tonality and emotion; some areas of the brain are involved in both the processing of music and the processing of emotion. Swedish researchers have described six mechanisms that could be involved in the induction of emotions when listening to music. These are (1) brainstem reflexes, (2) evaluative conditioning, (3) emotional contagion, (4) visual imagery, (5) episodic memory, and (6) musical expectancy.[41] These varied mechanisms are, in the view of the researchers, enough reason to cause confusion in the interpretation of experimental data about music and emotion. Thus they suggest that in future research on links between music and emotion, experimenters attempt to discern which mechanism is involved when a particular emotion is induced. This should aid a finer discrimination of the results of the research and lessen its ambiguities.

Participants in experiments about emotional arousal by music become moved by music (i.e., have an emotional response to it) at the same times. Their response sensitivity is much the same as that of their co-participants, but what they feel the music is about is markedly different from what other participants feel. So music can elicit emotional arousal, but the type of emotion aroused seems to be a function of memory and meaning, a cognitive function.

In his section on music that attempts to present a theme, Percy Scholes, in the *Oxford Companion to Music,* gives the story of a composer who asked three "brother composers" to listen to a piece of music that he had composed and say what they thought it was about. He had been attempting to illustrate "the discovering by Pharaoh's daughter of the infant Moses in the bulrushes." The "brother composers" gave the following interpretations: "1) 'Daybreak as seen from the bottom gallery of a Welsh coal mine.' 2) 'A boar-hunt in Russia' and 3) 'An enamoured couple whispering love-vows.'"[42] Clearly, each of these listeners brought their own associations to the music. But associations can be guided by a prior "programming," which will set the scene and guide a listener in the "right" direction.

Conversely, some music has become well known and taken on associations that the composer had not intended. For example, anyone who has seen the film *Elvira Madigan* will forever listen to the *andante* movement from Mozart's *Piano Concerto no. 21 in C Major,* K467, now often called the Elvira Madigan concerto, with a "directed ear." The emotional story of the blighted lovers whose only recourse is death has imprinted itself on the listener and "colors" the music.

Art is similarly influenced by language or by story. Looking at Van Gogh's *Wheat Field with Crows,* knowing that it was the last picture he painted before he died by his own hand, it is impossible not to see it as dark and foreboding. The black crows become symbolic of death, and "clearly" they are receding. Yet many people who do not know its history love this picture because of its color and movement. For these viewers, the blackness of the crows adds a contrast that enhances the yellow of the wheat. The arousal comes first, the "meaning" later.

Having said this, it does seem as though there are certain aspects of music that can evoke certain moods. Low-pitched, slow sounds suggest depression and are found in elegies or requiems. Tones that descend so that the contour of the music is one moving irrevocably downward also suggest this mood. Lightness, brightness, or happiness is evoked by quick notes, high tones, and ascending movement.

The transmission of meaning, especially emotional meaning, in opera as in life is accomplished through at least three different modes. Some listeners give primacy to the verbal or "lexical" meaning that the words or language convey. This is especially so since the widespread use of surtitles, which enable us to focus on the words themselves rather than the meaning evoked by the music or the expressions of the artistes. As Daniel Stern points out, we are "verbal selves," but this reliance on one particular mode separates us from our totality.[43] Words are processed in the left side of the brain, in Broca's area, whereas the other modes of expression are processed on the right side of the brain. These other modes include the sound of the voice, its pitch, rhythm, and timbre; the expression of the face; and, to a lesser extent, expression by the body. These are all capable of displaying a huge range of subtly different emotions. These emotions are "felt" by the viewer or person receiving the communication.

There is also the not-yet-clearly-understood way that emotion is transmitted between analysand and analyst with nothing visible or audible to account for it. This has been called "projective identification," and analysts may feel something that they might interpret as, for example, "she needed me to feel what it was like for her as a child" or something similar. An emotion *is* transmitted, but this is done outside of conscious sensation, in the realm of intuition perhaps.

There is debate among those who do "teletherapy," an increasingly used way of doing analysis, for example via Skype. Some value the use of a camera and others feel that they can get more out of really listening to the voice of the analysand. The camera users want to "see" what is going on, whereas the "listeners" feel that they can gain a better "picture" through the voice itself.

In this area I have noticed how difficult it is, especially initially, to work with a person who speaks a different language and thus has a melodic contour to their speech that is different from what I am used to. Likewise, someone who has some speech impediment such as a cerebellar dysarthria that renders the speech nonfluent is difficult to understand; clues about the "nonlexical" meaning of a particular utterance are no longer decipherable. Another way of putting this is that each language or culture has its own musicality and that musicality helps transmit meaning to those who are accustomed to it. An analysis has been done of the musicality of a particular language and nationality and that has been compared to the musical contour of the compositions produced by composers of that nationality. The contours, melodic and rhythmic, tend to match.[44]

When we think about boarding schools and their effect on children, especially boys, it seems likely that in these schools the "lexical" meaning of language is overvalued. Boys are encouraged, implicitly and explicitly, to hide their emotions, but in hiding these emotions from others they hide them from themselves, for part of feeling an emotion is feeling how the facial and bodily musculature is arranged. If that is hidden from others it is also hidden from oneself and, quite literally, a person may not know what it is that he feels until he is taken by surprise as the "unfelt feeling" explodes into action.

There are certain types of sound that carry their own meaning, probably cross-culturally. For example, a scream expresses excitement or fear, a bellow may express rage, deep tones generate respect or fear, and the middle range of the human voice tends to be experienced as most comforting. High tones expressed though a wail suggest acute grief or loss, but the chronicity of the grief results in the low slow sounds of mourning or melancholia.

The abstract expressionist Theodore Rothko refused to give names to his works, except for naming the colors in them, as he did not want to limit the viewer's reaction to the paintings. Likewise, Henry Moore, the twentieth-century English sculptor, gave his works names such as *Reclining Woman 1927* or *Upright Form,* leaving viewers to find their own meaning(s) in them. Much music is written abstractly—that is, not according to a program—and, like many abstract paintings, it is named after its completion. An example is Schumann's *Scenes from Childhood.* Scholes quotes Schumann as saying that "the superscriptions came into existence afterwards and are, indeed, nothing more than delicate directions for the rendering and understanding of the music."[45] The performer notes the "delicate directions" and imparts her emotionality to the music, which aids the listener in his (emotional) understanding of it.

COLOR AND SOUND

Synesthesia (where a stimulus of one sense, such as sound, is experienced as sensation of a different sense, such as color) has received wider public attention recently through chapter 14 of *Musicophilia,* titled "The Key Of Clear Green: Synesthesia and Music."[46] Scholes, in a section on Colour and Music, discusses the relationship between sound and color: "In discussing painting, we speak of 'tones' ('quiet' or 'loud', or 'low' or 'high'); in the parlance of music, we make use of 'chromatic' or 'coloratura' (both of them implying the introduction of tints)."[47] Scholes also notes that words and numbers may evoke colors in some people, particularly children, and that composers and compositions may do likewise.

In a 1923 experiment that Scholes mentions, a group of students were played a theme and variations composed by Schubert and asked to write down any color suggestions they became aware of. There was agreement about whether a particular color evocation was vivid or pastel but no agreement about the color evoked.[48] Timbres too have been linked to color. For example, one conductor suggested "black for strings and voices, red for brass and drums, and blue for wood."[49]

There is clearly no link between color and pitch scientifically, in the sense that although they are both caused by variations in the frequency of wave forms, a particular sound does not universally give rise to the same color sensation. Neither is there a correlation between low-frequency colors (such as red) and lower pitches and high-frequency colors (such as violet) and higher pitches. Also a pure tone may give rise to the sensation of a tertiary color such as brown and vice versa, a chord or group of notes may be "seen" as a pure primary color. What does seem to be true is that for a particular person the color association for a particular note is constant and has presumably evolved through some associative process that began in early childhood.

Sacks indicates that synesthesia is common in infants and usually disappears at about three months of age. Initially there is hyperconnectivity among cerebral neurons, but the interconnections between neurons undergo a "pruning" process a few months after birth as different areas of the brain become more specialized for different tasks.[50]

Although true "secondary" synesthesia may occur later in life, transiently during temporal lobe seizures or under the influence of hallucinogens, and permanently following loss of vision, synesthesia waxes and wanes for some people. The psychologist and author Michael Eigen writes this: "I am also accessed by synesthetic movements which enrich my experiencing and open realities. Multi-modal would be one way of describing this . . . I sensed this was a precious capacity at an early age and realized I would have to cultivate it, partner it, learn to integrate it with other capacities, so that the various modes contribute in. . . . But it . . . has to be nourished, the garden has to be tended, worked, used, developed."[51]

The brain is a plastic organ capable of changing throughout the life cycle, and I like to think that while there may be a natural "pruning" process early in life, the brain is capable of making wide connections later on. These connections might enable it to reach out of the separate boxes of sensory categories and into a multimodal world where colors have a taste and sounds have color or smell. This world would be not unlike the richly creative worlds where associations are encouraged, the worlds of analytical psychology or psychoanalysis.

In reading Eigen's writings and musings one becomes aware of a mind that is able to see, hear, feel, taste, and smell what it comes in contact with. It works multimodally, through what Freud called "primary process," and yet it is a mind that can bring critical, analytic thinking to bear. That mix of capacities to see, hear, think, and analyze as well as to compose, improvise, and remain fluid (yet within a structure) is both truly musical and truly psychoanalytic.

RHYTHM

The words "'rhyme' and 'rhythm' derive from the Greek, carrying the conjoined meanings of measure, motion and stream."[52] This "articulate stream" carries one along and has been used by novelists such as Thomas Mann, whose prose suddenly breaks into a more rhythmic form to mark an increase in the action.

> An excellent example is in Thomas Mann's *The Holy Sinner,* when Gregorius' lone battle outside the city gates is described by another character, M. Poitevin. Poitevin's monologue imperceptibly changes its inner structure so that it becomes highly rhythmical, galloping along in a way that matches the action he is describing, and becoming filled with rhymes or "jingles" that the speaker seems unable to prevent.[53]

There seems to have been a transitional period between the early poetry of the great sagas such as *The Iliad, The Odyssey,* and *Beowulf,* and later prose pieces that broke into poetry at certain times. It was the musicality of those early works that made them so unforgettable: the rhythm and the rhyme connected with the emotional part of the brain, the right cerebral cortex, and, perhaps through its arousal aided memory too.

Sacks writes beautifully about another of music's powers. "Music, uniquely among the arts, is both completely abstract and profoundly emotional. It has no power to represent anything particular or external, but it has a unique power to express inner states or feelings."[54] He also raises the point that "while . . . music makes one experience pain and grief more intensely, it brings solace and consolation at the same time."[55] There is something so important about this statement, and it is something that the South African poet, Stephen Watson, has written about with regard to poetry. In an essay "Poetry and Absence: One Writer's Account,"[56] Watson makes clear that a poem, even about something frightening, such as death, can contain the emotion. Stephen Bloch suggests that music too performs a containing function.[57] I would suggest that music brings "solace and consolation," to use Sacks's words, because it can give one a feeling that someone knows what one is feeling or has felt, even if the expression of that knowledge is nonverbal. In fact, we probably are able to feel this precisely because the music is nonverbal.

I quizzed a particular patient of mine about music, thinking perhaps to suggest that he could soothe himself by listening to the sort of music that le Roux recommends. "Classical music precipitates my falling into the void," he responded. "When I feel really bad I listen to Jimi Hendrix singing Dylan's 'All along the watchtower.'" The psychotic wail of the electric guitar relieves the solitude of his inner "madness." He is no longer alone with it but senses, outside of language, that someone else has experienced something similar to what he has.

Sacks also makes the point that, for people with dementia, music therapy "is possible because musical perception, musical sensibility, musical emotion, and musical memory can survive long after other forms of memory have disappeared. Music of the right kind can serve to orient and anchor a patient when almost nothing else can."[58]

I would like to stress again the point that it is "music of the right kind" that is useful. But finding that music requires openness on the part of the therapist, for sometimes what relieves deep distress seems counterintuitive.

CONCLUSION

Music is an archetype that, like all archetypes, is incarnated in a particular form in each person who opens him or herself to it. The way it takes on form will depend on the particular makeup of each individual.

The idea that music is both constructive/creative and healing has a long history, and some analysts and therapists today not only try to find the "right" music for a particular patient but also see their clients in musical terms and listen to them with a musical ear. In this way they have started to redress that unfortunate imbalance whereby individuals were "seen" visually and "heard" only through the meaning of their words. It is salutary that, as Stern has said, it is through language that one can distort reality,[59] but if one can learn to "listen" past the words, and that usually means listening musically, one has a greater chance of being able to hear through the ego defenses and listen to that which is wholly true albeit wholly other.

There is a danger in thinking that one knows what is right for a particular patient and sometimes in "knowing" that patients must be protected from some aspect of music. The problem about "knowing" is that it is always a knowing of the "known," and that is an ego activity. That ego activity prevents the unconscious from speaking, and in that speaking creating something fresh and vital or, perhaps, something awful. From out of the unitary reality of the psyche as a whole can come either.

———————————

NOTES

[1] *Harmony: Webster's Quotations, Facts and Phrases* (San Diego, CA: ICON Group International, 2008), p. 1.

[2] *As It Is in Heaven,* dir. Kay Pollak, DVD, Kino International, 2004.

[3] H. E. Anderson, "Sounds Emanating from the Self" (M.A. diss., University of Cape Town, 2006).

[4] Oliver Sacks, *Musicophilia: Tales of Music and the Brain* (London: Picador, 2007), p. 94.

[5] A. N. Schore, "Commentary," *South African Psychiatry Review* 7, no. 3 (2004): 16. Schore is commenting on Annie Panzer and Margaretha Viljoen, "Dissociation: A Developmental Psychoneurobiological Perspective," pages 11–14 of the same issue of *South African Psychiatry Review.*

[6] Jacket blurb, Sacks, *Musicophilia.*

[7] Sacks, *Musicophilia,* p. xi.

[8] *Ibid.,* p. 240n3.

[9] Zadie Smith, "Always Another Word," *Harper's Magazine,* January 2009, p. 26.

[10] Martha Ainsworth, "Be Still, and Know That I Am God: Concert Halls Rediscover the Sacred," unpublished article, 2002, available at www.metanoia.org/martha/writing/bestill.htm.

[11] Arvo Pärt quoted in *ibid.*

[12] Kathryn Wood Madden, *Dark Light of the Soul* (Great Barrington, MA: Lindisfarne Books, 2008).

[13] *Into Great Silence,* dir. Philip Gröning, DVD, Zeitgeist Films, 2007.

[14] Ainsworth, "Be Still."

[15] Percy A. Scholes, *The Oxford Companion to Music,* 10th ed., ed. John Owen Ward (Oxford: Oxford University Press, 1970), p. 441.

[16] Ken Wilber, *A Brief History of Everything* (Dublin: Gateway, 2001).

[17] Madden, *Dark Light of the Soul.*

[18] C. G. Jung and Basilides, *Septem Sermones ad Mortuos* (1916), new ed., trans. H. G. Baynes (London: Stuart & Watkins, 1967).

[19] Liner notes on *A Feather on the Breath of God,* p. 2, CD, Hyperion Records Limited, CDA66039, 1994.

[20] Quotes from "The Sound of God," broadcast on the BBC on 27 October 2003. For the BBC's Web page about this interview with Noírín ní Riain, see "Theosony: The Sound of God," at http://www.bbc.co.uk/religion/religions/christianity/music/theosony.shtml#one.

[21] John Cage quoted in Stephen Davies, *Themes in the Philosophy of Music* (Oxford: Oxford University Press, 2003), p. 14n.

[22] Frances H. le Roux, "Pain Management and Music," *Journal of Pain SA* 3, no. 4 (2008): 5–7.

[23] *Ibid.*, p. 6.

[24] *Ibid.*

[25] *Ibid.*, p. 7.

[26] *Ibid.*

[27] Paul Newham, *Therapeutic Voicework* (London: Jessica Kingsley, 1998).

[28] *Ibid.*, pp. 189–194.

[29] Astrid Berg, "Talking with Infants: A Bridge to Cross-Cultural Intervention," *Southern African Journal of Child and Adolescent Mental Health* 14, no. 1 (2002): 5–14.

[30] Johan Norman, "To Talk with Infants: The Baby Analysand as a Starting Point for Understanding the Mother and Baby Relationship," paper presented at the forty-first International Psychoanalytical Association Congress, Santiago, Chile, 25–30 July 1999.

[31] Newham, *Therapeutic Voicework*, pp. 200, 204.

[32] *Ibid.*, p. 221.

[33] *Ibid.*, p. 338.

[34] *Ibid.*, p. 201.

[35] See Chalice of Repose Project, "The Voice of Music-Thanatology," 2003, at http://www.chaliceofrepose.org/music.htm.

[36] *Ibid.*

[37] Jane Theron, personal communication, February 2009.

[38] These sources include Sacks, *Musicophilia*; "The Brain and Music," n.d., available at www.childrensmusicworkshop.com/advocacy/brain.html (accessed February 2009); and John C. M. Brust, "Music and the Neurologist: A Historical Perspective," *Annals of the New York Academy of Sciences* 930 (2001): 143–152.

[39] Sacks, *Musicophilia*, pp. 89–97.

[40] Brust, "Music and the Neurologist," p. 149.

[41] P. N. Juslin and D. Västfjäll, "Emotional Responses to Music: The Need to Consider Underlying Mechanisms," *The Behavioral and Brain Sciences* 5 (31 October 2008): 559–575.

⁴² Scholes, *The Oxford Companion to Music*, p. 835.

⁴³ Daniel N. Stern, *The Interpersonal World of the Infant: A View from Psychoanalysis and Developmental Psychology* (New York: Basic Books, 1985), p. 162ff.

⁴⁴ Sacks, *Musicophilia*, p. 243n4.

⁴⁵ Scholes, *The Oxford Companion to Music*, p. 835.

⁴⁶ Sacks, *Musicophilia*, pp. 165–183.

⁴⁷ Scholes, *The Oxford Companion to Music*, p. 202.

⁴⁸ *Ibid.*, p. 203.

⁴⁹ *Ibid.*

⁵⁰ Sacks, *Musicophilia*, p. 181.

⁵¹ Michael Eigen, e-mail correspondence with the author, 15 April 2009.

⁵² Sacks, *Musicophilia*, p. 239.

⁵³ Paul W. Ashton, *From the Brink: Experiences of the Void from a Depth Psychology Perspective* (London: Karnac, 2007), p. 219.

⁵⁴ Sacks, *Musicophilia*, p. 300–301.

⁵⁵ *Ibid.*, p. 301.

⁵⁶ Stephen Watson, "Poetry and Absence: One Writer's Account," in *Evocations of Absence: Multidisciplinary Perspectives on Void States,* ed. Paul W. Ashton (New Orleans, LA: Spring Journal Books, 2007), pp. 10–32.

⁵⁷ Stephen Bloch, "Music as Dreaming: Absence and the Emergence of the Auditory Symbol" in *Evocations of Absence.*

⁵⁸ Sacks, *Musicophilia*, p. 337.

⁵⁹ Daniel N. Stern, *The Interpersonal World of the Infant* (New York: Basic Books, 1985), p. 182.

9

In You More Than You: The Lacanian Real, Music, and Bearing Witness

Lawrence A. Wetzler

The Unsayable

In his book *The Cruelty of Depression,* Jacques Hassoun describes the being of absence, the origin of meaning, and a founding moment of subjectivity in the following passage:

> Meaning, the instant of unbearable waiting? The instant of the flash? The infinite instant of the child who, having lost his transitional object, finds himself naked, abandoned, and defenseless? The instant in which the child flees sudden, inexplicable death? The twilit instant in which vision is beclouded, the images bent out of shape, peopled with ghosts and hallucinations of absence?[1]

Frosh notes how for the postmodernist, meaning is a potential that cannot ever be fully realized.[2] The capacity of words to convey meaning remains at best only partial, the "unsayability" of psychic life remaining core. Butler speaks of the "not-knowingness" of loss as follows:

> If mourning involves knowing what one has lost (and melancholia, originally means, to a certain extent, not knowing), then mourning would be maintained by its enigmatic dimension, by the experience of not knowing incited by losing what we cannot fully fathom.[3]

What is the unsayable that Wordsworth is saying in these lines from his "Intimations of Immortality?"

> It is not now as it hath been of yore;—
> Turn whereso'ere I may,
> By night or day,
> The things which I have seen I now can see no more. . . .
>
> Our birth is but a sleep and a forgetting . . .
> Heaven lies about us in our infancy . . .
> Shades of the prison-house begin to close
> Upon the growing Boy,
> But he beholds the light, and whence it flows, He sees it in
>   his joy . . .
> At length the Man perceives it die away,
> And fade into the light of common day. . . .
>
> Thanks to the human heart by which we live,
> Thanks to its tenderness, its joys, and fears,
> To me the meanest flower that blows can give
> Thoughts that do often lie too deep for tears.[4]

Wordsworth is evoking that ineffable but ubiquitous loss to which his words can only allude, something unsayable, heartfelt, and "too deep for tears." Music can become a similar opening into a dimension of experience beyond language. This essay will focus on the place music can have in our lives in the face of traumatic experience.

In another of his works, Wordsworth writes,

> 'Tis done and in the after-vacancy
> We wonder at ourselves like men betrayed.[5]

Where are we and who are we in that "after-vacancy" following a traumatic loss? And where and who is the other? How might music and its resonance enable us to find our way through this "after-vacancy," allowing us to dwell in that dimension of experience beyond the sayable?

I was born into a musical family. I can remember my mother singing Brahms's Lullaby to me when I was a toddler. Another early memory involves my standing in the tulip bed on the side of our home, listening to my mother sing songs from the show *Kismet* to my father's piano accompaniment. I was in sheer awe over the beauty I heard in her voice and dreamed of assuming my father's place at the piano. In college I regularly accompanied sopranos for their examinations and recitals, reliving those early moments of wonder.

When I was around four or five, my father informed me that his mother had been a concert pianist in Vienna prior to marrying his father, a businessman from a small town in Germany. A few years after my paternal grandparents' marriage and the birth of their first son in the early 1900s, they moved to the United States, eventually settling down in Baltimore, Maryland. Here my grandfather went into the clothing business and my grandmother gave birth to two more sons and a daughter while somehow maintaining her career as a pianist. She gave occasional piano recitals on WBAL Radio and performed in local chamber music groups. My father was the youngest of her three sons. He shared stories with me of how he and his mother would play piano duets together throughout much of his childhood and adolescence. He continued this tradition with me, the two of us reading from the same music he had read from with her.

I grew up hearing my father playing the solo piano music of Beethoven, Chopin, and Schumann. From early on, I found myself entranced by the beauty of these seemingly magical sounds, sounds which enveloped me and transported me into another dimension. Although we experienced a rather turbulent relationship with one another, blocked by pervasive misunderstandings and miscommunications, we did bond through music; my listening to him playing solo piano works, our playing piano duets with one another, or our listening to music together while attending concerts at the old Lyric Theatre in Baltimore. By my adolescence, we had played through most of the Beethoven symphonies transcribed for piano duet. The joy inherent in our making music together is beyond anything words can express. In one of my last visits with him, shortly before cancer claimed his life in 1990, I brought him from his hospital bed out to that same baby grand piano on which we had read through so many duets together and played for him much of the solo music he had played for me throughout my childhood and adolescence. Another moment of profound bonding beyond words.

Reaching to a place beyond language, music can move us in ways words rarely do. What is it about music, the voice, the voice of music, or the music of the voice that brings us to that place beyond? I invite you to consider the ways in which the impact of music can evoke overtones of something in us which we have lost, perhaps even sacrificed, in the name of our so-called development, something which we are continually trying to refind.

Daniel Stern has noted how with the emergence of language in the second year of life, the infant enters into a new domain of relatedness in which shared meanings and the communication of mutual experiences become possible.[6] However, simultaneous with its emergence into this social fabric, the infant finds him or herself faced with a traumatic loss in which certain qualities and modes of experiencing may become foreclosed and no longer shareable with him or herself or with others. The onset and acquisition of language results in an alienation from the global, amorphous, sensory immediacy of lived experience. Required to "say it in words," the infant/toddler is asked to filter his or her originary mode of experiencing for the sake of "communication." What might be lost in our learning to speak? What is that paradise we must relinquish in our coming into language?

In his essay on children's thinking, Winnicott appreciates the fundamental difference between babies who reach out for words and babies who continue to live in a more hallucinatory sphere.

> Some babies specialise in thinking and reach out for words; others specialise in auditory, visual, or other sensuous experiences, and in memories and creative imagination of hallucinatory kind, and these latter infants may not reach out for words. There is no question of the one being normal and the other abnormal. Misunderstanding may occur in debate through the fact that one person talking belongs to the thinking and verbalising kind, while another belongs to the kind that hallucinates in the visual or auditory field instead of expressing the self in words. Somehow the "word people" tend to claim sanity, and those who see visions do not know how to defend their position when accused of insanity. Logical argument belongs to the verbalizers. Feeling, or a feeling of certainty or truth or "real," belongs to the others.[7]

Insofar as so much of Winnicott's concern revolves around "feeling real," is he not implying that something of the latter may be lost in our "reaching out for words"? Perhaps a primordial rupture in one's going-on-being occurs with the onset of language. A two-year-old's temper tantrums may issue, at least in part, from a refusal of that necessary loss which inheres in learning to speak.

We read in the Bible that in the beginning was the Word. Willy Apollon[8] notes how in the beginning was the Voice. Language did not come onto the scene until some 200,000 years later. Prior to the advent of language, people followed their own hallucinations, the voices within, the group following the hallucination of the chief or master. With the creation of language, society or the social link came into being. Usurping the place of the voice, language came to define the nature of human reality, determining what was and wasn't receivable. Language informed us as to what we could and could not experience, the thinkable and the unthinkable, what could be spoken and what was unspeakable.

The functioning of society with its ideals, norms, and values demanded the repression of one's hallucinations, drives, and fantasies as well as the *jouissance* intrinsic to each.[9] With the advent of consciousness, one's hallucinations, drives, and fantasies continue to function, but now only from behind the newly instituted social scene, in that other scene, the ob-scene, or the scene of the unconscious. For Apollon, psychoanalysis works against society and the repression it demands, making a place for all that had been banished through the institution of language. Psychoanalysis works to unearth signifiers which manifest themselves in symptoms, fantasies, dreams, and other formations of the unconscious. These unconscious formations are *outside* the limits imposed by language and society, *beyond* the limits of the pleasure principle and the homeostatic "balance" the latter affords. Engaging in a Lacanian psychoanalysis, one is called on to risk knowing oneself outside of and beyond these now-taken-for-granted limits.

In exploring the madness of James Joyce and his daughter Lucia, Lacan states,

> How can we not all sense that the words on which we depend, are in a way imposed on us? This indeed is why what is called a sick person sometimes goes further than what is called a healthy man. The question is rather one of knowing why a normal man, one described as normal, is not aware that the word is a parasite? That the word is something applied. That the word is a form of cancer with which the human being is afflicted. How is it that there are some who go as far as feeling it?[10]

And later, perhaps in reference to Joyce's own writing and life trauma,

> It is difficult not to see that a certain relationship to the word is more and more imposed on him. Imposed to the point that he finishes by, by dissolving language itself . . . to impose on language itself a sort of breaking, of decomposition which means that there is no longer any phonological identity.[11]

Joyce and Lacan are pointing to ways in which words constrict. In writing *Finnegan's Wake,* Joyce dissolves language into neologisms which transport us to some other scene. How might our own lives be truncated by the very language we speak? Creating a language of his own and clinging to his hallucinations and delusions, the psychotic is refusing to be a part of that taken-for-granted fullness of everyday speech, a fullness that masks a void he knows intimately. Living with a profound unconscious knowledge of the fundamental absence of the other, the psychotic spends a lifetime trying to repair the void that most of us would rather not know.[12] Unlike the neurotic, the psychotic is acutely aware of the parasitic nature of language.

EXILED FROM OURSELVES

In his description of how a Lacanian analysis brings the analysand face to face with his symptoms and fantasies, Zizek notes that

> at the beginning, the patient wants to retain the consistency of his Self and merely get rid of the embarrassing symptoms which disturb this consistency; in the course of analysis, however, it is the patient's Self which dissolves, while the patient is directly confronted with his symptom, deprived of the protective shield of his Self.[13]

For Lacan, the Self or the ego is an imaginary fiction created from out of one's identification with others and what these others desire. It is constructed to repress the subject, constituting itself as the ideal object for the other (the ideal ego) and shielding one from the registration of painful truths,

> The ego is structured exactly like a symptom. At the heart of the subject, it is only a privileged symptom, the human symptom par excellence, the mental illness of man.[14]

We are born into a living network of desiring: our parents' desires, our culture's desires, the desires of our social group—and for each of these, desires that remain submerged, unspoken but that are nevertheless communicated. For Lacan, one's desire is to be desired by the other, to desire as the other desires, to desire what the other desires. It is important to note that when Lacan speaks of "the other," he is referring to a completely imaginary other, the other one experiences through a reflection and projection of one's ego.

> Which other is this, then, to whom I am more attached than to myself (*moi*), since, at the most assented to heart of my identity, he pulls the strings?[15]

The psychic transformation we undergo and bring about in ourselves in order to be desired by others leads to what Lacan refers to as the subversion of the subject. I do not speak so much as I am spoken and spoken for, my identity being outside of me with the Other or in a particular *relation* with an other. When Lacan speaks of "the Other" (as opposed to "the other"), he is designating a radical alterity that transcends the illusory otherness of the imaginary, the Other referring to the symbolic order itself, the unique language and law we find ourselves born into, inhabiting, and inhabited by.[16]

> The first thing that happens to the "virtual" subject is his being dashed by a wave of signifiers that, although allowing for his emergence, petrify him at the same time. . . . The subject appears at the cost of a disappearance.[17]

Is not Lacan pointing to how our being in the world is possible only through a fundamental loss; that is, through that inevitable sacrifice of *jouissance* that human being and being human calls on us to make? He speaks of the lethal aspect intrinsic to our fading into the symbolic register within which we must exist in order to function in the social link. We become strangers to ourselves through our entrance into language. This *aphanisis,* this fading of the subject, a disappearing that is intrinsic to our fundamental alienation from ourselves, takes place in each of the three registers.

Not only do we disappear into the symbolic systems into which we are born, a language that precedes our birth and that translates us to ourselves, but we also disappear into the image or images we have of ourselves, the imaginary Gestalts we cling to and present to ourselves and the world. Taking refuge within these constructed unities that provide us with a sense of stability and consistency, we find ourselves rudely awakened when trauma insinuates itself into the fabric of our existence.

For Lacan, the real presents itself in the guise of trauma. It is unassimilable, beyond our capacity to take in, digest, process, or make sense of. The real feels unreal: "This can't be happening to me." Lacan speaks of the real as an encounter, *tuché,* but a missed encounter, a failed encounter, an encounter that is not encountered. Forever eluding me, the real is something I will never know, even though it continues to know me and direct my existence. The real is the impossible. Impossible to say the whole of. Impossible to symbolize. Impossible to imagine. No matter how we manage to speak about the real, it continues to expand and to reduce us to the role of impotent witness. In a somewhat concrete but nonetheless horrifying analogy, Zizek compares the impact of the real to the uncanny specter of an "immaterial" war where the attack is invisible—viruses, poisons that can be anywhere and nowhere.

> On the level of visible, material reality, nothing happens, no
> big explosions; yet the known universe starts to collapse, life
> disintegrates.[18]

We don't know what hit us. There seems to be no way to know.

THE IMPOSSIBILITY OF KNOWING

Speaking on the taboo against knowing and yet the inescapable need to know what transpired during the Holocaust, Felman and Laub, quoting Maurice Blanchot (1980), ask

> How, in effect, is it possible to accept *not* to know? We read books
> on Auschwitz. The vow of everybody there, the last vow: "know
> what has happened, do not forget," and at the same time: "you
> will never know."[19]

And later, quoting Blanchot's memory of Lewenthal, whose notes were found buried near a crematorium: "Truth was always more atrocious than anything that might be said about it."[20]

For Lacan, "No praxis is more orientated towards that which, at the heart of experience, is the kernel of the real than psychoanalysis."[21] The real places reality in abeyance. With this experience of rupture, we are thrown back into that other scene, the ob-scene, the Un-conscious, whatever reality we have constructed in the social scene no longer providing sanctuary. We are unable to process our encounter with the real by means of the symbolic and/or imaginary "tools" at our disposal. Similarly, with music, we don't quite know what is happening to us, but we find ourselves reached, moved, transported. The "I" we have lived and lived from out of is no longer viable. For Freud, psychoanalysis was meant to be a practice of the real, a bridge through which we can begin to inhabit that other scene.

Zizek notes how what we call "reality" implies a surplus of fantasy filling out "the black hole" of the real. Questioning how real reality is, he states that what we understand as social reality, our social link, is

> nothing but a fragile symbolic cobweb that can at any moment
> be torn aside by an intrusion of the real. At any moment, the
> most common, everyday conversation, the most ordinary
> event, can take a dangerous turn, damage can be caused that
> cannot be undone.[22]

What we experience as "reality," consensually validated, taken-for-granted meanings within which we seem to have staked out our identities and identifications, can be upended, thrown into question, and, ultimately, destroyed by the intrusion of the real. Consequently, the subject, for Lacan, is a barred subject, the bar indicating a lack of any support that would offer the subject a positive, substantial identity. By identifying with some master signifier that would guarantee its place in the symbolic network, the subject tries to blind itself to this fundamental lack. The barred subject comes into being in response to the real and the failure of symbolic representation, the bar signifying the impossibility of "becoming oneself," of actualizing one's identity. Radically decentered, the subject is both overwritten and overridden by signifiers that belong to the Other and is subject to the traumatic *jouissance* of the other's desiring, a desiring that is manifested in the overwhelming impact of the other's presence to and/or absence from the subject.

Like the ongoing movement of music, whereby notes, phrases, and motifs exist merely in their relation to other notes, phrases, and motifs, the Lacanian subject, like the Freudian unconscious, is in perpetual motion, perpetually being created and destroyed in response to the ongoing impact of a chain of signifiers. The existence of the Lacanian subject throws into question the whole notion of identity. With respect to one's parents, a child may find itself asking, "Who do I need to be to survive in this family? In this world? How am I being created and destroyed by their desires and my capacity or lack thereof to respond in the ways they need me to respond to them and for them? And where am I in the mix?"

We may assume that we know ourselves as well as one another. However, for Lacan, what we experience as recognition is ultimately misrecognition (*meconnaissance*). Encounter is ultimately missed encounter. The gap separating the real from its modes of symbolization is irreducible. To be a subject is to be subject to, and, as Fink has noted, the subject is always suspended between language and *jouissance*, between the symbolic and the real, forging imaginary pathways to negotiate this gap, a gap providing the coordinates for the subject as desire, the subject as lack, the subject as existing only insofar as it can go on desiring, with fantasy filtering and filling in for the traumatic excess of the real.[23]

As Zizek states,

> the only proper attitude is that which fully assumes the gap as something that defines our human condition without endeavoring to suspend it through fetishistic disavowal, to keep it concealed through obsessive activity, or to reduce the gap between the real and the symbolic by projecting a (symbolic) message into the real. The fact that man is a speaking being means precisely that he is, so to speak, constitutively "derailed,"

marked by an irreducible fissure that the symbolic edifice
attempts in vain to repair.[24]

How do we assume this gap as core to our being? How do we allow
ourselves to find this gap living through us? How is this gap calling on us
to respond? Are we even aware of the gap's gaze and the ethical responsibility
that the latter implies? Lacan speaks of the unconscious as holding itself in
suspense in the area of the "unrealized" and the "unborn." Are we not being
called on to assume this very position, holding ourselves in suspense in
the area of the "unrealized" and the "unborn," not closing off the gap but
listening for its gaping?

Espousing an ethic of certainty through premature interpretations of
one's own life or the life of another forecloses primordial truths. Maurice
Blanchot has noted how the answer is the death of the question. Rather
than letting an experience grow, evolve, and come into its own, how often
do we interrupt the flow of our experience of ourselves in the ongoing
moment or the analysand's experience of him or herself in that moment?
How often do we break in on his or her music, a music in which the subject
is locating his or her own lostness? Lacan notes that

> perhaps it is part of the analyst's role, if the analyst is performing
> it properly, to be besieged—I mean *really*—by those in whom
> he has invoked this world of shades, without always being able
> to bring them up to the light of day.[25]

Dare we dwell in this world of shades? What is called for in allowing
ourselves to be "besieged" by the impact of those with whom we have
invoked that opening onto a darkness that may have enveloped them a
lifetime, a real beyond their capacity to imagine or symbolize? When
Shakespeare noted that "we are such stuff as dreams are made on and our
little life is rounded with a sleep," was he not pointing to that missed
encounter with the real, a real that jolts us out of our imaginary-symbolic
sleep such that all three registers overlap in a confusion of tongues, fracturing
the taken-for-granted balance we assumed held sway?

THE VOICE OF MUSIC

I would like to explore how the voice of music inhabits us, holding,
hearing, and responding to that "in us more than us." It provides an opening
through which we can begin to process an encounter with the real and it
memorializes the gap between the speakable and the unspeakable, the
thinkable and the unthinkable, the symbolic and the real. Lily Kraus, a
pianist arrested by the Japanese in the midst of a tour of Java during World

War II and kept in solitary confinement, sustained her sense of sanity as well as the will to go on being through hearing the Mozart piano sonatas in her mind, the voice of music providing a reason to continue living. During World War II, Gideon Klein, imprisoned in the concentration camp at Terezin and awaiting certain death, composed some of his greatest music—a piano sonata and a string trio, quartets, and choral works—the voice of music drawing out his own voice.

Growing up in my own family with a highly anxious mother who regularly communicated herself through angry screaming, I found myself unable to sense what I was feeling or thinking until I had played the piano. The music of Mozart, Chopin, or Brahms provided a space in which I could access my own voice in counterpoint to the emotional whirlwind I had just come through. Perhaps because of my own experience with the ways in which music allowed for a thawing of that frozen image imposed on me by a traumatized parent, I found myself using music with difficult-to-reach patients in situations where words (theirs or my own) seemed unable to access those dark places in which they found themselves immobilized and mute.

"Cheryl"

Some five years into her treatment, Cheryl, a 35-year-old woman who had been brutally incested and subjected to physical and emotional torture by each of her parents, came into her session sobbing uncontrollably, seemingly incapable of speech. After an extended period of anguished silence, I asked her if she would like to listen to some music. I played a recording of a piano transcription of the Bach cantata "Sheep May Safely Graze." Cheryl, feeling "buried alive" in the horror she was facing and experiencing so fully for the first time, found this music opening her onto a dimension of experiencing herself and her life which she no longer thought possible.

> That feels like there's something bigger in the universe. Such a sense of safety. I'm still floating. Like floating off to sea, but with hope. Like falling off to sleep and smiling. I feel like I'm being taken away somewhere . . . like I lost myself.

When I wondered if she might be finding herself in a different way, she nodded thoughtfully.

Listening to music seemed to enable Cheryl to bear witness to memories that up to that point had been unspeakable, as she came to more fully experience a real she had given up on ever being able to face. The slow movement of Mendelssohn's D minor piano trio evoked thoughts on the musicians on the *Titanic* who continued to make music while the ship was going down, the sinking ship becoming a metaphor for her life. She spoke of being an "inanimate object" on board, "gazing" at her own demise.

> What if I wrote a story about what it was like to be a deck chair on the Titanic? You're born into this world. You're given life. Out of the blue, you're supposed to be steady and sure. You hit an iceberg and sink so quickly. You just gather rust and become your own hidden city under the sea. Objects adapt to their underwater environment. Everything erodes. The sunken ship becomes a secret underworld. How can something that starts out so beautiful, new and great, through such a freak accident, just sink and have the life sucked out of it? (Now addressing me) You're the discoverer who found the sunken ship. You're bringing up little parts to the surface. You're trying to polish it so it can come back to life.

During a later session after a period of bearing witness to her overwhelming suicidal feelings, her anguished sobbing, and her desperate sense of helplessness, I again asked Cheryl whether she might want to hear some music. When she said yes, I played the slow movement of Mozart's *Sonata for Two Pianos in D Major*. When the movement ended, we shared an almost mystical silence. Cheryl then spoke.

> That puts everything in such a different place. You're transported someplace else. It opens time. Everything around just stops. It makes me feel that maybe I didn't lose my soul completely. I could listen to it over and over and feel a healing.

Cheryl felt reached and recognized by the music at a place she needed to be reached and to reach into, the music opening a field of experience that had been inaccessible for her up to this point.

Perhaps a primary mission of works of art is to bear witness to—and allow us to bear witness to—the real of our experience, opening a dream space in which we can begin to nibble on the indigestible, to use Michael Eigen's phrase. What might it mean to appreciate literature, painting, and music as a "testimony," inviting us to be with that which is beyond signification but which nevertheless exists and inside of which we find ourselves existing? How do we find ourselves questioned by works of art? How do we allow the impact of these works to matter? What might works of art teach us about psychoanalysis? Perhaps these works embody the missed encounter, inviting us to experience that gap between the real and the symbolic, calling on us to allow for and acknowledge a decentering which opens us onto something in us more than us.

On the evening of 9/11, I found myself at the piano, repeatedly playing the Bach Fugue in F-sharp Minor from Book I of the *Well-Tempered Clavier,* a profound dirge where the voices sigh as they weave their way through a landscape of deep sorrow. I could hear the voices of the dead and dying reaching into an other-worldly beyond. I must have played this fugue over and over for a good hour, the music allowing me to begin to fathom the unspeakable horror of what had just transpired. Zizek speaks of music as an act of supplication, a humble entreaty imploring the Other to respond, not as the symbolic Other but in and through the real of his or her being.[26] An attempt to reach for and encounter the real, music can be heard as a questing, an exploring, an infinite longing.

Rousseau claimed that music should be given the right to "speak for itself," noting that, in contrast to deceptive verbal speech, in music it is the truth that speaks. For Schopenhauer, music directly expresses the noumenal Will while speech remains limited to the level of phenomenal representation. According to Zizek:

> What music expresses is . . . the underlying "noumenal" flux of *jouissance,* beyond linguistic meaningfulness. . . . It is the inexpressible excess which forms the very core of the subject.[27]

Perhaps for the composer, performer, and listener, music may be understood as bearing witness to a real, offering itself as a medium through which one can begin to enter into that region of experience beyond the imaginary and symbolic. Music invites us into a place that is beyond words. Perhaps music incarnates that primordial Voice prior to the Word, inviting us to return to and recover our fundamental hallucinatory mode of being, a capacity we necessarily sacrificed with the advent of language in order to create and sustain the social link and all that society has come to imply. Perhaps music, the voice of music and the music of the voice, all call on us to begin to know that massive void in humanity that Freud addresses in *Civilization and Its Discontents*, inviting us into an encounter with the real, an encounter which our imaginary and symbolic modes of experiencing life necessarily miss.

ADDENDUM:

The following is drawn from Dr. Wetzler's thoughts on the music he performed following his delivering this paper as part of a workshop for the Object Relations Institute in New York City. It is included here to give the interested reader a taste of what music can evoke for the listener or performer.

Bach's *Toccata in E Minor,* BWV 914, begins with what can be heard as Bach speaking to God, two voices in a solemn back and forth. This is followed by a sense of wandering, the next section evoking a deep sense of sorrow. The Toccata concludes with a fugue in which three voices engage in a lively interplay.

Bach's *Toccata in D Major,* BWV 912, begins with a lively flourish, which, again, one can hear as Bach addressing God. The next section can be heard as God laughing, only to be followed by a questioning and an exploration of the darkness. A recitative serves as a transition, which opens onto a fugue expressing a sense of unbridled joy.

In his music, Bach seems to be sanctifying the voice in its many modalities: making a statement, calling out, crying, sighing, laughing, questioning, alone or in conjunction with one or more voices circling around a given motif.

Brahms's *Phantasien,* opus 116, consist of a series of *capriccios* and *intermezzi.* In the *capriccios,* Brahms seems to be exploring his own private madness, the turmoil inherent in each *capriccio* contrasting dramatically with the dreamy sadness of the *intermezzi.*

The "Presto energico" of the *Capriccio in D Minor* seems to express a sense of turbulence, agitation, and turmoil.

The "Andante" of the *Intermezzo in A Minor* brings out a deep sense of sadness along with a wandering in search of home.

The "Allegro passionato" of the *Capriccio in G Minor* punctuates outer sections expressing turbulence with a middle section evoking hope.

The "Adagio" of the *Intermezzo in E Major* opens onto a sense of nostalgia, a dreaming of what might have been.

The "Andante con grazia ed intimissimo sentimento" of the *Intermezzo in E Minor* evokes the pure terror of the Uncanny, sounding in music what can never be registered in speech.

The "Andantino teneramente" of the *Intermezzo in E Major* is a standing in the Holy, a tasting of the Sublime.

The final *capriccio* in D minor, "Allegro agitato," returns to a terrifying turbulence with darkness descending, ending with the bells of Fate.

RECORDINGS

Bach, J. S. *Toccata in D Major,* BWV 912, on *Glenn Gould/Bach Toccatas, Vol. 1,* CD, Sony Music, 2001.

———. *Toccata in E Minor,* BWV 914, on *Glenn Gould/Bach Toccatas, Vol. 2,* CD, Sony Music, 2001.

———. "Sheep May Safely Graze," on *Leon Fleisher: Two Hands,* CD, Vanguard Classics, 2004.

———. *Prelude in F# Minor,* on *The Well-Tempered Clavier, Book 1, Andras Schiff (Piano),* CD, Decca, 1984.

Brahms, J. *Phantasien,* opus 116, on *Brahms: Works for Solo Piano, Julius Katchen,* CD, Decca, 1997.

Mendelssohn, F. "Andante con moto tranquillo," on *Felix Mendelssohn Bartholdy: Piano Trio Nr. 1, opus 49 in D Minor (1839), Piano Trio Nr. 2, opus 66 in C Minor (1846),* Arden Trio, Canal Grande, 1991.

Mozart, W. A. "Andante," from *Sonata for Two Pianos,* K. 448 (375a), on *Mozart: The Music for Piano Duet: Klaviermusic zu vier Handen,* Christoph Eschenbach and Justus Frantz, Deutsche Grammophon, 1972. Reissued in 1990 on two CDs.

NOTES

[1] Jacques Hassoun, *The Cruelty of Depression: On Melancholy* (Reading, MA: Addison-Wesley, 1997), p. 20.

[2] Stephen Frosh, "Melancholy without the Other," *Studies in Gender and Sexuality* 7, no. 4 (2006): 363–378.

[3] Judith Butler, "Violence, Mourning, Politics," *Studies in Gender and Sexuality* 4, no. 4 (2003): 12.

[4] William Wordsworth, *Ode: Intimations of Immortality from Recollections of Early Childhood* (Boston: D. Lothrop and Company, 1884), p. 40.

[5] William Wordsworth, *The Borderers,* in *The Complete Poetical Works of William Wordsworth,* vol. 1, *Early Poems* (Boston: Houghton Mifflin, 1919), p. 179.

[6] Daniel L. Stern, *The Interpersonal World of the Infant* (New York: Basic Books, 1985).

[7] D. W. Winnicott, "New Light on Children's Thinking," in D. W. Winnicott, Clare Winnicott, Ray Shepherd, and Madeleine Davis, *Psycho-Analytic Explorations* (Cambridge: Harvard University Press, 1989), p. 155.

⁸ Author's notes from Apollon's Lacanian psychoanalytic seminar "The Clinic of the Symptom," Quebec City, Canada, 2005.

⁹ When Lacan speaks of *jouissance*, he is referring to an enjoyment that is transgressive (i.e., the *jouissance* intrinsic to a symptom). *Jouissance* breaks through the homeostatic balance intrinsic to the pleasure principle, partaking of a certain excess that opens onto death. *Jouissance*, which is often spoken of as an excess enjoyment, is that which works in us "beyond the pleasure principle."

¹⁰ Quote from pages 115–116 of an unpublished translation by C. Gallagher of Jacques Lacan, *Le seminaire of Jacques Lacan,* livre XXIII, *Le Sinthome* (1975–1976). This translation was made from unedited French manuscripts that were later published as Jacques Lacan, *Le sinthome: 1975–1976* (Paris: Editions du Seuil, 2005).

¹¹ *Ibid.,* p. 118.

¹² Author's notes from Apollon's Lacanian psychoanalytic seminar "Clinical Strategies and Psychic Structures," Quebec City, Canada, 2001.

¹³ Slavoj Zizek, *The Plague of Fantasies* (New York: Verso, 1997), p. 83n15.

¹⁴ Jacques Lacan, *The Seminar of Jacques Lacan,* Book 1, *Freud's Papers on Technique, 1953–1954,* ed. Jacques-Alain Miller, trans. John Forrester (New York: W.W. Norton, 1991), p. 16.

¹⁵ Jacques Lacan, *Ecrits: The First Complete Edition in English,* trans. Bruce Fink (New York: W.W. Norton, 2006), p. 524.

¹⁶ Lacan speaks of three orders or registers of reality: the imaginary, the symbolic, and the real, each of which is elaborated as this essay unfolds. Originating with our mirror image and the ways our image is reflected back to us by significant others, the imaginary consists of those fantasies of wholeness, stability, and consistency through which we negotiate our lives and mask the horror of what we cannot digest. The symbolic is essentially a linguistic dimension, modulating the imaginary through a system of preestablished modes of thinking and understanding into which we are born. Triadic in its structure, as opposed to the dyadic "you-me" structure of the imaginary, the symbolic opens onto the realms of lack, absence, and death. The real is outside language and cannot be symbolized. Lacan has spoken of the real as trauma that cannot be assimilated, the symbolic prematurely foreclosing and thus misrepresenting the impact of the real.

¹⁷ Robert Harari, *Lacan's Four Fundamental Concepts of Psychoanalysis: An Introduction,* trans. Judy Filc (New York: Other Press, 2004), p. 245.

¹⁸ Slavoj Zizek, *Welcome to the Desert of the Real! Five Essays on 11*

September and Related Dates (New York: Verso, 2002), p. 37.

[19] Shoshana Felman, and Dori Laub, *Testimony: Crises of Witnessing in Literature, Psychoanalysis, and History* (New York: Routledge, 1992), p. 116.

[20] *Ibid.*

[21] Jacques Lacan, *The Four Fundamental Concepts of Psychoanalysis* (New York: Norton, 1981), p. 54.

[22] Slavoj Zizek, *Looking Awry: An Introduction to Jacques Lacan through Popular Culture* (Cambridge: MIT Press, 1992), p. 17.

[23] Bruce Fink, *The Lacanian Subject: Between Language and Jouissance* (Princeton, NJ: Princeton University Press, 1995).

[24] Zizek, *Looking Awry,* p. 36.

[25] Lacan, *The Four Fundamental Concepts of Psychoanalysis,* p. 23.

[26] Zizek, *The Plague of Fantasies.*

[27] Slavoj Zizek, *The Parallax View* (Cambridge, MA: MIT Press, 2006), pp. 229–230.

10

An E-Mail Interview with Michael Eigen

Stephen Bloch

Michael Eigen is the author of eighteen books, including *Flames from the Unconscious: Trauma, Madness and Faith*; *Feeling Matters*; *The Psychoanalytic Mystic*; and *The Sensitive Self.* He has led a seminar on Bion, Winnicott, and Lacan for over thirty years. He is on the faculties of the National Psychological Association for Psychoanalysis and the New York University Postdoctoral Program in Psychotherapy and Psychoanalysis.

Stephen Bloch: Your writing seems so intrinsically musical. As others have commented, you write in a powerfully evocative manner, often from within a musical psyche rather than about it. Psychologist Aner Govrin, for example, has reflected on the musicality of your writing. Can you give us some thoughts on how you respond and feel yourself musically in the analytic encounter?

In *Toxic Nourishment,* you wrote that "very often deeply damaged people reach for something musical in the therapist and hope that the latter will respond to something deeply musical in themselves" (p. 82). I have carried this quote in me for a long time. Perhaps you can take further what this musical core is. Where are you in the room musically? Does this refer to specific works, themes, or auditory images or to a broad musical sensibility?

Michael Eigen: I don't think I especially think of music or think I'm tuning in to something musical in sessions, although sometimes I hum a tune or sounds come by themselves or I sing a bit of a lyric. Occasionally someone asks me to sing a lullaby like a mother might her child and I may do that, quietly, not knowing what will come out, a mixture of sound, word, hum. At such moments, I feel my chest quivering, resonating heart to heart, and bordering on tears. It is often a Jewish melody I make up, and the person I sing to weeps deeply, as if long waiting to be touched this way, scarcely believing that it's happening.

There is, too, the innate musicality of speaking/pausing, like notes and rests, intervals, rhythms, all that happens by itself, and there is much to be said for this kind of "dance." Since I was a jazz musician, improvisation is natural in sessions, and I can feel syncopated rhythms, jerks and pushes, fast runs, and legato. All this and more happens implicitly and rarely is centered in attention. I don't think one is unaware of these shifts and their musicality, but they are not usually focused on.

Music is in the skin, the feel of a moment. I have often been told that the tone of my voice touches someone inside, as if my soul is in my tone. Voice varies and sometimes is more musical than at other times. One goes through a lot of changes. The changes a baby goes through in a few hours would exhaust an adult—if an adult went through what a baby does he'd have to go to bed for a month to recover.

I mention these things, but they and others like them are not my focus of the moment. I want to bring out something deeper; you mention a musical core. There *is* a musical core. Perhaps more than one. For example, the sound of a session. How the session or a person sounds. People have, so to speak, smells—psychic smells—and they have sounds. The word sound, too, also connects with how sound one is—the soundness of mind or body or judgment or intention—hinting that in primordial language, feeling sounds. A popular song speaks of the sound of silence. There are also the sounds of feelings.

But here I want to go further and touch a soundless sound. There is soul music, inner music, akin to the music of the spheres. You can hear it. Yet it has no sound at all. Profoundly silent. Yet this silence sounds. It is deeply musical. Keats writes of "spirit ditties of no tone." There are moments when this no-tone is the inaudible tone of the universe. Poets often use words to communicate wordless realities. We speak of vibrating to one another or a bell ringing inside or my bell ringing your bell or yours ringing mine. What is it that rings? You can hear it or almost hear it—by what sense? Does quiet have a sound? My quietness and yours—hush, listen. Often we are told in the Bible, listen, hear.

Hear, O Israel, be quiet, listen, and you will hear God. Not simply a still small voice or a voice in the whirlwind but the voiceless. The purest music that sets the heart aquiver, heart to heart. In some sense, perhaps, the music of the spheres was a "projection" of music of the heart. Heart-music pervading, informing human life. Why not? Why so much cacophony? I once heard a bell made in Ireland arouse a taste of this purity. Pure sound. A divine tone in the flesh, mediated by the ear, the ear-soul or ear-heart connection. The word heart has ear in it, hear. An intimacy between ear and tear, to be touched by what one hears, moved to tears. We have a very musical body, a very musical mind. Yet there is music that hides this fact and music that shows it or is it. Voice, sound, impact, emanation. For Milner, places in the body were very important. Both Milner and Bion painted. Yes, painting is visual and an externalization of body elements as well. But it is also more and may come from body tonalities and give the latter expression via visual bodies. Some painting is musical. Kandinsky's (and perhaps Miro's) consciously so. In some way, if only at moments, we have a musical body.

Perhaps music is even a basic structure of our bodies, our rhythms, timing of processes. Perhaps there is a special ear that "hears" body times, rhythms, tonalities and builds on them, with them, an inaudible kind of hearing that feeds sound.

S.B.: I am struck by how early in your response you have foregrounded silence and its place in music (or music's place in silence). I think of two contemporary composers—John Tavener and Arvo Pärt (the so-called holy minimalists)—who deliberately use and relate to silence. A book of interviews with John Tavener is entitled *The Music of Silence*. Arvo Pärt in "Cantus in Memory of Benjamin Britten" begins the work with three "beats" of silence, bringing silence into the conscious awareness of the musicians and then the audience.

S.B.: Your reflections on music and Bion's notion of alpha function are a particular area I would like to explore.

M.E.: As mentioned near the end of my last response, music can show, music can hide. One can go further. Music can foster music or kill music. By that I mean, too, music can mediate psyche or kill psyche. We recoil at suicide but we are suicide-prone beings. We all kill ourselves one or another way.

One thinks of the huge importance to U.S. veterans that soldiers missing in action had. After the Vietnam War, obsession with combatants missing in action mounted. In retrospect, part of this must have had to do with a deeper sense that soldiers who returned were also "missing in action." A recent movie, *Waltz with Bashir,* shows the blotting out of vast areas of self and experience in face of war horrors. A lesser-known recent movie, *Leave No Soldier,* also focuses on this theme. The human psyche has the capacity to blot itself out in order to survive. We have defenses ranging from ignoring, numbing, deleting, dissociating, blotting out, killing off— killing off parts of ourselves or our capacities in order to go on living. Music plays a complex role in this too, as the soundtracks for the two movies I mentioned show.

Much hinges on how we use our capacities and ourselves, how functions are used. They can be used in nourishing and/or destructive ways. The same capacity, for example thinking or feeling or imagining or acting, can be used to enrich or impoverish living, to add to life or add to deprivation. Emotional starvation and emotional overeating are both real, depending, in part, on how emotions are used, how we relate to them, our modes of approach.

In the hands of the Nazis, music became an organ of the state to incite, cajole, push people past natural inhibitions to the point of aiding atrocities on a massive scale. This kind of use of music is not unusual, although in Nazi Germany the scope and horror of its use reached new levels. Music helped people go past the horror barrier and do things that might otherwise repel them. This is not what I call alpha use of music, not music for psychic nourishment in the profound sense. Perhaps you might call it ersatz nourishment, but that is too weak. Mock nourishment, demonic nourishment? There is such a thing as feeding devils, and music can play a role. But alpha music?

What can I mean by alpha music? In a chapter called "A Little Psyche-Music" in *The Sensitive Self,* I note that a ball player can make a great catch one moment and drop the ball the next. One moment, alpha body, the next a beta moment, one moment flowing, the next blocked, paralyzed. Likewise dancing. One moment you move fluidly and freely, dancing is wonderful; the next you are all left feet and stumble over yourself or your partner. Alpha movement one moment, beta another. So with any activity or capacity. Jazz musicians speak of being in the zone and at other times it's cliché. Alpha one moment, loss of alpha another.

An important aspect of alpha function is the role it plays in emotional digestion. When music is musical and music-ing, when it is alpha-ing, it not only mediates, conveys, and stimulates emotion, it also plays a role in processing, digesting, creating it. It is an important quality of alpha music that digestion and creation go together, that creation is a form of digestion and vice versa. The same happens, say, in Rilke's poetry, where an alpha word opens reality, creates reality, and at the same time begins the digestion of its creative transformations.

S.B.: The idea of opening and digesting experience is a powerful way of understanding a helpful analytic interpretation.

M.E.: Jesus signaled something like this when one moment he praised his student, saying "He is with God," the next moment saying of the same disciple, "You're of the Devil." This is a matter of spirit, some say intention, or, as I've sometimes called it, affective attitude. There are affective attitudes that act as viable frames of reference and modes of approach to experience that enrich the human spirit and life, mediate the creation and digestion of experience. And there are attitudes that poison experience. The Bible is always asking us to choose between sin and goodness, alternative paths of being. Perhaps what it is getting at over-literally also has to do with quality of feeling attitude, quality of heart-mind, or, in Bion language, quality of heart alpha, mind alpha. "Thou shalt know them by their fruits," says Jesus of prophets or, in this Bion moment, thou shalt know them by their alpha, by the way capacities are used.

S.B.: You are highlighting the fact that music can be destructive as well as constructive. This is an important caution against a too-sentimental understanding of the relationship between music and psyche. Some writers, in their enthusiasm, focus only on music's beneficial aspects. However, Gurdjieff, in writing about "objective music," stated: "There can be such music as would freeze water. There can be such music as would kill a man instantaneously" (quoted in Ouspensky, *In Search of the Miraculous*, p. 296). I am obviously not concerned with any physical claims here, but the thought of music that can block emotional sensitivity ("freeze water") and deaden aliveness is powerful. This is obviously close to your concerns in *Psychic Deadness* and "Killers in Dreams" (*Emotional Storm*).

M.E.: That is a wonderful quote.
Yes, it is said of God and Medusa that seeing either of them can kill you. "I die, I die" is a common saying when one is under the sway of deep feeling, erotic or sheer poetic musical beauty.
One feels one will go under, under the impact of unbearable beauty.

It is also true that music can function as a toxin. But it is also true that its power or beauty can destroy your usual way of organizing experience, destroy your own cliché, or habitual style, a radical revision of the psyche just by hearing a few notes. I was destroyed by the beginning notes in Beethoven's String Quartet No. 14 and by a few sounds the first time that I heard Bartok as a very young man. My approach to sensitivity underwent radical reworking in an instant. What I was moments before no longer existed, except perhaps as a dull shell that would haunt me like a ghost, skin that can't ever quite be shed but that was already dead, gone, old and buried. What the quartet and Bartok opened carried me into the me of the future—then!

S.B.: Would you share with us some of your thoughts on Freud and music?

M.E.: Everyone knows Freud said music wasn't his thing. His writing wasn't especially flowery, but there was a poetics to it, a deep music. The biggest award he got in his lifetime was a Goethe award for literature. There is deep music to his thought, and his clinical theory has to do with listening, hearing. He is rightly famous not for discovering the Oedipus complex but for using the Oedipus story to aid in discovering psychoanalysis (as Bion points out). Too many of his followers soon enough used psychoanalysis to reduce the arts. But the deeper truth is that the arts opened and continue to open psychoanalysis.

In one of Freud's later works, "Analysis Terminable and Interminable," there are two or three pages packed with musical possibility, suggesting an inherent rhythm of the psyche that can go wrong. In condensed fashion he brings together a number of tropes to evoke a sense of a stuck psyche, sticky or inert libido, something resembling entropy, a loss of psychic energy (he notes that the psyche has a fixed amount of energy, but via the death drive some can be lost in a fashion that is not known). In one or another way, loss or presence of vitality was a theme throughout his work from the beginning, when he wrote of loss of energy, weak libido, neurasthenia. My chapter on Freud in *Psychic Deadness* goes over this in detail and the chapter on Freud and Sade in *The Electrified Tightrope* adds [more].

What I want to bring out here is his noting in "Analysis Terminable and Interminable" that in the case of stuck libido something is off with the rhythm of the psyche. He speaks of timing, rhythm as basic to psychic function and experience. To be sure, one can make a case for the possibility, even likelihood, that he had Fliess's male-female biorhythms in mind. But I suspect this does not cover the ground, although it may play a subrole.

Freud is writing about a certain rhythm gone wrong, stopped, blocked, a paralysis, a loss of rhythm and flow and is doing so near the end of his life, when his own rhythms are challenged by disease, loss, and the desolation of war besetting Europe, European culture imploding-exploding in hideous ways with more on the horizon. The death drive formulation comes toward the end of his life and what may have looked like the end of an era of European civilization. Paradoxically, the Second World War led to a more united Europe in certain ways, but the problem of destructive force or energy still looms large in human life across the globe.

I am interested in Freud's referring to something malfunctioning in the rhythm and timing of the psyche when he speaks of death drive, masochism, inert, sticky libido, or a destructive force, essentially a self-destructive force. Something off in the music of the psyche. I feel that with his cultural background, which includes ancient Greek literature and philosophy, he is quasi-consciously/unconsciously also referring to the music of the spheres, which earlier I described as a projection of music of the psyche. We have a musical psyche, a rhythmic psyche. As world music and breakthroughs in modern music show, there are rhythms we do not know. Some get revealed/created as we experiment, as we listen and play and work. The emphasis on arrhythmia extends the horizon of what rhythm can be, surprise becoming a studied art.

When Bion was in New York, the only paper by a once New York based analyst he referred to was Theodore Reik's paper on surprise. Bion felt surprise was a constitutive dimension of psychic unfolding, rhythms of unfolding. It seems resonant that physicists speak of infinite dimensions enfolded in one another, implicit rhythms of enfolding-unfolding, akin to Cabalistic formulations of above in below, below in above (as above, so below; as below, so above), intricate interweavings of psychospiritual functions with emergent (surprising) possibilities. No accident that one of Bion's last seminars explicitly viewed psychoanalysis as akin to art (the Paris Seminar, 1978).

The music of the psyche, the rhythm of the psyche, can be a rhythm of surprise, a rhythm that plays against and breaks rhythm—that opens new rhythmic possibilities. Thus rhythm is not necessarily a homeostatic thing. There are rhythms that destroy homeostasis, break new experiential ground. There are really amazing jazz drummers today who never seem to play the same thing twice, even when they do. Something keeps varying in thrilling ways, sometimes tone or emphasis or texture, but often sequence and pulse of whatever the drums pull out of themselves. When I was younger, playing in college bands, my favorite time was the end of the job when our drummer would play for us with his hands, no sticks or brushes, back to the hands—such a soft touch he had—and the rhythms never stopped changing. I could weep listening, my whole body mesmerized, needy, wanting more and more. No matter how long he played, I never wanted him to stop. My sense now is that this is what psychic processing is like, what alpha is like, an ever-changing rhythm, the depths and scope of which we scarcely can imagine. It is part of emotional life that we can express or narrate or convey only a bit of what we feel. We do not know the whole of it. There is always some frustration built in. It is like swimming in the ocean. We can never take in the whole ocean all at once. But we do swim in part of it, and the water we swim in, while not the whole ocean, is real water.

In my chapter "A Basic Rhythm" in *The Sensitive Self,* I try to bring out rhythmic variations having to do with coming through destruction and use Winnicott's "use of the object" formulation, passages from Henry Elkin's work, and a Bion passage having to do with being murdered and being all right. Coming through destruction, a basic theme and rhythm. So much derives from it, including versions of rebirth, renewal, a new heart but also a new realism, seeing things as they are. There are no contradictions when it comes to human capacities. Our job is to learn if it is possible and how it is possible to live in such a way that our diverse capacities are mutually nourishing and that all together they nourish life.

Bion writes of common sense and by this he means many things. The senses may not work in tandem. They may tear each other apart. And agreed-upon common sense between human groups may not work in tandem but may heighten destruction via alliances (banding together in order to destroy targets). Shakespeare describes alliances as a way to jockey for power and destroy "enemies" or "obstacles." Links to destroy other links. Sometimes Shakespeare's logic is so black (Lear, for example), that destruction has the final word, with the exception that the viewer suffers a kind of "renewal" at seeing a truth of the psyche, a fact of life. The coming through comes not in the play where all is nullity, but in the viewer. One goes through the experience and comes back for more. When it comes to making contact with life through Shakespeare, one always comes back for more. The rhythm of coming through lives through those who undergo Lear and receive the transmission and go on experiencing what Lear opens up.

Freud takes the music of the psyche forward by variations on the theme of life and death and death and deadness. One who is dying may find in the process how alive he is at the moment of truth, instants before the light goes out (as Tolstoy depicts in *The Death of Ivan Ilyich*). Death makes me more alive, stimulates new rhythmic possibilities.

Freud speaks of consciousness as a psychic sense organ, a sense organ of psychical qualities. Language, too, can be viewed as a sense organ when used expressively, evocatively, when the concern is giving voice to feeling, letting feeling speak. Sense is a packed word, spanning many levels, from traditional references to sensory experience to sense as meaning, common sense and a certain "realism," and this amazing meaning Freud touches, consciousness itself as a kind of sense organ, a sensing of psychic qualities. We have a sense of psychic smell and taste, the taste and smell of experience. We smell and taste each other's psyches, psyche to psyche, like dogs smell assholes. We smell and taste each other's personalities. "Follow your nose," we advise someone who needs to use intuition. We mean a psychospiritual sensing. We speak of animal sensing, as when we sense danger or safety, sense the possibility of nourishment, sense a good or bad day, sense a storm, sense a moment of peace. What is this sense organ? Why call it an organ? Organic? Spontaneous? Something intrinsic?

Music is part of this domain of sensing, a special sensing that invisibly permeates our bodies, becomes our bodies. Music is part of poetry and art, rhythm and timing and color and sound. But something else too, something ineffable, a sense or feel, a musical feel, a musical sense. As you bring out, the possibilities of what is musical changes with time, age, culture, history. To what extent does music follow history, to what extent does it lead history? Herbert Read wrote that image precedes verbal idea by about 200 years. And music? We certainly are aware of correlations between forms of music, architecture, writing, and politics of an age. And Spengler writes of souls of cultures. The role that music plays in creating the tone or even forms of culture—more can be done. Music as a sense organ, like an animal senses scents in the wind, only more so, more fully, bringing into being worlds of experience that otherwise would have been silent or not been born at all.

S.B.: I feel a basic rhythm in the image of the Black Sun. This is a symbol with multiple resonances. On the one hand it is an image of a "destructive force" in the psyche. Taking it further, if one thinks of blackness as a negating force, then the black is the force of nullity, evacuation, and emptying out. The Black Sun, for me then, is a pulse between emptiness and form, absence and presence. In an auditory channel the earliest origins may be in the sound, in utero, of the mother's heartbeat, an oscillation between nullity (absence) and connection (presence).

M.E.: Coming through destruction, a basic rhythm. Yes, but we come through only partially. We are engaged in lifelong births and abortions. Our coming through is partial. When there is rebirth it is partial. Some rebirths seem total and change the direction of a life. But lifelong work on oneself continues in light of the new revelation. Every birth on the psychospiritual plane is also a partial abortion. And work on oneself continues little by little, day by day (sufficient unto the day is the evil thereof). There is beatific experience, revelation, a change of the Archimedean point of soul or spirit. But there is endless mop-up work, working with one's character and personality, struggles with barriers and toxins. Near the end of *Feeling Matters,* there is a chapter called "The Annihilated Self," wherein variations of annihilated aspects of personality are expressed. Rebirth is partial birth and partial abortion. In *Coming through the Whirlwind,* I speak of rebirth as a basic structure or psychic movement and experience, but often rebirth rhythms are aborted and one keeps trying to right it, whether realistically, demonically, by varied mixtures. Look what hells rebirths have wreaked. Yet it is a basic experience that uplifts the soul. One we need to learn how to work with, an essential movement or rhythm we need to partner and develop.

S.B.: I have a simple curiosity as to the music that has meant a lot to you. What is the music behind you?

M.E.: I was pretty much born into music. My mother played piano, my father fiddled. I started piano lessons pretty young and played my first recital when I was six. When I was maybe seven or possibly eight, a man came around to the Catskill hotel we were at one summer, put a hat on the ground, took out black parts, assembled them, started to play. Blew my brains out, no, my heart, tore my heart and lit me up. It was, you guessed, a clarinet and he played Yiddish music. It was the most exciting thing that had happened to me since I saw stars in the night when I was a bit over two and died inside. I mean died of joy, amazement, happiness, love. I couldn't stop staring. They lit my heart up. Now years later I can look back and also say that part of what I felt was love that such things could be. I fell in love with the universe, a love that remains, although I know how horrible this world can be and is.

At about seven or eight I started clarinet lessons and studied piano and clarinet throughout childhood. My clarinet teacher would play a little after lessons and I would laugh and laugh. He threatened time and again to stop playing if I laughed. But I could not help it. It was one of my greatest pleasures, to hear the sounds he made and laugh and laugh, they tickled me so.

As teens approached I felt I wanted to play tenor sax. I think it was sex. The deep sound of the tenor, sensuous, sexy, full, heavenly. It didn't light me up like stars or the clarinet sound, but it was part of growing up for me, going with girls, playing in bands. I think in 8th grade I started my first band and we played at a "Y" dance and stunk. I never played in a band that stunk again. I bought my own tenor and played until I was good. Sort of the way I learned to ride a motorcycle years later. I somehow or other managed to get it where I lived and rode it all night, falls and all, and by morning I was a cyclist.

I played sax through high school and college and a bit after. I heard Bird and saw Miles when he was just starting with Bird, then saw Miles as he developed all through, saw everybody I could in those days, listened, imitated, tried things. Bud Powell became my favorite piano player, but I also loved Erroll Garner and for a time in college Dave Brubeck. I started playing piano more. One day the piano player was sick and didn't show up for a job and I sat in and, in time, that's what I ended up playing for the rest of the time I played, through my mid-twenties. I was getting deep into psychoanalysis by then and it is a regret that I did not keep on playing too. I plunged into psychoanalysis, hooked by psychic life, and never came out. When my kids were growing up, one played bass, the other drums, so I played piano with them. It was a thrill playing jazz with my kids.

As hinted earlier, when I was young I loved Bartok, Stravinsky, James Joyce (speaking of music!), Klee, Kandinsky, but also Bach and especially Vivaldi. Vivaldi lit me up for a time like the clarinet and stars once did, and I felt it was the most centered music I had ever heard. My taste now is pretty old-fashioned. When I put on a CD it tends to be Bach (solo violin sonatas), Beethoven (late quartets, chamber groups), Haydn, Mozart, Handel (solo piano). I'll listen to and dig anything you play for me but when alone my taste would seem pretty conservative to you now. When I play piano, it's my version of jazz. I say my version because I fear I don't know any better. Now and then my son the bass player plays with me, and he's played with some really good pianists and I am grateful he tolerates me. There's nothing like hearing a bass when you play.

When I write I see colors and hear music, or maybe I should say hear the words musically, as color and sound. I think I may have been in my early thirties when I dreamt that I should paint small, not large canvasses. You could see the canvasses in the dream. I took this to mean I needed to pour my creativeness into smaller frames, smaller work, and my first psychoanalytic writing involved shortish papers. I also published a short story and some poems. The idea that I was to do smallish things was freeing, took a lot of pressure off. I could compress a lot into small spaces. This led to writing being less fragmenting, depressing, injurious. I could write in small doses and condense the intensity, and this enabled me to survive the process better in the long run. It takes a lot to learn what might work for one. In time, I found as a therapist that dosing things out was a key, at least for me.

The other day when I was thinking of words and wordlessness, the following came, two little bits:

> words as waves and wind
> ear to them
> listening to words as
> a sea shell
>
> hearing sea
> in the silence
> of words

Paul Ashton: I had heard about the film *Into Great Silence* two years before it came to South Africa and expected that I would love it. When I finally saw it I had just come back from a two-week winter safari with my wife and daughter. We had lived close to the "ground" and experienced storms, floods, cold; wide, wide spaces; towering mountains; and an ever-changing night- and day-time sky. When I did see the film, apart from the long held shots of simple objects, suggesting mindfulness, I found it lacking. I wondered if this had something to do with the fact that we had experienced "God's Cathedral" and the film was about "man's monastery." The silence imposed on the monks is very different from the silence of the cosmos, which evokes something like "the absence of God in God's presence." Would you comment on this?

M.E.: Our experiences, Paul's and mine, are very different. I loved *Into Great Silence*. I had an immediate sense of recognition. The movie touched something in my spiritual core and had the effect of diminishing shame. When I saw the faces in prayer and meditation, I felt shells of shame begin to fall off my soul and inner body. Their faces were the way I felt, and seeing them gave a kind of permission to live that part of me more fully, less apologetically, less defensively.

In our society, to be a man was to be aggressive, achieving, out for power, sex, money. Yet these faces, these supplicants—unashamed of the deep intimacy with God they touched and courted. To court God in deepest intimacy. Supplicants—a word resonating with supple. Instead of harsh, to be supple. To unabashedly spend time with Intimate Presence, as much time as one wants or can. It helped free me to meditate and pray for longer periods, following the moment, on my knees, standing, sitting, head in hands, hands uplifted, head bowed, head lifted, heartfelt, ordinary, bored, caring. Whatever. It is a wonderful thing to give oneself this time, this contact with the Deep One. Perhaps at my age and condition time is more precious and the need for the Deepest of All is pressing.

I needed the faces of these monks but didn't know it. As soon as I saw them, I knew my own face, my inner face. I'm far from being psychologically blind, so I know the monks have problems, serious problems, perhaps with no way to address them. I take for granted we are all quite mad and wounded and have ways that work and others that fail to address our beings. For me, all this goes into parenthesis. I do not need to know their bag of worms. I know what worms are like. What the faces of the monks who allowed themselves to be photographed gave me is what I needed this moment of my existence, permission to come out of closets I didn't quite know I was in, spiritual closets. To come out in the open— again, in new ways.

There is a silence deeper than music. Perhaps not even music goes all the way. Music can distract from this silence. There are times listening to music or playing it brings me deeper into contact with deepest silence. There are times it is an imposition, takes me away from it. It takes time and experience to be able to link up with how you feel from moment to moment. When to stop playing or listening, when to turn the CD off, when to fall on your knees or stand in hushed attention listening to —?

Zen has an image of cutting a thread that holds everything. You cut this thread and words like "stillness," "silence" don't come close. Some call it absolute samadhi. It is breathtaking. But words like this are silly. As Zennists say, you have to experience it and experience it your way. When you know your samadhi, no one can talk you out of it. You impose nothing on others or yourself. And when you come back, you say thank you. Bow. Care. Life is in full bloom.

The deepest processing goes on in this silence. I don't know whether or not it is musical or music reaches it. More likely, music grows from it.

Music that grows from it and mediates it processes deep emotion as part of its work. To process feeling is one of the great tasks facing us as evolving beings. As one of my book titles says, *Feeling Matters*. Our ability to produce states is way ahead of our ability to process them. Music creates experience but also plays a role in processing experience. As other creative arts do too. Dance creates experience and catalyzes body processing of it at the same time. One might say dance is part of music or music grows out of dance or is dance. We can argue about primacies for the rest of our existence, which might be fun. There are networks of possibilities creativity opens. We do not know the beginnings or ends of these networks, which keep growing.

Any moment of art can take us closer or farther, open or act as barrier to the Deep Silence that prayer and meditation mediate. As mentioned above, Keats has a phrase, "spirit ditties of no tone." Yet it is not simply this Deep Silence that we are after. We love the color of sound. It opens us, soothes, excites, dumbfounds, thrills, nourishes. It can express catastrophe, faith, horror, foreboding, and presentiment in instants. Silence and the color of sound further each other, extend nuances and possibilities of both. They can, too, compete with and deform each other. So much depends on encompassing attitudes, implicit affective frames that are part of the background of creative work.

The night before I was to be on a panel discussing *Into Great Silence,* the following words came to me. Don't expect too much from them, just a little sharing of a passing moment. They came after an hour or so of sitting quietly.

> weight lifts, oppression lifts
> heaven, hell and purgatory lift
> beyond distinction and no distinction
> beyond self and God.
> great is Your faith
> to live in Your faith

The words grew out of sitting for an hour but refer to a Hebrew prayer said upon awakening. The prayer, loosely translated, goes something like: Thank You for restoring my soul, Presence in all, great is Your faith. At first glance, it might sound odd to praise God for His faith. Isn't my faith what's at risk? Then I realize, perhaps this means God has enough faith in me to give me another day. Another chance to make something of the time I have, to move someone, light someone, bring life to another place. God has enough faith that I might come through, worms and all. A communication one wants to share. The phrase "to live in Your faith" may touch another line from the morning prayers, "In Your light do we see light." The variation my words produced: "In Your faith do we live faith." This faith is deeply musical. It is such deep music that it takes us beyond music, if that is possible.

In *The Psychoanalytic Mystic,* I write that psychoanalysis is a form of prayer. Music can be too. This does not mean prayer is all that psychoanalysis or music is. Far from it. But the link is worth entering. In my own life, they (music and prayer—psychoanalysis came later) grew together. I could fantasize that they have roots in my mother's musical voice when I was a baby. But then I would have to say that her musical voice had roots in—love.

BIBLIOGRAPHY

Bion, W. R. "A Seminar Held in Paris." July 10, 1978. Originally published in French in *Revue Psychotherapie Psychanalytique de Groupe* in 1978. Published in English on the British Psychoanalytical Society Web site at http://www.psychoanalysis.org.uk/bion78.htm.

Eigen, Michael. *Coming through the Whirlwind.* Wilmette, IL: Chiron Publications, 1992.

———. *Emotional Storm.* Middletown, CT: Wesleyan University Press, 2005.

———. *The Electrified Tightrope.* 1993; repr., London: Karnac Books, 2004.

———. *Psychic Deadness.* 1996; repr., London: Karnac Books, 2004.

———. *The Psychoanalytic Mystic.* London: Free Association Books, 1998.

———. *The Sensitive Self.* Middletown, CT: Wesleyan University Press, 2004.

Freud, Sigmund. "Analysis Terminable and Interminable (1937)." In *The Standard Edition of the Complete Works of Sigmund Freud,* vol. 23, *Moses and Monotheism,* ed. James Strachey et al. London: Hogarth, 1974.

Govrin, Aner. "The Area of Faith between Eigen and His Readers." *Quadrant: Journal of the C. G. Jung Foundation for Analytical Psychology* 37, no. 1 (2007): 9–27.

Ouspensky, P. D. *In Search of the Miraculous: Fragments of an Unknown Teaching.* New York: Harcourt and Brace, 1949.

Read, Michael. *Icon and Idea: The Function of Art in the Development of Human Consciousness.* Cambridge: Harvard University Press, 1955.

Tavener, John. *The Music of Silence.* Ed. B. Keeble. London: Faber and Faber, 1999.

11

The Music of Unthinkable Anxiety and Nameless Dread

LAWRENCE A. WETZLER

When listening to a psychotic discourse I discover with continual astonishment the extent to which it discloses a measure of ultimate truth that appears to be inaccessible to ordinary humans, perhaps because it is incompatible with the illusions we all maintain in order to invest life with meaning.—Piera Aulagnier[1]

REACHING FOR THE AGONY

Through much of his writing, Winnicott concerns himself with evacuated human beings . . . those who, having never found a home inside their parents, can never find a home within themselves. Psychosis is understood as the premature organization of agony, a precocious structuralization of the personality that is a complex defense against an agony that cannot be experienced and agonized over. The work of the analyst involves giving agony a home.

Winnicott describes the enormous damage that occurs when one is born into an environment that is unable to support one's development. "When there is not good enough mothering, the infant is not able to get started with ego-maturation or else ego development is necessarily distorted." He speaks of the baby "as an immature being who is all the time on the brink of unthinkable anxiety." Falling into this state is only forestalled by the mother's capacity "to put herself in the baby's place and to know what the baby needs in the general management of the body, and therefore of the person."[2] When the mothering one is absent, preoccupied, or overwhelmed by her own emotional state of being and unable to provide what the baby needs for its own development at that stage of absolute dependence, the baby is catapulted into a state of unthinkable anxiety.

For Winnicott, every infant has a fundamental need to experience a beginning phase of life, which he calls "unintegration." Being in this originary state of unintegration is experienced as relaxation by the infant. As the mother's ego-supportive functioning can be taken for granted, there is no felt need to integrate. The baby is able to be totally dependent while being totally unaware of being dependent. Without the experience of this originary unintegration, there is no resting place, no home, and one is never able to truly rest, feel safe, or be at home with oneself or with another. In his later writing, Winnicott associates unintegration with regression to dependence: "The patient regresses because of a new environmental provision which allows of dependence."[3] Unintegration manifests itself as a state of being, achieved in analysis by those patients who are able to reach into, and rest in, that place where their psychic development originally got derailed, irreparably damaged, or deformed while in the very process of being formed.

Winnicott conceives of this originary point of breakdown as "a fact hidden away in the unconscious." Although patients may desire to remember this original experience of primitive agony and are always reaching into that place where their psyche's development became derailed, "it is not possible to remember something that has not yet happened because the patient was not there for it to happen to."[4] Blown to bits in the very process of its own development, the psyche undergoes a breakdown in an integration that has not yet happened.

Winnicott speaks of psychosis as an illness that has its point of origin in the stages of individual development prior to the establishment of an individual personality pattern. Psychosis results from a loss, break, or rupture in continuity prior to the development of the capacity to bear such a disruption. He claims that it is not useful to think of psychosis as a breakdown. Rather, it is a defensive organization relative to a primitive agony or what he ultimately refers to as a state of disintegration. Disintegration is understood as "an *active* production of chaos in defense against unintegration in the absence of maternal ego-support, that is, against the unthinkable or archaic anxiety that results from failure of holding in the stage of absolute dependence."[5] This "*organization towards invulnerability,*" this active creation of chaos, protects the patient from a state of being that would be much more terrifying and unbearable.[6]

Winnicott takes note of the relationship between a patient's fear of breakdown and the fear of death.[7] Some patients seem compelled to look for death and seem strangely drawn to deathlike images. He understands this movement as a search for the death that has already happened but was not experienced, as the patient was not yet mature enough to experience psychic death. Such a death has the impact of annihilation. He notes how many people spend their lives wondering whether to find a solution by suicide—that is, sending the body to a death that has already happened to the psyche.

Perhaps Freud's notion of the death instinct was created to substitute, at least in part, for recognition of a death that has already happened to all of us but that may be too unbearable for us to experience or acknowledge. Winnicott is describing a psychic death one can neither comprehend nor escape from and in response to which one can live a lifetime with the feeling that one has not yet begun to exist.

In a later work, Winnicott notes the relation between the fear of madness and the fear of dying without anybody being there at the time, that is, "with nobody there who is concerned in some way that derives directly from the very early infant-parent relationship."[8] Eigen has noted how we all die alone many times as babies and come back from the dead to talk about it.[9] How often are our patients saying to us in so many ways, "Can't you see how I have died and am dying . . . in these ways . . . with you . . . here . . . at this moment?" We are being called on to appreciate how exhausting our patients' self-holding patterns have become and how they long for (and are terrified of) moving toward that state of unintegration in the transference, from out of which they may experience, for the first time, their original breakdown. Recall Freud's report of that dream in which a father's dead child wakes him, whispering reproachfully, "Father, don't you see I'm burning?"[10] The dead child behaves in the dream as if he were once more alive.

How can we recognize our patients' dying while honoring the exquisitely personal nature of the event? For Winnicott, the preservation of personal isolation through what he refers to as "the incommunicado self" is part of the search for identity as well as for the establishment of a personal technique for communicating that does not lead to violation of the central self.[11] Although it may be a tragedy never to be found, perhaps it is an even greater tragedy to be found before being there to be found. We are challenged to be there with our patients as they circle round their personal madness. Winnicott states that whenever we reach into these core places, we know there is some ego organization that is able to suffer. And this means going-on-suffering so as to become aware of suffering. The original madness, or breakdown of defenses, if it were to be experienced, would be indescribably painful. The nearest one can get to one's core madness involves experiencing whatever is available of psychotic anxiety as it emerges in the transference.

It is very painful to be with ourselves and our patients in those moments when they are reaching into their madness, allowing themselves to be mad in the analytic setting, engaging in a reliving in the transference, which is the nearest they can ever get to that point where their psychic development ended and disintegrative defenses took the place of true growth. According to Winnicott, any attempt on the part of the analyst to be sane or logical destroys the only route the patient can forge back to their madness.[12] This is a madness that needs to be recovered in experience because it cannot be recovered in memory. The analyst has to be able to tolerate whole sessions or even periods of analysis in which logic is not applicable in any description of the transference. Consequently, an analyst needs to consider the fact that there are ways of interpreting a patient's experience that are devastating and that cover over the embryonic emergence of a madness that simply must be experienced. Interpreting a patient to himself or herself can prematurely move that patient onto a symbolic level, derailing the patient from an agony he or she may be struggling to reach.

Winnicott believes that the patient is under a compulsion to get to the madness; and this compulsion is slightly more powerful than the need to get away from it. The patient is forever caught up in a conflict between the fear of madness and the need to be mad. Cure comes only if the patient can reach to the core anxiety around which the defenses were organized; that is, to the original state of breakdown. Winnicott refers to this state of affairs as X. What is absolutely personal to the individual is X. Patients are repeatedly reaching toward X in the transference. As the patient is able to be more and more mad in the treatment, the analyst is called on to allow this madness to become a manageable experience from which the patient can make a spontaneous recovery.

THE MUSIC PRIOR TO WORDS

It has been said that music sounds like feelings feel. Tensions build and resolve, rise and fall, expand and contract. Music can communicate on profound levels without words. Mothers sing lullabies to their babies. Babies woo their mothers with their cooing. Eigen has noted that very often deeply damaged people reach for something musical in the therapist and hope that the latter will respond to something deeply musical in them. At such moments, how we sound to each other is a gateway to how we taste emotionally.[13] Aren't we always playing on one another's psyches? The patient does something to the analyst and the analyst does something to the patient. Are we attuned to the music of the session? Can we hear the music of our patients' lives, which may be an ever-present background and, hence, contextual for whomever they are able to be with us now? Are we not all born into and do we not already find ourselves inhabiting and inhabited by an ever-present music of sorts . . . cultural, familial, linguistic, emotional?

I experience my work with patients along musical dimensions. I listen to myself and to them from within the music we make together. Such a listening allows for a hearing of the fluidity of interweaving voices in the affective presence they embody with us and we with them. I see myself as helping patients sing their song and give voice to a music that may have been long submerged in the cacophony of a confused and deeply pained experience growing up in their family of origin. I am deeply moved by Winnicott's description of the psychic death patients undergo early in their development and the courageous efforts they make to reach into that most personal, inviolable place in order to retrieve, in the transference, a sense of their core agony and resume a growth process that had ceased.

What does it mean for the analyst to stay alive in the face of death, the patient's or his or her own? Perhaps the analyst, like the patient, is being called on to grow the capacity to suffer madness, to partner with the patient as well as with him/herself in wonder, reverence, and awe as this incommunicado dimension of experience finds its place in the treatment. Remember, if you would, Winnicott's prayer, "Oh God! May I be alive when I die."[14]

At one point, Winnicott refers to the "silent scream" in his work with a patient who somehow knows that not-screaming is the theme behind all the material she produces.[15] The great *non-event* of every session is screaming. The child cried and the mother did not appear. The scream that the patient is looking for is the last scream just before hope was abandoned.

Schubert's *Erlkönig* is a song that incarnates the unheard scream. It also embodies what Bion has referred to as a failure in reverie, whether between parent and child, analyst and patient, or conscious and unconscious. The music and words tell of a father riding through the night with his young son, the horse galloping headlong into the unknown, the boy calling out to his father that Death is coming for him, the father seemingly oblivious to his son's cries for help. Consequently, the boy dies alone, unheard, in his father's arms. Again, we may be reminded of how

our patients are calling out to us to see that they are dying, beckoning us
to recognize what they are undergoing and to be with them in their daring
to experience and own a core madness against which they have erected a
lifetime of brittle defenses.

I find myself in the midst of such an emotional storm with Cheryl.
She is being carried through the darkness by the couple we have become
and we are both being swept along by a dark force that seems greater than
either of us. At times I get the sense that Death has descended. Entire
sessions are filled with a sobbing that spills over into a hiccuping with Cheryl
gagging for breath, her anguish accompanied by a seeming refusal to speak.
Cheryl simply shakes her head in hopelessness at my feeble attempts to
make contact with her. She is without words for what she is going through.
And so we sit together in a pained silence, her sobbing punctuating the
sense of dread I am experiencing. For the most part, I am unaware of what
has triggered this state of utter despair.

At one point, in the midst of Cheryl's anguished sobs, I found myself
thinking the words from the 23rd Psalm, words that somehow transformed
the situation I found myself in. "She leadeth me beside the still waters" .
. . the river, Lethe? . . . "she restoreth my soul" . . . there was something
healing about her sharing her agony with me in this moment . . . healing
for each of us, even though we were without words for what was happening.
"Yea, though I walk through the valley of the shadow of death, I will fear
no evil" . . . Cheryl seemed to be re-experiencing her deepest agony in my
presence and felt safe enough to allow a psychic bleeding in the moment,
trusting that I would be with her in her agony. "For thou art with me; Thy
rod and Thy staff, they comfort me." I could sense how I *was* with Cheryl
in the darkness enveloping us both. And so the dimension of *faith* emerged
for me as I sat with Cheryl through her tortured periods, believing that I
was providing a home for an unbearable pain that I may have unwittingly
triggered and for which I would try to stay present. I found myself enveloped
both by her heaving sobs and my own inner terror.

CAN YOU FEEL WHAT I FEEL?

In understanding projective identification as a realistic activity we all
engage in as well as a rudimentary mode of communication between
mother and child, Bion speaks of the latter as consisting of behavior
intended to arouse in the mothering one feelings that the infant wishes to
be rid of.[16] If the infant fears that it is dying, it can arouse fears that it is
dying in the mother. A well-balanced mother can accept these
communications in a manner that makes the infant feel that it is receiving

its frightened personality back again but in a form that it can tolerate; that is, the fears become manageable by the infant personality.

If the mother cannot tolerate these projections, the infant is reduced to continued projective identification carried out with increasing force and frequency, and the infant's fear that it is dying is denuded of meaning. It therefore reintrojects not a fear of dying made tolerable, but a nameless dread. If the mother cannot be present to her infant, "the infant takes back into itself the sense of impending disaster which has grown more terrifying through the mother's rejection and through its own rejection of the feeling of dread. . . . Matters get worse and worse until the infant cannot stand its own screams any longer. In fact, left to deal with them by itself, it becomes silent and closes inside itself a frightening and bad thing, something which it fears may burst out again."[17] This new, terrifying, internal object is referred to as the murderous superego.

The infant has introjected "a peculiar form of primitive superego hostile to projective identification even as a method of communication, and so, by extension, to all forms of communication."[18] The infant's attempts at seeking are traumatized and its capacity to communicate are mutilated. According to Bion, the infant is left with "the semblance of a psyche," the predominant characteristic of which is "without-ness."[19] In the violence of the unresponded-to scream and the forcefulness of the projection, the infant virtually evacuates its whole personality, including its will to live, collapsing into itself as if into a black hole. The result of the mother's rejection of the infant's projective identificatory communications is disaster, the infant remaining catastrophically unborn; that is, in a state of frozen unintegration.

After describing the devastating impact of the mother who cannot tolerate her baby's prerequisites for growth, Bion asks whether the analyst can tolerate growth. Can the community tolerate growth? Can a nation tolerate growth? Or does it get so frightened of it that it has to say, "Thus far and no further"? When does the analyst find himself or herself paralyzed with a sense of unthinkable anxiety and/or nameless dread? When does the analyst close down and reject the patient's projective identifications? How often do we unconsciously replicate a patient's primal trauma, leaving him or her with feelings that cannot find feelings in us, insides that can't find our insides? People who come for treatment are seeking an analyst for whom projective identificatory communication will be a genuine possibility. The seeker is a projector and projection seeks an object. Bion concerns himself with the analyst's dread both of experiencing the mental turbulence a patient communicates and recognizing the black hole into which the patient's existence has collapsed.

> Can he "detect" turmoil? We are unlikely to welcome the capacity
> to do so. This continuing mental activity can be so hated or
> feared that the person who experiences it thinks that he is having
> what he calls a "mental breakdown". The practicing analyst must
> get hardened to mental breakdown and become reconciled to
> the feeling of continuously breaking down; that is the price
> which we have to pay for growth. We cannot fall back on the
> idea of being cured, because that is an old-fashioned and
> inappropriate term. We have to be reconciled to the feeling that
> we are on the verge of a breakdown or some kind of mental
> disaster; we have to have a certain toughness to stand this
> continuing experience of mental growth. . . . So you can take
> your choice; mental stagnation and decay on the one hand, or
> perpetual upheaval on the other—like living in the middle of a
> mental breakdown, without being clear whether one is breaking
> up or breaking down.[20]

Gustav Mahler's "Adagietto" from his Fifth Symphony seems to incarnate this sense of the unborn straining to be born, reaching out, seeking what Bion has referred to as "tropisms" that in certain circumstances may be too powerful for the modes of communication available to the personality. We sometimes experience moments in our work where speaking seems to be a barrier to what needs to be communicated, covering over a turbulence that would be experienced were nothing said.

> Patients often want to tell you something, but all they have
> available are the remnants of articulate speech. So the first
> thing you are confronted with are the remains of a culture
> or civilization.[21]

Bion has described one patient's speaking as "doodling in sound." Another patient informed him that if he would only stop talking and listen to him play the piano, his analyst might learn something of who he is. Believing solely in the efficacy of talking, Bion forfeited an opportunity and thereby missed out on what might have been an essential part of the treatment. Ultimately, Bion acknowledges that it "seems extremely unlikely that psychic reality bears any resemblance to articulate speech."[22] Rather, psychic reality is "won from the void and formless infinite." In a letter to Lou Andreas Salome, Freud noted that when he was investigating a very dark subject, he sometimes found it illuminating to investigate it by artificially blinding himself. Bion suggests that we bring to bear "a penetrating beam of darkness: a reciprocal of the searchlight." If we did so, perhaps "the darkness would be so absolute that it would achieve a luminous, absolute vacuum. . . . Thus a very faint light would become visible in maximum conditions of darkness."[23]

On occasion, I have found myself hearing Mahler's Adagietto when I am in the dark, listening to patients seeking, struggling to find words for a deep ache, a secret yearning that even they may not be conscious of as they reach into that region of experiencing that brings to our work a musical sense of the psychic disaster that has befallen them. Through its shimmering texture and melodic line, this music incarnates a tentative reaching from out of the darkness, a reaching that bears one's suffering in fear and trembling, in the hope that something transforming will transpire.

When Being Born Is a Crime

Cheryl was an unwanted child who has invested most of her life in an effort to compensate her parents for the anguish her very existence had caused them. She was abused physically, emotionally, and sexually by each parent and quickly learned to dissociate from the horrific scenarios she was subject to, leaving her body behind and viewing the abject treatment she underwent from above. What went on inside the family was never to be divulged and what transpired outside the family was not to be trusted. Consequently, the toxic atmosphere in which she lived felt "normal," as any sense of herself apart from her parents and their devastating acts slipped into oblivion.

Each parent suffered from poor health and was intermittently hospitalized. Her mother had frequent bouts of pancreatitis and came down with a virulent case of breast cancer when Cheryl was nineteen. She died two years later. Her father suffered from diabetes and lost his sight for nine years, ultimately dying from throat cancer when Cheryl was in her early forties. Each parent was prone to sudden outbursts of rage and violence. Rather than providing Cheryl with the basic emotional nutrients required for her own psychic growth, they used her to satisfy their own sexual and aggressive needs, emotionally cannibalizing her with their predatory and parasitic hungers.

In her words: "I've built an armor . . . and survived a war. If I let my guard down, I won't see the attack coming. I'm up all night waiting for the attack . . . always ready for the attack." These attacks, which initially came from her mother and father, she now expected from her therapist as well as from other significant people in her life. All the while she engaged in relentless self-attacks.

During the first two of our five years together, Cheryl experienced almost every session as her last, believing that I wouldn't want to see her again. She seemed convinced that in sharing her nightmarish existence she had pushed me away. She found herself terrified of her growing dependence on me and did not want to let me matter so much to her. At the same time, she was convinced that she did not matter to me, that I would not think of her between sessions and that I would cringe in disgust over having to be in the same room with her, looking at her heavy body and listening to her sobbing session after session. Afraid of meaning too little to me, she seemed even more frightened of being experienced as too much for me or for any other human being. Convinced that she was draining me, Cheryl blamed herself whenever I came down with a cold.

Cheryl meets with me four times a week. She experiences a sense of hopelessness and futility between sessions, convinced that I no longer want to see her after one of her many emotional upheavals and believing that neither of us can bear the emotional strain of the work. Worried that she will overwhelm me in the ways her father overwhelmed her, Cheryl attacks herself for experiencing a deep ache that won't go away. When she leaves the office, she feels as if she is going to die, and she has asked me to tell her that I don't want her to die. Cheryl engages in a ritual of standing by the door and, with tears streaming down her face, shaking her hands in a downward flicking motion as if she were trying to shake me off as well as any painful experience she may have allowed herself to undergo in our time together. Whatever contact we have made with one another feels unreal for her as soon as she has walked out the door. She would rather be numb than continue to experience that agony that surfaces when we are with one another but that she finds unbearable to be with alone.

Cheryl continually experiences the close of many sessions as an attack. Saying goodbye has come to mean that she's been duped again, her existence obliterated in my mind as she walks out of the room, only to be replaced by another patient. She is haunted by images and bodily sensations that resonate with how her father would use her, only to toss her aside. She experiences a similar scenario with me. At times she seems convinced that our work together is merely a business and that my sole concern is money.

Often I have found myself feeling electrified when listening to Cheryl speak, each of us seeming to move into a profound state of reverie as she finds the courage to reach into core anxieties that manifest in her dreams, fantasies, and everyday interactions at work. The sense of at-one-ment that seems to exist between us in those moments seems to melt into a sense of atonement. In her pained speaking, Cheryl seems to be reaching out for and finding a sense of forgiveness, both from herself, as she finds words for her agony, and from me, in the listening presence I am able to bring to our work.

The Andante movement from Schubert's first piano trio resonates with a sense of forgiveness, a felt sense that can emerge for patient and analyst at those moments when they are reaching and reaching into those intimate and inviolable incommunicado places. The piano, cello, and violin mirror, deepen, and bring out the essence of one another, as each instrument voices a theme that recurs in different forms. Perhaps this music gives voice to a way of being and being with that unspeakable, unthinkable anxiety and nameless dread.

There are times when it seems as if Cheryl and I are killing one another, our capacity to come through these agonizing moments ultimately seeming to bring us to another level in our work. Cheryl engages in a self-deadening process, attacking herself as she seems to swallow and even choke on her words. I find myself falling into a semi-stuporous state, straining to keep my eyes open as her speaking seems to communicate an orgy of procrastination. I am then struck with a screeching sensation as Cheryl's words embody for me a simultaneous pushing me away and pulling me toward her, as if she were putting on the gas pedal and the brakes at the same time. Her halting train of words appears to be Cheryl's attempt to "get rid of the evidence," obliterating any sense of the pain she is on the brink of entering into, destroying herself and the analytic couple we have become.

When she confronts me on my seeming so exhausted, blaming herself for "sucking me dry," I am able to recognize how Cheryl is letting me know what it feels like to be her, terrified and constrained by the oppressiveness of her parents' demands, numbed out by the toxic bonds she did not dare to transform or escape from, unable to find her own voice in the midst of her agony, and having to remain emotionally unborn so that her parents could "live." Finding ways to experience, acknowledge, and communicate these states has brought our work to a deeper place.

CREATING AND RE-CREATING CIRCULATION

Bion speaks of a psychotic and non-psychotic part of the personality.[24] Hopefully, we are able to allow for a flow between these two poles of experience and modes of being in the world, both within ourselves and within those with whom we work. This back-and-forth flow is also present in the way that Bion understands the paranoid-schizoid and depressive modes of organizing experience as oscillating with one another, enriching one another in a dissolving and coagulating, dissolving again, and coming together anew.

At one point, Winnicott asks us to consider whether sanity is a defense or an achievement. He sees those who attempt to avoid their madness as avoiding what is most personal in themselves. One who does not reach into his or her madness cannot feel real. In his essay on children's thinking he distinguishes babies who reach out for words from babies who are more invested in sensory experiences of a hallucinatory kind. Those in the latter group who may never develop the words to defend their hallucinatory experiences may be considered mad. Yet whereas verbal logic may characterize the word people, "a feeling of certainty or truth or 'real' belongs to the others."[25] Here Winnicott is pointing to the inherent limits of words while inviting us to consider the importance of recognizing and perhaps even learning to develop the capacity to think hallucinatorily, a capacity that will enable us to be more at home with archaic anxiety, internal chaos, and disintegrative tendencies in ourselves and in others.

According to Freud, there may be more truth in Schreber's delusions than we want to admit and more delusion in science than we are willing to acknowledge. Bion speaks of the destructive effects of sanity and the creative effects of insanity.[26] Unlike the neurotic who fears making the unconscious conscious, the psychotic, or psychotic part of the personality, fears allowing the conscious to become unconscious. To do so is tantamount to losing consciousness forever, or death. Desperately holding together improvised fragments of himself or herself, the psychotic or psychotic part of the personality is hyperconscious, hypervigilant, and overly guarded, unable to digest his or her experience and allow unconscious processing to happen.

For Bion, the primary work of the conscious is to protect the unconscious, to be a background environment and supportive presence for unconscious work. But how can the capacity for unconscious functioning grow if the experience of unintegration was prematurely disrupted or never allowed for or if one's primitive projective identificatory communications were rejected and/or met with insult? For the person who undergoes this disaster, the world becomes a persecutory womb, constituting the murderous superego, which one is terrified of facing as an intrinsic part of oneself. Blood and death may appear everywhere.

For Bion, the analyst's work involves dreaming his or her patients and providing a space in which the patient can dream his or her madness; that is, the murderous superego. This internal object is hostile to projective identification and has damaged the patient's capacity for dreamwork and hence for storing, making use of, and learning from experience. The murderous superego has emerged as a hatred of reality, the refusal and consequent inability to digest experience, the continued evacuation of experience, and an ongoing destruction of whatever links may be forming, within oneself or between oneself and others. Perhaps we might begin to think of music as offering us a medium through which we can engage in dreamwork insofar as music creates and opens us onto an emotional landscape in which we can gather and begin to digest experience that has been exiled from our everyday lives.

Bion speaks of the analytic session as an opportunity for patient and analyst to create that dream that the patient is too terrified to dream alone. Dreaming this dream with our patients, we are called on to enter into that profound sense of insecurity and turbulence our patients bring with them into their sessions without prematurely foreclosing the space for this dreamwork to happen. The analyst is called on to develop the capacity to sustain and suffer experience which has always been indigestible for the patient and which could only be evacuated.

Together we are called on to become, rather than to merely know, the ultimate emotional reality of the session.

Thus, my work with Cheryl goes on as we continue to dream together the horrors of her existence, hearing in her music ways of beginning to think unthinkable anxiety and name nameless dread.

Recordings of Works Mentioned

Mahler, G. "Adagietto," on *Mahler: Symphony No. 5,* Riccardo Chailly conducting the Royal Concertgebouw Orchestra, CD, Decca, 1998.

Schubert, F. "Andante un poco mosso," from *Trio for Piano, Violin and Cello No. 1 in B flat major,* op. 99, D, 898, Odeon Trio, on *Franz Schubert: Oktett (D. 803) / Klaviertrios Piano Trios Nos. 1 and 2,* CD, Capriccio, 1996.

————. *Erlkönig,* on *An Die Musik: Favorite Schubert Songs,* Bryn Terfel and Malcolm Martineau, CD, Deutsche Grammophon, 1994.

Notes

[1] Quoted in Joyce McDougall and Nathalie Zaltzman, "New Preface," in Piera Aulagnier, *The Violence of Interpretation: From Pictogram to Statement,* trans. Alan Sheridan (Hove, East Sussex: Brunner-Routledge, 2001), p. xxiv.

[2] D. W. Winnicott, "Ego Integration in Child Development" (1962), in *The Maturational Processes and the Facilitating Environment* (New York: International Universities Press, 1965), pp. 57–58.

[3] D. W. Winnicott, "The Concept of Clinical Regression Compared with That of Defence Organization" (1967), in *Psycho-Analytic Explorations* (Cambridge, MA: Harvard University Press, 1989), pp. 193–199.

[4] D. W. Winnicott, "Fear of Breakdown" (1963), in *Psycho-Analytic Explorations* (Cambridge, MA: Harvard University Press, 1989), pp. 87–95.

[5] Winnicott, "Ego Integration in Child Development," p. 61.

[6] Winnicott, "The Concept of Clinical Regression Compared with That of Defence Organization," p. 198. Winnicott's emphasis.

[7] Winnicott, "Fear of Breakdown."

[8] D. W. Winnicott, "The Psychology of Madness" (1965), in *Psycho-Analytic Explorations* (Cambridge, MA: Harvard University Press, 1989), p. 124.

[9] Eigen made this statement in 1997 at his ongoing seminar on Bion, Winnicott, and Lacan.

[10] Sigmund Freud, *The Interpretation of Dreams,* in *The Standard Edition of the Complete Psychological Works of Sigmund Freud* (London: Vintage, 2001), p. 509.

[11] D. W. Winnicott, "Communicating and Not Communicating Leading to a Study of Opposites" (1965), in *The Maturational Processes and the Facilitating Environment,* see p. 187.

[12] Winnicott, "The Psychology of Madness," pp. 119–129.

[13] Michael Eigen, *Toxic Nourishment* (London: Karnac Books, 1999), p. 82.

[14] Winnicott, *Psycho-Analytic Explorations*, p. 4.

[15] D. W. Winnicott, "Additional Note on Psycho-Somatic Disorder," in *Psycho-Analytic Explorations* (Cambridge, MA: Harvard University Press, 1989), pp. 115–118.

[16] W. R. Bion, *Learning from Experience* (1962; repr., Northvale, NJ: Jason Aronson, Inc., 1994).

[17] Wilfred R. Bion, *Brazilian Lectures: 1973 São Paolo, 1974 Rio de Janiero/São Paolo* (London: Karnac Books, 1990), p. 54.

[18] W. R. Bion, *Cogitations,* ed. Francesca Bion (London: Karnac, 1992), p. 35.

[19] W. Bion, *Learning from Experience* (1962; repr., Northvale, NJ: Jason Aronson, 1997), p. 97.

[20] Bion, *Brazilian Lectures*, p. 203.

[21] W. R. Bion, *Bion in New York and São Paulo* (Perthshire: Clunie Press, 1980), p. 20.

[22] Bion, *Brazilian Lectures,* p. 49.

[23] *Ibid.,* pp. 43–64.

[24] W. R. Bion, "Differentiation of the Psychotic from the Non-Psychotic Personalities" (1957), in *Second Thoughts: Selected Papers on Psycho-Analysis.* (Northvale, NJ: Jason Aronson, Inc., 1993), pp. 43–63.

[25] Winnicott, "New Light on Children's Thinking," p. 155.

[26] W. R. Bion, *Transformations: Change from Learning to Growth* (1965; repr., London: Karnac, 1984); and Bion, *Cogitations.*

12

"Night Is a Sound": The Music of the Black Sun

STEPHEN BLOCH

Intense light; intense black; nothing between; no twilight. Harsh sun and silence; black night and violent noise. Frogs croaking, birds hammering tin boxes, striking bells, shrieking, yelling, roaring, coughing, bawling, mocking. That night, that is the real world and real noise.[1]

This is Bion's graphic description of a tiger hunt in India during his childhood. It is important because it captures his relationship to darkness, which can be traced as a theme in his writings.[2] It is also significant because of his movement from the visual to the auditory as a way of capturing his experience. It is as though the sounds of his experience are more precise descriptors than the visual. He evokes the night by its sounds.

Sound has an immediate, embodied sense, often expressing emotional states more directly than the visual or intellectual. Sound also reaches into archaic depths as our auditory capacity exists prenatally, from around four months. The sounds in the uterine environment may be the earliest sense of the other.

Moreover, in the mythology of many cultures, sounds created existence and the world. These sounds may have been a cry, thunder, a song, or, as in a Kabbalistic legend, laughter. "Before shapes and faces," Maiello writes, "the gods were rhythms and melodies."[3]

This essay, then, will follow Bion's movement from the visual to the auditory. The enigmatic yet compelling image of the Black Sun will be explored through musical examples. This involves a deliberate synesthesia, where senses combine in experience, the arcing from sight to sound allowing a more embodied and emotionally precise involvement with the image. This essay is an exploration of what it means to participate in an image acoustically rather than visually, allowing (one would hope) a deeper opening into its nature. Music also allows the more destructive and desolate aspects of Black Sun imagery to be contained and find creative expression.

In his book, Stanton Marlan explores various dimensions of the Black Sun.[4] Using his analysis as a grid, I will explore various aspects and interwoven meanings of this image, adding insights from object-relations psychoanalysis. Five aspects of Black Sun symbolism will be explored:

1. Black Sun and descent
2. Black Sun and destruction
3. Darkness as lens
4. Vivid darkness
5. Blackness, no-thing, silence.

THE BLACK SUN AND DESCENT: DOWLAND

The image of the Black Sun was first used by the seventeenth-century alchemist Mylius. Jung understands the image as a general image of the unconscious, an understanding that is too broad to be clinically useful. When the Black Sun is linked to the alchemical stages of *nigredo*, putrefaction, and mortification its relevance begins to emerge. These stages are associated with experiences of rot, decomposition, sickness, failure, and dying. In classical Jungian analysis these represent the initial descent into the unconscious. The containment in the therapeutic setting allows this descent to be transformative and facilitates its integration.

The experience of blackness in the *nigredo* is expressed in John Dowland's "In Darkness Let Me Dwell." Dowland, the influential seventeenth-century lutenist, was absorbed in his own melancholy and the melancholy of his age. Much of his work deals with sadness and loss and seems at times strangely contemporary in its concern with depression and alienation. His work *Lachrimae, or Seaven Teares,* for example, constitutes a progressive exploration of tears and sadness, suggesting that psychological work necessitates an ongoing development of the capacity to tolerate loss and grief. This may be a consequence of inevitable life experience but also indicates that any shift in the sense of self brings about a loss of and mourning for the old sustaining identity. There are suggestions, not improbable, that Dowland was knowledgeable about alchemy. Certainly the images in "In Darkness Let Me Dwell" seem very close to those in alchemical illustrations.

A particular rendition of "In Darkness Let Me Dwell" by the Dowland Project portrays these themes. The Dowland Project consists of John Potter (tenor), Stephen Stubbs (lute), and Maya Homburger (baroque violin) as well as jazz musicians John Surman (saxophone) and Barry Guy (double bass). This unique line-up allows an interplay between classical structure and improvisatory freedom. The aim of the musicians was to reclaim and engage with the music as Dowland's colleagues might have done as well as to bring its concerns into the present. As Robert White comments: "What his [Dowland's] age knew and we sometimes lose sight of, is that meditating on a beautiful expression of sadness can help to provide a thoroughly uplifting sense of consolation."[5]

The following description of Dowland's song by the English lutenist Diana Poulton meets the beauty of the music with its own elegance and highlights the music's timeless relevance:

> In the greatest of his songs, "In Darkness Let Me Dwell,"
> Dowland freed himself from almost all of the conventions of
> his time. The strange and beautiful melody rises from the words
> with a sense of inevitability, while the demands of verbal rhythms
> override conventional bar-lines. Biting discords from the lute
> enhance the tragedy in the words, and chords with augmented
> and diminished intervals are used to express emotional intensity
> to an extent unsurpassed in any other song at that time.[6]

The work is characterized by indeterminacy—staggered rhythms, harmonic uncertainty, and an unusually unresolved conclusion.[7] The delicate interchange between lute and tenor is set against the chthonic bass grounds which deepens the text, eliciting a sense of descent, opening to intensity and holding the darkness. The searing background accompaniment expresses the more directly painful experience of the engagement with unconscious experience. The interplay is between containment and descent, as well as structure and improvisation. Their rendering of Dowland translates darkness into sound, extending awareness beyond the words yet simultaneously maintaining the meaning. The sound of the delicate lute strings captures an experience that is present in any serious therapeutic encounter—the uncertainty as to whether the fragile process will snap under the tension or move onward to a resolution.

The Black Sun and Destruction: George Crumb

A major aspect of Black Sun symbolism revolves around traumatized aspects of the psyche. Where life-giving energy is undermined by annihilatory tendencies, blackness often reflects these deathly, stuck dimensions.

Marlan notes that traumatized children have used black sun images in their drawings. He cites a schizophrenic patient of Laing, who, in the terror of destruction, claimed that she was "born under a black sun."[8] Moreover, Kristeva's classic exploration links the Black Sun to depression and melancholia.[9] Kristeva's account describes a depression at the edge of that which can be spoken about but that can be conveyed in artistic and creative expression. She discusses the artist Hans Holbein the Younger, the poet Gérard de Nerval, and authors Fyodor Dostoevsky and Marguerite Duras in this regard. She distinguishes early narcissistic depression (melancholia) from later objectal depression (occurring after weaning and even post-oedipally where language and subject-object distinction has occurred). Both types inhibit the capacity or willingness to speak or find artistic or (in the terms of this essay) musical expression.

De Nerval's poem "The Disinherited" ("El Desdichado") reflects narcissistic depression and the movement from this state to a sense of music, with the implicit suggestion that the experience of the Black Sun reaches toward a musical resolution. Kristeva comments on De Nerval's poem as follows:

> As a result of the absorption of the "dead star" into the "lute", the "Black Sun" of "Melancholia" emerges. Beyond its alchemical scope, the "Black Sun" metaphor fully sums up the blinding force of the despondent mood—an excruciating lucid affect asserts the inevitability of death, which is the death of the loved one and of the self that identifies with the former (the poet is "bereft" of the star).[10]

Kristeva also comments on De Nerval's "psyche struggling against dark symbolism"[11] and his experience of the opposites: presence and absence, "abolishment and song." (This rhythm of no-thing and presence anticipates a key aspect of Black Sun symbolism that I will discuss later in this essay.)

The threat of psychic annihilation can be metabolized by music and poetry:

> By means of a leap into the Orphic world of artifice (of sublimation) the saturnine poet, out of the traumatic experience and object of mourning, remembers only a gloomy or passional tone. He thus comes close, through the very components of

language, to the lost Thing. His discourse identifies with it, absorbs it, modifies it, transforms it: he takes Eurydice out of the melancholy hell and gives her back a new existence in his text/song.[12]

As with Bion's description of the tiger hunt, a deepening sense of the Black Sun moves out of silence into sound and tone. It is the evolution into symbolization, and specifically music, that opens the possibility of shifting the subject's attachment to the Black Sun as "the most archaic expression of an unsymbolizable, unnameable narcissistic wound."[13] The Black Sun occupies a position beneath representation and meaning, and in its destructive aspects it undermines the very possibility of symbolization.

The sense of a sun as potentially destructive and annihilatory, as opposed to life-giving and generative, is disturbing, yet it expresses a truth of psychological experience. The light of consciousness becomes excessive and therefore damaging, in the same way that the sun can be experienced in the case of global warming. The scorching, burning aspects of hypertrophied light are captured here. The Black Sun can also suggest an overcritical aspect of the psyche as in the savage super-ego that incinerates and immobilizes psychic aliveness. The sun has destructive aspects within it, and von Franz points out that Apollo was not only god of the sun but also of rats and wolves.[14]

The Black Sun can further be regarded as an imaginal representation of the tension between Eros and Thanatos, the blackness representing the death force operating at the origins of psychological existence. The death instinct is the impulse toward disintegration and self-destructiveness and "hatred of life."[15] The drive toward death and against life was postulated by Freud, who nevertheless felt that there was little clinical evidence to validate the hypothesis. However, if the death instinct was clinically "silent" to Freud, it was, as Hinshelwood states, "noisy" to Klein.[16] Again it appears that an acoustic representation more precisely fits subjective experience, especially when trying to articulate death and blackness.

With regard to destructive forces in the psyche, Klein wrote of anxiety arising from "the operation of the death instinct within the organism"[17] and of a "primary anxiety of being annihilated by a destructive force within."[18] Primary aggression at the beginning of psychic life is, in the Kleinian view, an expression of the death instinct. The origins of the super-ego are based on this aggressive impulse. The central role of envy was, to Klein, a particular manifestation of the death instinct. Envy in the original setting can be understood as destructive impulses toward the source of life itself. The fear of counter-envy similarly undermines and subverts life-giving impulses.

The Black Sun also reflects infantile experiences of the breast as intrusive, impinging, or toxic. Eigen writes of these situations as being characterized by toxic nourishment and writes "We nourish ourselves by the very things that poison us and poison ourselves by what nourishes."[19] Intrusive parental needs, as opposed to containment, can result in this situation. There is attachment and bonding even to parents who are abusive and damaging. Much therapy consists in disentangling these connections.

This confluence of destruction and nurturance is captured in Paul Celan's image of Black Milk. Emerging from the annihilatory experience of the Holocaust, Black Milk reflects the sense of poisonous destructiveness in that which should be life-giving or soothing. This can be experienced not only in trauma but also in the persecutory experience of absence (or no-thing) where something should be present. Boris writes:

> Human beings have a kind of *black-night* to their spectrum of experience. For us there is no such thing as nothing, only a no-thing where something should have been. And there is no such thing as a no-space, only a hole or a blank or a piece of darkness where something should have been. Black milk, where milk was to be. Black holes where time should have been.[20]

George Crumb's *Black Angels* renders these dimensions of the psyche into music. The work was originally composed as a reflection on the Vietnam War and depicts a voyage of the soul through three stages— Departure (fall from grace), Absence (spiritual annihilation), and Return (redemption). I focus on the second movement (Absence) for our purposes. It is a striking depiction of destructive and persecutory forces in collision with cohesive and healing forces, annihilation competing with the good. The contiguity of "Black" with "Angels" (as a traditional, if sentimental, image of goodness) is heard throughout as attempts at cohesion are met by discordant fragmentation. "Things were turned upside down," George Crumb writes. "There were terrifying things in the air . . . they found their way into Black Angels."[21]

The sounds of the "terrifying things" are shouts, chants, whistles, whispers, and gongs, all on the cusp of the preverbal and verbal. Crumb also employs numerological and musical principles often associated with negative forces. These are specific lengths and sequences of notes, groupings, and repetition, which are often regarded as "fateful." There is also the tritone interval, the so-called *Diabolus in musica,* or the devil's trill. The attempt to reach coherent grief is continually undermined by primitive states of mind which override mourning. The work depicts a primitive terrain where loss is experienced as persecutory; lack as an attack.

George Crumb further explored the nature of darkness in *Night Music* (1963) and in the austerely beautiful *Songs, Drones, and Refrains of Death* (2006), the latter involving "Lorca's dark imagery."[22] Crumb has often used Lorca's poetry as a basis for his compositions. *Songs, Drones, and Refrains of Death* is an evocation of nascent life confronting death, the conflict of Eros and Thanatos. The loss and desolation of Lorca's poetry finds acoustic expression in this work. There are long drones representing death, while dissonant, agitated, and disconnected sounds prevail throughout. The composition can be understood as a sonorous landscape of aspects of the paranoid-schizoid psyche. A primal sense of annihilatory dread pervades it. Fragmentation and disaggregated sounds characterize the composition. Part-object sounds emerge from and disappear back into silence.

Primitive chants and strident phrases emerge and conflict. Urgent, at times desperate, voices sound at the edge of what can be verbalized. The piece features intense and sudden developments of musical dynamics, which subside and dissolve into silence. However, it also includes approaches toward integration and cohesion that fluctuate and reflect the difficult to-and-fro movement from part-object to whole-object relating. The difficulty in this transition may be in the struggle to come to terms with destructiveness.

The movement toward integration occurs at the same time that sounds hang isolated in a slow atmosphere. A sense of background containment is carried by silence and in the holding (rather than the ominous) aspect of the drones. Malevolent sounds do not develop into threat, while soothing sounds decay. The listener is left uncertain whether sounds are exploring a void or if silence is containing the tentative development of sound. All the while a dark instinctuality pervades. In describing the work Crumb quotes a line from Lorca's "Malagueña": "Black horses and villainous people move along the deep paths of the guitar."[23] The work is a dreamlike sound-world of blackness and emergent precarious life, finding its way through "nocturnal murmurs" and "white death."[24] An unusual vividness pervades the work, and in fact by rendering primitive experience into sound, the overall effect is containing rather than disintegrative.

In analysis, these aspects of the Black Sun can be seen in forces that oppose and compete with psychological growth. For some patients, all possibility of movement seems blocked; while in other cases initial gains are reversed. New potential aspects of the self or other relationships are experienced as threatening or dangerous. These states can be experienced in terms of blackness and deadness. Waska describes how there is an absence of security and support when nourishment has been withdrawn by the abandoning object. In this abandonment, internal persecutors destroy the ego in a negative void, and rescue seems impossible.[25]

Riviere described this desolated state of mind in the following way, capturing a significant aspect of the Black Sun: "all one's loved one's *within* are dead and destroyed, all goodness is dispersed, lost, in fragments, wasted and scattered to the winds; nothing is left *within* but utter desolation."[26]

Waska delineates many of the anti-growth impulses that can occur and form barriers against the good. The patient may be mistrustful of the good object, defending against the possibility of loss. He or she may also feel that accepting a good object will lead to the collapse of a coping self. Envy toward the analyst also makes it difficult to make use of containment and interpretation. Envy may also operate intrapsychically where emerging aspects of the self are intolerable to an older, more encrusted sense of self. The therapist may be too alive for deadened aspects of the patient.[27]

DARKNESS AS LENS: GAVIN BRYARS

Hillman objects to a developmental model of alchemy and psychological development where blackness is regarded as a stage that needs to be worked through and resolved. He regards this as a "Salvationist" model in which *nigredo* tends toward whitening and resolution.

Marlan comments on this sequential model as follows:

> One of the dangers of placing blackness into a process of development is the tendency to move too quickly away from its radicality, its blacker-than-black, its depth, its severity and the suffering associated with it. . . . This runs the risk of not seeing with that dark eye that sees blackness for itself and not simply as a passage to whiteness, change, and generation.[28]

Hillman and Marlan are suggesting that not all blackness can or indeed should be assimilated. Casey reminds us that "a symbol is not what we see but how we see."[29] Archetypal psychology suggests that we see by way of darkness using it as a perspective or lens. *Nigredo* is therefore an achievement and an accomplishment rather than an initial stage. The value of blackness is that it involves endurance, holding, not acting out by reaching for premature understanding. For Hillman, blackness warns, dissolves, and "sophisticates the eye."[30]

One could add that blackness sophisticates or develops not only the eye but also the ear. Indeed, blackness may allow hearing to emerge as the crucial sensory modality.

There is a striking convergence here between the post-Jungian archetypal approach and that of Bion's post-Kleinian view. Bion describes a dark light in a number of places. In the Brazilian lectures, Bion described a "diminution of light" as a "penetrating beam of absolute darkness" that is a "reciprocal of the searchlight" and becomes a "luminous, absolute vacuum." In this way "a very faint light would become visible in maximum conditions of darkness."[31] Grotstein's notes add nuance to Bion's thoughts. He recollects Bion's loose translation of Freud's letter to Lou Andreas-Salome: "When conducting an analysis one must cast a *beam of intense darkness* so that something which has hitherto been obscured by the glare of the illumination can glitter all the more in the darkness."[32]

Bion wrote of artificially blinding himself "to focus all the light on one dark spot."[33] He referenced the blind poet Milton, who wrote of "the rising world of waters dark and deep, won from the void and formless infinite."[34] A forced blindness, was, to Bion, a methodology, a way of opening to internal experience and ultimately to the void and O.

This dark perspective suggested by Hillman and Bion nevertheless remains in a visual arena and discourse. What is not elaborated is the way the inhibition of vision opens to other senses, notably the auditory. In *The Black River,* Gavin Bryars allows an immersion and participation in blackness and creates an auditory lens that filters perception through an acoustic channel. Bryars is a contemporary and often radical British composer. His work is characterized by a unique perspective on sound. Ondaatje comments on the impossibility of categorizing Bryars's work and refers to his ability to capture "primal emotion."[35]

The slow contours of his music often express primitive and preconscious experiences, images, and memory. Indeed, this work, which was composed for organ and voice, creates a sense of the immensity of the unconscious and challenges the listener to tolerate a radical blackness that cannot be assimilated. The composition develops sound in terms of textures, densities, and slowly forming soundscapes. Usual constructs of space and time are shifted, opening interior terrains. Bryars's work is composed in B minor, which according to the liner notes was Beethoven's black key, and E minor, which was the key of the Crucifixion for Bach.[36]

The unhurried and sustained chords of *The Black River* slow the imagination at the same time as they contain the listener. Bosnak refers to this "slowing of the imagination" as an essential step in the embodied movement of imaginal content. He differentiates two types of imagination. The one he terms confabulation. This is characterized by a speeding fantasy production and hypothesizing in the patient. The second and more important mode of fantasy is an embodied and moderated entering into the image. The latter approach leads to more substantial shifts in the patient. He notes how free association can occur in a rapid disembodied state and contrasts this to psychotherapeutic work where the patient experiences a "compressed" felt sense. He writes, "Embodiment requires intense restraint or the natural speed of the imagination will surf on and on."[37] I am suggesting that the perspective of blackness facilitates this restraint. Blackness acts as a gravitational pull, allowing compression and greater participation in the image by the subject.

Gavin Bryars's *The Black River* provides an experience of a viscerally slowed imagination, a process that allows imagery to deepen and mature. It demands that the listener sacrifice rapid psychic movement and loose free association.

Vivid Darkness: Piazzolla

Marlan develops a further dimension to our understanding of Black Sun symbolism. By not evading it, but embracing or holding to a radical and unassimilable darkness, the darkness develops a light of its own. In this way it becomes a luminous darkness. This "light of darkness," in Marlan's phrase, is linked to the alchemical search for a light embedded in nature.[38] The light of nature, the *lumen naturae* is not a light split off from darkness. The *lumen naturae,* Jung writes, is "the light of darkness itself, which illuminates its own darkness, and this light the darkness comprehends. Therefore it turns blackness into brightness."[39]

This incinerating light is involved in processes that burn away the redundant and the inessential. Kali, who is invoked in Tantric rites, has a similar function and is also described in terms of a shining fiery blackness. This dark light is not transcended but is integrated into a psyche and body that contain dark and light simultaneously.

Black Sun imagery lies at the roots of tango music and its development into the *tango nuevo* of Astor Piazzolla. Its beginnings were in the brothels of Buenos Aires, as Jorge Luis Borges noted. This world of bordellos, with the association of sexuality and violence, can be viscerally felt in Piazzolla's music.[40] In the way that Piazzolla has developed the tango into an art form,

the shadow, borderland sexuality develops into a complex marriage of
opposites; the tango as *coniunctio* lifting shame into dance.

The other significant origin of tango is in the struggles of Argentinean
immigrant communities. In fact, in the symbolism of the tango the woman
often represents Argentina while the man is the arriving immigrant:

> Traditional tango captures the dislocation of the immigrant
> porteño, the disillusionment with the dream of a new life,
> transmuting these deep and raw emotions onto a personal
> plane of betrayal and triangular relationships. Piazzolla's
> genius comes from the fact that, within the many layers and
> changing moods and pace of his pieces, he never betrays the
> essence of tango—its sense of fate, its core of hopeless misery,
> its desperate sense of loss.[41]

However, from within these dark themes Piazzolla liberates a vibrancy
and vitality. In doing this he expresses musically Bion's and Eigen's
reflections on how life often emerges from the same place as a person's
damage and emotional turmoil.[42] I suggest that Piazzolla's darkly ecstatic
compositions are the auditory counterpart of radiant darkness, the
"darkness that shines." Astor Piazzolla's tango compositions are an aural
and visceral counterpart to this aspect of Black Sun imagery. Many of the
tango titles themselves suggest darkness and vitality, for example, "Midnight
in Buenos Aires" and "Oblivion." However, it is the work "El Tango,"
especially the rendition by Gideon Kremer, that particularly captures the
themes of this essay.

"El Tango" emerged from a collaboration between Borges and Piazzolla
in 1965. It consists of a poem by Borges that is spoken against the
background of a *milonga,* with typical Piazzolla glissandos and musical effects
that continually undermine order and create erupting aliveness. The poem
in Spanish recounts a fratricide. However, to listen to the piece without
understanding Spanish is an experiment with listening to timbres, rhythm,
and textures underneath the verbal. This is the resonant field of
communication happening continually in analytic sessions, and this work
can help sensitize therapists to this level of communication.

The work is volatile and energetic and, at the same time, grave and
mournful, the severity of the poem reaching a peak of turbulence in the
engagement of words and music. At a crucial point, silence punctuates
the intensity. In the stillness one confronts all that has gone before, the
shock of the murder and its implications, but it is also a stillness that allows
one to absorb the poem and is followed by a more resigned, sadder
reflection. Violence has evolved into acceptance.

Honesty may well be the counterpart of light in the psyche. It would be contemptuous to inform a patient in a major depression that his or her darkness is in fact shining. However, in a depression the undefended confrontation with what seems like an irreducible truth may be the equivalent of light in the psyche. Bion was particularly concerned with how truth allows the psyche to develop, while, conversely, lies undermine thought and destroy psychic growth. The congruence between truth, beauty, and psychic aliveness are all aspects of this insight. Piazzolla's "El Tango" is a work of insistent, relentless honesty, mining the Borges poem for every facet of its emotionality. Its aliveness is based on this authenticity.

BLACKNESS, NO-THING, SILENCE: ROBIN WILLIAMSON

The core of emptiness evokes the most radical aspect of blackness— its representation of no-thing, nullity, and the void. Hillman regards black as the color that negates, dissolves, and deconstructs. It is the quality that breaks down cohesiveness and structure. Hillman illustrates the nullifying and negating aspects of black in various polarities: where knowledge is good, black is unknowing; where morality is good, black is evil, and where life is good, death is depicted as black. These binary relationships underscore the process whereby black moves being into non-being and presence into absence. Black, to Hillman, is also outsiders—as he puts it, the color of Goths, Satanists, and hit men. In his reflections, Hillman asserts that through its negation and deconstruction, black is an essential aspect of change and the destruction of fixed states. In its most radical action, black dissolves form into formlessness and therefore into emptiness, no-thing.[43]

In *Transformations,* Bion explores the nature of no-thing, and Eigen extends its clinical implications in "Bion's No-Thing" and "Two-Kinds of No-Thing."[44] Bion, using geometrical metaphors, demonstrates how a sense of absence is the context of a presence, how a position an object occupies always carries with it a sense of the position it does *not* occupy. It is the absence, the no-thing, that is a critical element in the relationship with an object's presence. Bion's insights are a meditation on presence and absence. The crucial issue is the way we relate to this no-thing in its various grades and qualities.

In his papers on "no-thing" Eigen shows how a tolerance in the individual for no-thing allows the psyche to evolve, to move and "play" with absence. The creative use of absence and no-thing involves tolerating the gap between them emotionally, allowing the strain of lack of stimulation and nothingness to be endured so that a symbol can develop.

If, on the other hand, the no-thing is denied, creative symbolic capacity is undermined. As Eigen points out, at this point the object is reduced to something that must be controlled and manipulated. The absence, which in the original situation is the absent breast, can be attacked, hated, or denied. Indeed, one can attack and deny the emotional capacity to acknowledge this absence.

The denial of absence leads to a premature movement toward insight, a confabulated understanding. The symbol is used negatively when it forecloses and nullifies emotional reality. Eigen comments that rebirth symbols, for example, may be used to undermine and degrade psychic reality by preventing the experience required to ground it. Eigen writes: "A truncated time and space, moralistic causality (blaming) and definitions that cancel rather than open life are rigid remains of what might have been a rich and open psyche."[45]

Symbolic consciousness is possible only when image and non-image, known and unknown, are held in simultaneous awareness. The Black Sun, in combining the opposites of presence and absence, becomes the portal to symbolism, and the ability to hold its paradoxical nature becomes the essential psychic capacity. The Black Sun tempers precocious resolution and develops the capacity in the individual to tolerate experience long enough for a symbol to develop.

The acoustic counterpart to blackness is silence. The ear works around silence as the eye does around blackness. Various contemporary composers such as Arvo Pärt, Toru Takemitsu, and John Tavener have explored the interaction of music and silence. The Estonian composer Arvo Pärt, having withdrawn from Serialism in the 1970s, returned to composition after investigating contemplative and religious music. For Pärt, music not only involves contemplative silence but silence is the creative core in the composer from which music emerges. Silence as the creative context of music can be heard in the way the music emerges and disappears in *Tabula Rasa*. In "Cantus in Memory of Benjamin Britten" there is a deliberate and conscious scoring of three beats of silence that must be "played," thus bringing silence into the awareness of performer and listener. The Japanese composer Takemitsu is another modern composer who has directly evoked the use of silence through the concept of "*ma*." "*Ma*" refers to the space, the empty nothingness between words, images, and objects, and in music, the silence between notes. It is linked also to the qualities of this space. "*Ma*" is the gap, the open space between notes that is an area of freedom and the creative void that is potential space. The presence of "*ma*" permeates most of his compositions, including his film music.

These composers have portrayed silence as the context of music—the ground from which it emerges and to which it returns. Silence can also be the potential space where new acoustic images and rhythms can emerge. This is true in improvisatory jazz but also in music therapy and in verbal therapies. Julie Sutton suggests a further aspect of the relationship between silence and music.[46] She notes how in mother-infant interaction silence may be the downtime where the integration of stimuli and information occur. At these places there is a slowdown of interaction, and silent periods allow the mother and child to digest the impacts of stimuli. Stern terms these "time-out episodes,"[47] pointing out that the infant needs them to regulate his or her affective states. Silence therefore digests sound and noise.

Silence has to be tolerated. Before its sublime aspects can be held in consciousness, a threatening void has to be confronted and negotiated. The relationship with absence and the "gap" reaches into the essence of Bion's concerns. Bion is asking the core question as to how we are able to endure experience so as to allow meaning and thought to develop. At the root of this issue is how we can endure and experience no-thing and absence. The original Ur-absence is the no-thing of the absent breast. Thinking develops out of the need to make sense of this gap. It is facilitated by the reverie and dreamwork alpha of the mother.[48] The crucial aspect is how no-thing is related to. Thought can then emerge from no-thing and absence rather than being evacuated or imploding in emptiness. Grotstein, for example, differentiates a primary meaninglessness (the emptiness that must be experienced) from secondary meaninglessness where there is a negation of meaning that is the "disintegrative nothingness of the 'black hole.'"[49]

Silence in music therefore has a range of meanings and effects on the listener. At its most sublime and ineffable it is stillness and the creative void out of which sound emerges. But silence can also strain and torment a listener who is used to an overproduction of notes. This type of silence disturbs. This range of responses to silence can be heard in the pure silence that surrounds Arvo Pärt's minimalist compositions. The disintegrative destructive aspects of silence can be heard, for example, in Leonardo Balada's avant-garde *No-res (No-thing)*.[50] The latter is an expression in sound of a persecutory void and the loss and absence of a containing other/mother.

Silence as the context of music reveals the catastrophic no-thing, which to Bion is at the origin of psychological experience. Music is at the same time a significant channel in which silence is contained and responded to by the mother. Music dreams (in Bion's sense of performing psychological work) no-thing, allowing a persecutory void to evolve into a symbol. Music metabolizes absence, as much as silence is the background from which music emerges.[51] Music metabolizes the silence of absence at the same time that silence digests the impacts of experience and sound.

Music and silence therefore share interdependence. This can be experienced in psychotherapy with different qualities of silence and the responses to it. In particular, there is a crucial distinction between silence that is productively worked with and silence that is denied or manically filled.

Robin Williamson's "To God in God's Absence" captures many aspects of Black Sun imagery, especially its relationship to no-thing. Williamson was a founding member of the influential countercultural group The Incredible String Band. He later moved on to a solo career and recently has released three notable CDs on the ECM label, which combine poetry (Dylan Thomas, Blake, and Whitman, among others) with postmodern jazz settings.[52] The extended three-stanza version of "To God in God's Absence" on *The Iron Stone* reveals an intensity and severity in Williamson, even as it moves to a statement of faith and openness. On this track Williamson delivers his melismatic singing accompanied by Celtic harp. The harmonic background is provided by the free improvising of violist Matt Maneri, multi-instrumentalist Ale Möller, and bassist Barre Phillip.

The song-prayer begins with the pathos of a lament in which Williamson's Irish and Scottish roots are quite evident. Carried by a pulsing bass the song develops gravitas and becomes an incantation, a Gnostic hymn traversing emptiness and fullness, radical interiority and being.

Williamson's voice hovers between notes and tonalities and he moves freely in and around time signatures. His singing is in a liminal space as he searches for the sound that captures in-betweenness and the tension between presence and absence.

The first stanza, in which Williamson invokes and engages with absence, has many images congruent with the Black Sun. He sings of "the unlit dark and the snuffed flame" and refers to "the murder of my words."

> I Pray to God in God's absence
> Honouring the unlit dark and the snuffed flame.
> I sing to send songs back to themselves,
> Seeking no sanctuary more than the world is home.
> What safety is there if we are not kin
> To the killed and plentiful, blinded in full-view,
> Mated to the soothe of thunder?

> To own the mammal horn and the murder of my words
> I venture the significance of being born.

In the second stanza he counters with his sense of presence and a collective sense of psyche, suggesting that fullness is revealed in relationship.

> I pray to God in God's presence humanly
> And most of all in love
> I sing to us in our ship, in our night
> In our common fear and laughter . . .

Through holding these opposites in awareness, and, crucially, engaging with no-thing, Williamson emerges in the third stanza with a vision of the creative mystical void. He calls to the "bright unknowing" and the song resolves with the following evocation:

> I sing to the textless pure
> And the unborn.[53]

These are descriptions of the fertile Emptiness; *sunyata* in Buddhism and the Ein Sof in Kabbalah. It is the unforeclosed potential carried within the mystical aspects of Bion's O.[54]

The short bridge between the second and third stanzas is characterized by an urgent, grinding interplay of instruments (viola and bass). This interaction, which continues in the third stanza, reveals the effort demanded in integrating and combining the elemental opposites of presence and absence. Although Robin Williamson's lyrics liberate a redemptive conclusion, the colors and shapes of the background improvisations reveal that this resolution cannot be taken for granted. The abstract and oblique harmonies express the alienation and stalling ironies that can occur in the interweaving of absence and presence, losing and finding. The complex instrumental accompaniment carries this struggle and "dreams" the material in the sense used by Bion, namely as the process that works on and metabolizes raw impacts of experience and facilitates an evolving psyche.

CONCLUDING REMARKS

This chapter has explored the soundscape of the Black Sun. It was heard in Dowland's descent and the fragmented thanatos of George Crumb's compositions. Bryars's slowness revealed blackness as lens or perspective. The vitality of Piazzolla's tango music reflected the luminous darkness, while Robin Williamson's song revealed an evocation of absence, presence, and the creative void. Although the Black Sun may carry destructive aspects, other dimensions reveal a redemptive quality and a perspective that is essential to the analytic process.

The musical examples facilitate an embodied participation with the dimensions of the Black Sun as well as a salvific expression of it. One experiences the images rather than merely perceiving them. The initiation is carried by the music but also by the specific nature of the image. Darkness and blackness mark the edge of the visual and confront it with its limits. The dominance of the eye is defeated, and the visual surrenders to the auditory. This movement was expressed in Bion's quote which began the essay and is echoed by Peter Hoeg: "Night is not a time of day, night is not an intensity of light, night is a sound."[55]

RECORDINGS OF WORKS MENTIONED IN THIS CHAPTER

Balada, Leonardo. *No-res (Nothing): An Agnostic Requiem,* CD, Naxos, 2005.

Bryars, Gavin. *The Black River,* CD, ECM New Series, 1993.

Crumb, George. *Black Angels,* CD, Elektra Nonesuch, 1990.

———. *Songs, Drones, and Refrains of Death,* CD, Naxos American Classics, 2006.

Dowland, John. "In Darkness Let Me Dwell," on *In Darkness Let Me Dwell,* CD, The Dowland Project, ECM New Series, 2000.

Pärt, Arno. "Cantus in Memory of Benjamin Britten," and "Tabula Rasa," on *Tabula Rasa,* CD, ECM New Series, 1984.

Piazzolla, Astor. "El tango," on *Astor Piazzolla: El Tango,* CD, Nonesuch, 1997.

Williamson, Robin. "To God in God's Absence," on *The Iron Stone,* CD, ECM Records, 2006.

NOTES

[1] Wilfred R. Bion, *The Long Weekend, 1897–1919: Part of a Life* (Abingdon: Fleetwood Press, 1982), p. 18.

[2] James S. Grotstein, *A Beam of Intense Darkness: Wilfred Bion's Legacy to Psychoanalysis* (London: Karnac Books, 2008).

[3] Suzanne Maiello, "The Sound Object," in *Developments in Infant Observation: The Tavistock Model,* ed. Susan Reid (London and New York: Routledge, 1997).

[4] Stanton Marlan, *The Black Sun: The Alchemy and Art of Darkness* (College Station: Texas A&M University Press, 2005).

[5] Robert White, CD liner notes for *John Dowland: In Darkness Let Me Dwell,* ECM, 2000.

[6] Diana Poulton, in *The New Grove Dictionary of Music and Musicians,* ed. Stanley Sadie (Washington, D.C.: Grove's Dictionary of Music, 1980).

[7] Peter Holman and Paul Odette, "Dowland, John," in *The New Grove Dictionary of Music and Musicians,* 2nd ed., ed. Stanley Sadie and John Tyrell (London: Grove MacMillan, 2001).

[8] Ronald D. Laing, *The Divided Self* (Baltimore, MD: Pelican Books, 1965).

[9] Julia Kristeva, *Black Sun: Depression and Melancholia,* trans. Leon S. Roudiez (New York: Columbia University Press, 1989).

[10] *Ibid.,* p. 151.

[11] *Ibid.*

[12] *Ibid.,* p. 160.

[13] *Ibid.,* pp. 12–13.

[14] Marie-Louise von Franz, *Alchemy: An Introduction to the Symbolism and the Psychology* (Toronto: Inner City Books 1981).

[15] R. D. Hinshelwood, *Clinical Klein* (London: Free Association Books, 1994), p. 36.

[16] *Ibid.,* p. 140.

[17] Melanie Klein, "Notes on Some Schizoid Mechanisms," in Melanie Klein, Paula Heimann, Susan Isaacs, and Joan Riviere, *Developments in Psycho-Analysis* (London: Hogarth, 1952), p. 296.

[18] *Ibid.,* p. 297.

[19] Michael Eigen, *Toxic Nourishment* (London: Karnac Books, 1999).

[20] Harold V. Boris, "Black Milk," in Boris, *Envy* (Northvale, NJ: Jason Aronson, 1994), p. 54.

[21] Quote by George Crumb on "The Compositions: Black Angels," available at http://www.georgecrumb.net/comp/black-p.html.

[22] CD liner notes, p. 2, on *George Crumb: Songs, Drones and Refrains of Death,* Naxos, 2005.

[23] *Ibid.*

[24] Garcia Lorca, "Casida of the Boy Wounded by the Water," quoted in *ibid.,* p. 3.

[25] Robert Waska, *The Danger of Change: The Kleinian Approach with Patients Who Experience Progress as Trauma* (London: Routledge, 2006).

[26] Joan Riviere, "A Contribution to the Analysis of the Negative Therapeutic Reaction," in Joan Riviere, *The Inner World and Joan Riviere: Collected Papers 1920–1958,* ed. Athol Hughes (London: Karnac Books, 1991), p. 144.

[27] Michael Eigen, *Psychic Deadness* (Northvale, NJ: Jason Aronson, 1996).

[28] Marlan, *The Black Sun,* p. 189.

[29] Edward S. Casey, "Towards an Archetypal Imagination," *Spring* (1974): 1–32.

[30] James Hillman, "The Seduction of Black," in *Fire in the Stone: The Alchemy of Desire,* ed. Stanton Marlan (Wilmette, IL: Chiron, 1997), p. 9.

[31] Wilfred R. Bion, *Brazilian Lectures: 1973 São Paolo, 1974 Rio de Janiero/São Paolo* (London: Karnac Books, 1990), p. 21.

[32] James Grotstein, *A Beam of Intense Darkness* (London: Karnac, 2009), p. 1.

[33] Wilfred R. Bion, *Attention and Interpretation: A Scientific Approach to Insight in Psycho-Analysis and Groups* (1970; repr., London: Karnac Books, 1984), p. 57.

[34] John Milton, *Paradise Lost* (1667), lines 11–12, in John Milton, *Paradise Lost and Other Poems,* ed. Edward Le Comte (New York: Mentor, 1961).

[35] Michael Ondaatje quoted on Gavin Bryars's Web site, http://www.gavinbryars.com/Pages/biography.html (accessed 26 April 2010).

[36] CD liner notes for George Bryars, *The Black River,* ECM, 1993.

[37] Robert Bosnak, *Embodiment: Creative Imagination in Medicine, Art, Travel* (London: Routledge, 2007), p. 75.

[38] Marlan, *The Black Sun,* p. 97.

[39] C. G. Jung, *The Collected Works of C. G. Jung,* vol. 13, *Alchemical Studies,* trans. R. F. C. Hull (Princeton, NJ: Princeton University Press, 1967), pp. 160–161.

[40] Simon Broughton, Mark Ellingham, David Muddyman, and Richard Trillo, eds., *World Music: The Rough Guide* (London: The Rough Guides, 1994).

[41] Jan Fairley, "Astor Piazzolla," in *World Music: The Rough Guide,* ed. Broughton, Ellingham, Muddyman, and Trillo, 582.

[42] Eigen, *Toxic Nourishment,* pp. 187–204.

[43] Hillman, "The Seduction of Black," 42–53; and Paul W. Ashton, *From the Brink: Experiences of the Void from a Depth Psychology Perspective* (London, Karnac Books, 2007).

[44] Eigen, *Psychic Deadness,* pp. 45–48 and 55–67.

[45] *Ibid.,* p. 55.

[46] Julie P. Sutton, "The Air between Two Hands: Silence, Music and Communication," in *Silence, Music, Silent Music,* ed. Nicky Loseff and Jenny Doctor (Hampshire: Ashgate, 2007), pp. 169–204.

[47] Daniel N. Stern, *The First Relationship: Infant and Mother* (Cambridge MA: Harvard University Press, 1992).

[48] *Editors' note:* These themes are explored in greater detail in Chapters 10 and 16 of this volume.

[49] James S. Grotstein, "Nothingness, Meaninglessness, Chaos and the 'Black Hole,' I," *Contemporary Psychoanalysis* 26 (1990): 257–289.

[50] Leonardo Balada, *No- res (Nothing): An Agnostic Requiem,* CD, Naxos 2005.

[51] Stephen Bloch, "Music as Dreaming: Absence and the Emergence of the Auditory Symbol," in *Evocations of Absence: Multidisciplinary Perspectives on Void States,* ed. Paul W. Ashton (New Orleans: Spring Journal Publications, 2007).

[52] Robin Williamson, *The Seed-at-Zero,* CD, ECM, 2000; Robin Williamson, *Skirting the River Road,* CD, ECM, 2002; Robin Williamson, *The Iron Stone,* CD, ECM, 2006.

[53] "To God in God's Absence," on *The Iron Stone.* Lyrics reproduced with the kind permission of Robin Williamson.

[54] While the song evolves to this conclusion, Williamson passes through the primitive agony and fear of falling forever ("falling, falling") and a sustaining sense of continuity in his plea "Live on, live on." These have resonance with Winnicott's concepts of primitive anxiety and "going-on-being." There is also an expression of gratitude in "O the kindness I have been shown."

[55] Peter Hoeg, *The Quiet Girl,* trans. Nadia Christiansen (London: Wavill Seeker, 2006), p. 151.

13

Can Music Save the World?

Melinda Haas

Introduction[1]

"It was the best of times; it was the worst of times." This is certainly as applicable to today as it was to 1775 France in Charles Dickens's *A Tale of Two Cities*. It is the best of times for ego, and it is the worst of times for psyche. It is the age of technology, directed linear thinking, and black and white judgment. Even the quotation comes out of the binary, either/or thinking of ego. But where *is* the age of wisdom?

I have never really considered myself a student of culture in the sociological sense but have always been a student of music. This moment in Western culture and American culture in particular leads me to notice and encourage the conjunction of culture, depth psychology, and music. Jung's thinking began with the individual and moved out into the culture. By 1936 he had no choice but to write "Wotan" as a response and warning to the crisis that permeated *his* culture. We too might be at such a moment, when the *Zeitgeist* (crisis in our time) demands that our gaze include a larger view as well as the individual one. The overvaluation of life lived solely through ego without regard for the depth and all-inclusiveness of psyche is, in my opinion, the crisis of our time. This imbalance is reflected at the individual level because it is pervasive at the collective level; it is as much an interpersonal and cultural crisis as it is an intrapsychic and individual one.

The purview of this chapter is to posit music's potential to address what I see as the crisis in our culture. I will attempt to critique only American culture, though Western culture at large is, I believe, similarly implicated. There is much interesting new research and thought concerning the brain and music, including the work of Daniel Levitin and Oliver Sacks. For this chapter, however, I have a different focus. And unlike Daniel Levitin's new book, *The World in Six Songs,* I have elected to use as examples music *without* words. This choice allows us to experience music's abstraction. As we strip away verbal language, we interrupt our habitual mode of meaning-making, laying bare a different kind of meaning. We begin to find access to the symbolic that before was not available to us. Now we start to speak the language of psyche.

The essay is laid out in three parts. Part I will address what I see as the crisis in our culture. In Part II, I will tell you about a socioeducational experiment that has been going on for thirty-four years in Venezuela. If music might be a way to shift our culture's priorities, it is useful to look at a system that has had an impact on the social fabric of an entire country. Part III will discuss why/how music, as one avenue to the transcendent, could address the crisis we are in.

PART I: AMERICA

Philip Zabriskie wrote in *Quadrant:*

> Every impression of America as a land of opportunity and new beginnings has been matched by a parallel account of America as a land without culture and given to restless violence—a superficial civilization of high technology, but without wisdom, subtlety, or depth.[2]

He added: "One-sided accent on newness and innovation and the future is purchased at the price of a sense of history, a sense of the weight and value and seriousness of the past."[3]

Jeremy Shapiro, who teaches philosophy, sociology, and information systems at the Fielding Institute in Santa Barbara, California, hears the American condition in the opening of Copland's *Appalachian Spring*:

> It is the loneliness of being an American. . . . It is what is symbolized by the Wild West, plains, canyons, mountains, and deserts. All of these are external representations of that essential American loneliness. . . . The loneliness of a Jew is the loneliness of never fitting within what is taken for granted. The loneliness

> of a European, for at least a modern European, is that of
> reconciling contradictions, the loneliness of irony; of living out
> a particular blend of enlightenment and tradition, industrialism
> and pre-industrialism, or urban and agricultural existence, of
> bourgeois and anti-bourgeois values. The loneliness of
> Americans is entirely different. It is the loneliness of people who
> do not know that they are lonely but bear it constantly upon
> their faces. It is the loneliness of people lost in space, projected
> out of history, condemned to naïveté.[4]

Zabriskie attributes this one-sidedness to the archetypal hero and *puer* energy constellated in the experience of exploration and openness found in the "new world." The ego development necessary to fill that outer space has consumed all time, energy, and interest, leaving none for interior exploration. We could say that Shapiro describes that same solo archetypal energy from the perspective of feeling. Suppose we take as a working hypothesis the position that in our culture, ego dominates experience. It wills experience into existence; ego defines, judges, and compares, whether or not its subject fits into a linear grid of cause and effect. It analyzes and partializes (it also differentiates, separates, and distinguishes). It infuses experience with this masculine energy, replete with its shadow. Where does that leave those experiences that emerge from psyche and belong to psyche, that lie outside ego's purview? The neoclassical Jungian perspective would have it that experience is processed (at times co-opted) by ego such that an experience of and in psyche is no longer able to be experienced *without* ego, outside of ego. We eschew and dismiss other kinds of consciousness. We ignore our bodies, senses, feelings, intuition, the ineffable. In short, we live almost exclusively in Personality #1. In *Memories, Dreams, Reflections,* Jung says:

> The play and counter-play of personalities No. 1 and No. 2 . . .
> is played out in every individual. In my life No. 2 has been
> of prime importance, and I have always tried to make room
> for anything that wanted to come to me from within.[5]

Herein lies the crisis. We have created a way of life without the means to listen to "anything that wants to come from within."

I am not alone in thinking that we could call America the ADHD (attention deficit hyperactivity disorder) nation. Images flash on the computer screen, multiples per second. News and information enter our consciousness in sound bites instead of paragraphs. Even dial-up connections are far too slow. From the outside, it would seem that shopping at Wal-Mart, which contains *all,* would be like entering psyche. But in truth it is a product of postmodern multiplicity, little bits of everything, with no depth. Curiously, the specialization of the butcher, the grocer, the baker was, in previous times, not so much a part of ego specificity as it was the vendors' connection to both nature and the human relationships they developed with their customers. The split between the superficial aspect of the horizontal and the depth connection of the vertical is in full evidence even in our shopping patterns!

We have little time or money for arts education in our school systems. Many parents don't have the patience or interest to urge their children to leave their computer screens and begin the arduous process of learning to play an instrument. Nor do most of us have the attention necessary to sit and listen to one piece of music that lasts for sixty-eight minutes, like Mahler's *Symphony No. 5,* an hour that takes one on a journey through a vast range of human emotion and experience.

John Adams figured his generation like this: "He had to study politics and war, so that his sons could study mathematics and philosophy, in order to give their children a right to study painting, poetry, music and architecture."[6] His son, John Quincy, carried on his father's vision when he called for "'laws promoting . . . the cultivation and encouragement of . . . the elegant arts, the advancement of literature and the progress of the sciences.' Failure to exercise constitutional powers for the elevation of the people 'would be treachery to the most sacred of trusts.'"[7] We have surely breached that trust. John Adams's grandchildren have not been given the right to develop their individual and collective relationship to psyche.

Jeremy Shapiro notes this problem: "I am deeply concerned with the one-dimensionalization and trivialization of experience endangered by our society, which endangers the capacity to experience individuality and complexity." Yet he is not without hope: "I deeply believe that listening to music can help restore this capacity."[8]

PART II: VENEZUELA

In 1975, Venezuelan José Antonio Abreu started a youth orchestra to give professional opportunities to talented young classical musicians. At the time, there were only two orchestras in the whole country. Abreu's sights were set much higher than on this one orchestra. He wanted to create many orchestras, in order to "give access to music to poor people." He asked, "Why concentrate in one class the privilege of playing Mozart and Beethoven?" He felt that "the high musical culture of the world has to be a common culture, part of the education of everyone."[9] In 1977, his orchestra succeeded brilliantly at an international competition in Scotland and the Venezuelan government began fully financing it. Abreu explains his commitment this way: "An orchestra is the only group where people get together to reach agreements and they reach agreements producing something beautiful."[10]

Today, thirty-four years later, more than two million children have studied music in the National System of Children and Youth Orchestras of Venezuela, commonly known as *el sistema*. Across Venezuela, *el sistema* has established 246 centers and more than 600 orchestras. These employ 15,000 teachers for children between the ages of two and eighteen. At any one time, 250,000 children are studying music. Typically the children practice three to four hours a day, six days a week, and they are playing in orchestras from the very beginning of their music experience. "In an orchestra," says an administrator of the government-funded program, "everybody respects meritocracy, everybody respects tempo, everybody knows he has to support everyone else, whether he is a soloist or not."[11]

Abreu, a classical musician and economist, envisioned music as an agency of social change. Javier Moreno, the general manager of *el sistema,* describes that vision. "We're interested in creating citizens with all the values they need to exist in society: responsibility, teamwork, respect, co-operation and work ethic."[12] To carry that philosophy even further, now a pilot project involving three prisons (two men's, one women's) is receiving $3 million from the government. "We start with the simple idea that performing music lifts the human being to another level," says the lawyer who helped create the prison orchestras.[13]

El sistema's flagship orchestra is the Simón Bolívar Youth Orchestra in Caracas. Its members range in age from fifteen to twenty-five. It has been led by one of its own, Gustavo Dudamel, since he was fifteen. Dudamel, who grew up in *el sistema,* became the principal conductor of the Los Angeles Philharmonic in September 2009 at the age of twenty-seven. The youth orchestra and its conductor have a recording contract with Deutsche Grammophon and have produced, to date, recordings of Beethoven's Fifth and Seventh Symphonies and Mahler's Fifth Symphony. In recent years, the orchestra has toured Europe and America, including a series of concerts at Carnegie Hall in 2007. The youngest member of the Berlin Philharmonic, a bassist who was seventeen when he entered, comes from the Simón Bolívar Youth Orchestra.

Inspired by its new conductor, the Los Angeles Philharmonic has introduced a program called Youth Orchestra LA that is directly modeled on *el sistema.* The program began with children ages eight to twelve from a disadvantaged district of the city of Los Angeles, but the grander scheme is "to provide a musical instrument and a place in a youth orchestra for every young person in Los Angeles County who wants one."[14] On the East Coast, Marin Alsop, principal conductor of the Baltimore Symphony, has used some of her symphony grant money to develop a similar program in the public schools of Baltimore. Further afield, the Scottish Arts Council has recently begun a similar pilot program.[15]

El sistema now has a new eleven-story, $25 million building, the Center for Social Action through Music, on the outskirts of Caracas. The Inter-American Development Bank helped to underwrite it and is putting $150 million toward seven regional centers throughout Venezuela. The bank, which usually funds infrastructure development such as sewers and roads, was initially wary about this kind of funding until it did some research about *el sistema*. One study showed that more than two-thirds of the 2 million children served by the system were from poor backgrounds. Other studies linked participation in the program with improvement in school attendance and declines in juvenile delinquency. As *New York Times* journalist Arthur Lubow concluded, "Weighing such benefits as a falloff in school dropout rates and a decline in crime, the bank calculated that every dollar invested in the sistema was reaping about $1.68 in social dividends."[16]

The system has weathered ten governments, from extreme right to extreme left, in its thirty-plus year history. How? From the beginning, it fell under the dominion of social services ministries rather than the ministry of culture. The social welfare element is fundamental to Abreu's philosophy, so this arrangement has been very successful, particularly since many government bureaucrats see social services as far less "disposable" than the arts. But might it also be the case that this particular process and product is able to reach some kind of metalevel, enabling it to hold its psychic ground above the wiles of politics?

PART III: MUSIC IN A TIME OF CRISIS

I am well aware that Venezuela is not America and that the social crisis *el sistema* has helped address is not the psychic crisis I am referring to in our own technologically sophisticated culture. However, I believe that the reason that music is able to influence delinquency and truancy is precisely because it reaches under the social/collective layer of society into the archetypal ground of humanity. It is there, in that common space, that healing can take place, no matter how diverse the outer symptoms are.

Hegel wrote in *The Philosophy of Fine Art* (1831) that "sound liberates the ideal content from its fetters in the material substance . . . permitting the echo and reverberation of man's emotional world through its entire range of feelings and passions."[17] Gustavo Dudamel echoes Hegel when he talks about Mahler's *Symphony No. 5*:

> One has to think of the structure as a whole, of how it is possible that a work that begins with a funeral march develops into a second movement filled with despair, then turns into a third movement filled with joy and happiness, which then grows and connects with love in the Adagietto, and then by the end of the fifth movement, has arrived at hope. . . . Some people say that you have to have lived many years to have experienced all that emotion and be able to communicate it. I believe the most important thing is simply to feel it and play.[18]

If one listens to the opening of the second movement of Mahler's Fifth Symphony, we hear in the span of two minutes a journey across an entire universe. (Listen to the Simón Bolívar Youth Orchestra's recording of Mahler, *Symphony No. 5*, Movement 1, section 2 [0 to 2:13 on the CD]. If you're listening with the score in hand, this would be to Rehearsal Number 6.)

We turn to Schopenhauer, who wrote in *The World as Will and Idea* (1819):

> [Music] stands alone, quite cut off from all the other arts. In it we do not recognize the copy or repetition of any Idea of existence in the world. Yet it is such a great and exceedingly noble art, its effect on the inmost nature of man is so powerful, and it is so entirely and deeply understood by him in his inmost consciousness as a perfectly universal language, the distinctness of which surpasses even that of the perceptible world itself, that . . . we must attribute to music a far more serious and deep significance, connected with the inmost nature of the world and our own self.[19]

And now we turn to Jung, who rarely spoke of music, so I take the liberty of quoting what he writes about poetry as though it were about music.

> We would do well to think of the creative process as a living thing implanted in the human psyche. . . . We would have to be prepared for something suprapersonal that transcends our understanding to the same degree that the author's consciousness was in abeyance during the process of creation. We would expect a strangeness of form and content, thoughts that can only be

> apprehended intuitively, a language pregnant with meanings,
> and images that are true symbols . . . bridges thrown out towards
> an unseen shore.[20]

This bridge toward an unseen shore is our connection to psyche. The arts are eminently equipped to be that bridge. Music stands at the ready.

When Daniel Barenboim talks about harmony in music, not only in the musical sense but in the harmony one experiences of thought and feeling, we could say that he is speaking of ego and psyche and masculine and feminine. He implies that masculine and feminine energies coexist in music when he refers to "that absolutely necessary relationship between manipulation [the penetrating and differentiating of the masculine] and yielding [the receptive of the feminine], which to me is the basis of all music-making, in fact, of human existence."[21]

When one listens to a Beethoven symphony, one moves from the first theme to the second, from angularity to roundness, from heroic to lyric, from masculine to feminine, with an awareness of the layering and juxtaposition of the two. The relationship to time also taps into an experience of ego and psyche, of masculine and feminine. Unlike the visual arts, music takes place in time, over time. With the exception of some contemporary music, time is measured and divided. We experience its linear march, the horizontal sequence of melody and rhythm. But at the same time we experience the vertical element of harmony, the chords that sound notes simultaneously. We turn again to Barenboim: "In this respect, music is exactly like history, which has to be lived both simultaneously and subsequently."[22] We might consider the concurrent perception of the present moment and the passage of time to be a sensory *coniunctio*, particularly through music's use of silence and its hint of eternity. Dudamel told his orchestra that "Stravinsky once said . . . that time is . . . in space. And when a musician makes music he takes it from the time he is living in."[23] In the opening of Beethoven's *Symphony No. 7* we hear a stunning example of the horizontal and vertical experience of time. We can discern the difference between and the juxtaposition of the verticality of the chords, notes sounding at the same time, and the melody that flows out of those chords unwinding over time in its horizontal path. (Listen to Beethoven's *Symphony No. 7*, Movement 1 [0 to 1:30 on the CD]; measures 1–26 in the score.)

When we take in what Barenboim says next, we get closer to the territory that we must approach in our culture:

> Music is so very important and interesting to me because it is at
> the same time everything and nothing. If you wish to learn how

to live in a democratic society, then you would do well to play in an orchestra. For when you do so, you know when to lead and when to follow. You leave space for others and at the same time you have no inhibitions about claiming a place for yourself. And despite this, or maybe precisely because of it, music is the best means of escape from the problems of human existence. [24]

We hear in this quotation intimations of the wholeness and totality of psychic experience. Now we are invited beyond the both/and of masculine/feminine, ego/psyche, causal/acausal dichotomies (even if they are joined) into the all-containing and accepting land of psyche herself. In this territory, the horizontal and vertical, time and the timeless, are experienced as a totality rather than separate parts conjoined. We begin to achieve a sense of the *whole* piece, the whole spectrum of emotion and experience, not merely a set of strung-together movements. (Listen to Beethoven's *Symphony No. 7,* Movement 3 [0 to 1:30 on the CD], then Movement 4 [0 to 2:13 on the CD]. On the score, measures 1-180 of Movement 3 and measures 1-124 of Movement 4.)

If one listens to the opening minutes of both Movements 3 and 4 of Beethoven's 7th Symphony one is able to discern a vast variety of texture, timbre, sound quality, density, rhythmic complexity, harmonic tension and release. And one hears the span of suggested emotions—from excitement to anticipation to surprise to playfulness to tenderness—to say nothing of the technical prowess it takes to execute these varieties and subtleties.

There is a continuing discussion among arts educators in America about the need for multicultural representation and equality. Inherent in this discussion is our ongoing struggle as Jungian analysts between the literal and the symbolic, the external and the internal, and even the partialized and the whole. Once again we are pressed to reach beyond the tension of the opposites and even beyond the binarism of both-and to the energy of psyche that holds all and accepts everything. Maybe we need to strive to become the "post–both-and era" at this time in our sociopsychological development.

Kwame Appiah's recent book *Cosmopolitanism* addresses the pull between identity and multiculturalism that is embedded in any discussion of culture:

If the argument for cultural patrimony is that the art belongs to the culture that gives it its significance, most art doesn't belong to a national culture at all. Much of the greatest art is flamboyantly international; much ignores nationality altogether. [25]

And further:

> One connection—the one neglected in talk of cultural
> patrimony—is the connection not *through* identity but *despite*
> difference. We can respond to art that is not ours; indeed, we
> can fully respond to "our" art only if we move beyond thinking
> of it as ours and start to respond to it as art.[26]

In the context of Appiah's comments about cultural patrimony, what
do we make of the fact that 2 million children in Venezuela are playing
Mozart and Beethoven as well as orchestral transcriptions of more
indigenous Venezuelan music? Is Venezuela secure enough in cultural
homogeneity that it can "risk" stepping outside its culture to "dabble" in
European expression? Or might there be something specifically about this
classical *orchestral* music that itself stands outside its own culture? And if
so, might the freedom of being culturally unbound be the result of an
intimate relationship with psyche and the archetypal layer of existence?

If one agrees with (or at least follows) my working hypothesis, then
one recognizes that ego has taken center stage, at the very least in the culture
of the United States. It must begin to share the stage. It must be relativized
if we are to survive as the deep and complicated human beings that we
are. Music has the ability to relativize the ego both for player and listener
by engaging each in an active experience of psyche. Because music exists
outside verbal language it has the possibility of circumventing the part of
our thinking function that sets ego into its overachieving motion. But let
us not discount ego's role in music-making. The technique and analysis
required to master an instrument and play in an orchestra rely heavily on
an array of ego functions. That is part of what makes music a uniquely
probable example of psyche—it contains *all*, ego and non-ego alike—and
if anything is missing, then the music *itself* will be missing.

John Russell, the late art critic for the *New York Times*, wrote:

> When art is made new, we are made new with it. We have a
> sense of solidarity with our own time, and of psychic energies
> shared and redoubled, which is just about the most satisfying
> thing that life has to offer.[27]

Gustavo Dudamel speaks of this newness (and thus the potential for
the constellation of psychic energies) when he says: "A professional orchestra
has played these symphonies hundreds of times. For us it's new music."[28]
When listening to the opening minutes of the second movement of
Beethoven's *Symphony No. 7,* as recorded by the Simón Bolívar Youth

Orchestra, one should bear in mind that these musicians were fifteen to twenty-five years old and that their conductor was only twenty-six when this recording was made. (Listen to Beethoven's *Symphony No. 7*, Movement 2 [0–3:07 on the CD]. On the score, measures 1–101.)

Think for a moment about what it took to execute the first three minutes of this music. As they move into adulthood, these young people now have, through their bodies and their experience, access to many life lessons. They have learned something about patience, the ability to tolerate tension, the subtle understanding of building something beautiful from the bottom up, and a connection to the many layers that make a whole.

In my next example, these same young interpreters are being asked to be supple and flexible, to garner entirely different energy almost instantaneously. As a result, whole worlds materialize simultaneously. Through the use of the fugue, Mahler achieves a layered texture that builds intensity. Then the abrupt textural changes alternate between sharp and smooth, angular and legato. These juxtapositions might well imply the masculine/feminine elements that I believe Barenboim alluded to when he spoke of manipulation and yielding. However, the overall effect is not either/or, nor is it both-and, but rather a kind of all-encompassing totality. This excerpt is part of the fifth (and final) section of the third movement of Mahler's Fifth Symphony. (Listen to Mahler's *Symphony No. 5*, Movement 3 [7:30 to 9:22 on the CD]. On the score, measures 417–537 of section 5 of the third movement, or from six measures before rehearsal number 17 to rehearsal number 24.)

Let us return for a moment to Shapiro's American loneliness. Or that sense of lack of history that Zabriskie spoke of. How could participation as listener or player speak to these gaps in our culture? Edward Said wrote that "music, in some profound way, is perhaps the final resistance to the acculturation and the commodification of everything."[29] The holes, the emptiness, the absence of depth are felt individually, collectively, and intrapsychically. They are the space we left when we abandoned our connection to psyche and thus to the possibility of the transcendent. When we built a life and culture defined and proscribed by ego, we created gaps in ourselves and a gap in our ability to come to our deep selves as the primary resource in our lives. Paradoxically, because classical orchestral music exists outside the literal, it has the potential to fill those gaps with the wide-open limitless space of psyche. Because it exists outside the verbal, it crosses cultures and spans geographical borders.

In closing, I would like to quote Susanne Langer's eloquent understanding of music. Here is a perfect description of a consciousness that rests in psyche and outside ego, linked to imagination and connected to the whole of life:

> The assignment of meanings is a shifting, kaleidoscopic play, probably below the threshold of consciousness, certainly outside the pale of discursive thinking. The imagination that responds to music is personal and associative and logical, tinged with affect, tinged with bodily rhythm, tinged with dream, but *concerned* with a wealth of formulations for its wealth of wordless knowledge, its whole knowledge of emotional and organic experience of vital impulse, balance, conflict, the *ways* of living and dying and feeling.[30]

(Listen to the "Adagietto" of Mahler's *Symphony No. 5*—Movement 3, section 4.)

NOTES

This chapter was first presented as a paper at the North American Conference of Jungian Analysts & Candidates, Sebasco Harbor Estates, Maine, 18–21 September 2008. The theme of the conference was Explosions and Containment: Our Worlds in Crisis.

[1] It is the author's hope that the reader will listen to the Simón Bolívar Youth Orchestra of Venezuela's recordings of Beethoven's *Symphony No. 7* and Mahler's *Symphony No. 5* in their entirety. They can be found on *Beethoven 5 & 7: Gustavo Dudamel and the Simón Bolívar Youth Orchestra of Venezuela,* CD, Deutsche Grammophon, catalog number 000689902, 2006; and *Mahler 5: Gustavo Dudamel and the Simón Bolívar Youth Orchestra of Venezuela,* CD, Deutsche Grammophon, catalog number 000983702, 2007. All of the in-text references to passages from these two works are from these recordings. The author suggests that readers begin their experience of this chapter by listening to the trumpet opening of Mahler's Fifth Symphony: Movement 1, Section 1, 0 to :42. (This is up to rehearsal number 1 if you're listening with score in hand.)

[2] Philip T. Zabriskie, "America as 'The New World,'" *Quadrant* 21, no. 2 (1988): 58.

[3] *Ibid.,* p. 58.

[4] Jeremy J. Shapiro, "My Funeral Music," in *Listening, Playing, Creating: Essays on the Power of Sound,* ed. Carolyn Bereznak Kenny (Albany: State University of New York Press, 1995), p. 264.

[5] C. G. Jung, *Memories, Dreams, Reflections* (New York: Vintage, 1961), p. 45.

[6] Arthur Levitt, Jr., "Introduction," in *Public Money & the Muse: Essays on Government Funding for the Arts,* ed. Stephen Benedict (New York: W.W. Norton and Company, 1991), p. 32.

[7] *Ibid.,* p. 33.

[8] Shapiro, "My Funeral Music," p. 259.

[9] Arthur Lubow, "Conductor of the People," *New York Times Magazine,* 28 October 2007, p. 36.

[10] Lisa Blackmore, "Redemption Songs: The Street Children Saved by Music," *The Independent* (UK), 17 August 2007, available at http://www.independent.co.uk/news/world/americas/redemption-songs-the-street-children-saved-by-music-461934.html.

[11] Lubow, "Conductor of the People," p. 35.

[12] Blackmore, "Redemption Songs."

[13] Simon Romero, "Amid Despair in a Venezuelan Prison, Strains of Hope from a Music Program," *New York Times,* 23 June 2008.

[14] Lubow, "Conductor of the People," p. 34.

[15] Blackmore, "Redemption Songs."

[16] *Ibid.,* p. 37.

[17] G. W. F. Hegel, *The Philosophy of Fine Art,* trans. F. P. B. Osmaston (London: G. Bell, 1920), 1:118–119, quoted in Lewis Rowell, *Thinking about Music: An Introduction to the Philosophy of Music* (Amherst: University of Massachusetts Press, 1983), p. 125. *The Philosophy of Fine Art* was published posthumously.

[18] Charlotte Higgins, CD liner notes for *Mahler 5: Gustavo Dudamel and the Simón Bolívar Youth Orchestra of Venezuela,* Deutsche Grammophon, 2007.

[19] Arthur Schopenhauer, *The World As Will and Idea,* trans. R. B. Haldane and J. Kemp, 6th ed. (London: Kegan Paul, Trench, Trubner & Co., 1907), 1:330–331.

[20] C. G. Jung, "On the Relation of Analytical Psychology to Poetry, 1931," in *The Collected Works of C. G. Jung,* vol. 15, *The Spirit in Man, Art, and Literature,* trans. R. F. C. Hull (Princeton, NJ: Princeton University Press, 1966), pp. 75–76.

[21] Daniel Barenboim and Edward W. Said, *Parallels and Paradoxes: Explorations in Music and Society* (New York: Vintage Books, 2004), p. 85.

[22] *Ibid.,* p. 148.

[23] *Tocar y Lucha* (To Play and to Fight), dir. Alberto Arvelo, DVD, Explorart, 2006.

[24] Barenboim and Said, *Parallels and Paradoxes,* p. 173.

[25] Kwame Anthony Appiah, *Cosmopolitanism: Ethics in a World of Strangers* (New York: W.W. Norton and Company, 2006), p. 126.

[26] *Ibid.,* p. 136.

[27] William Grimes, "John Russell, Art Critic for the Times, Dies at 89," *New York Times,* 25 August 2008.

[28] Shirley Apthorp, CD liner notes for *Beethoven 5 & 7: Gustavo Dudamel and the Simón Bolívar Youth Orchestra of Venezuela,* Deutsche Grammophon, 2006.

[29] Barenboim and Said, *Parallels and Paradoxes,* p. 168.

[30] Susanne K. Langer, *Philosophy in a New Key: A Study in the Symbolism of Reason, Rite, and Art* (Cambridge: Harvard University Press, 1957), p. 244.

14

Bonfire of the Vanities: Music, Playback Theatre, Xenophobia, and Trauma in a South African Township

Chris Wildman

In a church hall near the heart of Masiphumelele, a growing African township in greater Cape Town, an impromptu audience has been invited to watch a free show where they will provide true stories that can be acted out in front of them.[1] In Masiphumelele amenities are scarce: schools overcrowded, no police station, and an understaffed Day Care Clinic, while a possible 30–40 percent of the community is infected with HIV and/or TB.

In the hall the disparate audience consists of concerned members of the community, children with little else to occupy them except attending a free show, white community activists from more privileged neighborhoods, and a miscellany of journalists and interested visitors to this township. When the show starts they will sit in a semicircle around the performance space, which has no stage or set. Even in post-apartheid South Africa such a culturally diverse audience is a rare experience. Also rare is a culturally diverse company of actors, as Cape Town is still a very racially segregated city.

The Bonfire Theatre Company was founded in October 2005 by Paula Kingwill, Heather Schiff, Lesley Bester, and Kyle Hudson. Their aim was to provide a new form of theatre in South Africa based on the theatrical form of playback theatre developed by Jonathan Fox.[2] The purpose was to facilitate the healing of splits and divides in South Africa through the telling of stories that emerge from the daily lives of South Africans. The company explicitly aims to "create a space for healing of painful memories through sharing them with one's community" as well as encouraging "crossing divisions between race, class, gender and nationality so that we can undermine prejudice with knowledge of one another."[3]

Bonfire Company's members range in age from twenty-two to sixty and broadly represent the diversity of South African society. However, as Bonfire's policy statement makes clear:

> Transformation from an apartheid mentality is taking place at the level of government and institutions. However, transformation is a much slower process on the personal and individual level. In order for any change to be successful and healthy it needs to take place on all levels. Playback theatre is a powerful and accessible way to facilitate change of people's attitudes towards one another.[4]

The specific value of playback theatre in the researching of refugee stories in London has recently been validated by Erene Kaptani and Nira Yuval-Davis:

> Unlike in interviews and focus groups, the stories that emerge in Playback theatre are usually illustrative, focusing on particular moments of time and place, but encapsulating much wider insights regarding the participants' lives and situations. These narratives constitute, by the end of each show, what Freire[5] calls *generative themes,* as actors produce the main themes that emerged from their lived experiences.[6]

Here in Masiphumelele our form of playback theatre is seen as an appropriate way to engage with and reflect on the impact of this community's traumatic experience of xenophobia. It is November 2008. There have been terrible outbursts of xenophobic violence throughout South Africa in recent months and in Masiphumelele in particular. This show is part of a series of shows in the community that aims to discover a common humanity and build a unified community through storytelling.

PREPARATIONS

The Bonfire performers arrive from different parts of Cape Town. None of them originates from Cape Town and all have experienced the city from an outsider's point of view. This makes them sensitive to the anxieties experienced by immigrants and refugees who have been threatened, attacked, and chased out of the townships. Most of the performers, including myself, have been rehearsing and performing with the Bonfire Theatre Company for the past four years. We have done this in schools, workplaces, and theatres in Cape Town, Johannesburg, Port Elizabeth, Soweto, Botswana, Malawi, and Mozambique.

Masiphumelele is a noisy place. Outside the hall a scene not untypical of an early evening African township unfolds. People return from work. Before the show is due to start, the hall echoes with many voices in a clash of English and Xhosa. Children, chatting and squealing in Xhosa, run in and out of the hall. A woman selling soup at the door shouts to friends, some of whom may only enter for the soup and then leave. Outside many passersby take a stroll while it is still light and safe to be about. As the playback musician, unpacking and setting up my electric keyboard and percussion instruments, I am conscious of the loose acoustics yet enjoy the sense that this is a place that amplifies many voices and does not require the respectful vocal restraint that a conventional theatre might.

In a corner of the room I join the five actors and the conductor-director. We stand in a circle and acknowledge each other in a silent ritual that leads into the symbolic building of our "bonfire." The "logs" are the contributions and hopes we each put in to help the fire of tonight's show burn brightly. We hold hands and close our eyes and wait for the synergetic moment of ignition.

Next we set up. While the actors assemble a costume rack and a table of symbolic props, I place my keyboard and instruments as close to the acting space as I can. I also place it close to the audience so I can witness and reflect their facial expressions and gestures as carefully as possible. Above all I do not want the music to be too separate from the actors, as is the case with most conventional theatre music, because here the music must play an integral role in the action as it unfolds. For me the musician's role includes the freedom to intervene in the enactment as an actor might. I choose to play standing rather than sitting, so I can be more on a level with the actors and less like mere accompanist.

As I test out the keyboard sound and adjust volumes to match the acoustics of the hall, children and some local adults stop to watch as if I am a jazz performer getting ready for a gig. But despite having performed such gigs, I am not here either to display my talent or to play the role of mere accompanist. As a music therapist I bring many years of experience of reflecting the moods and feelings of both individuals and groups. Now I meet the exciting challenge of playing music inspired by the subjectivities of the people who will tell stories here this evening and the actors who will perform them.

Playback theatre has always relied on the presence of one or more musicians on stage, although very little has been written about the musician's role in a playback event. Music is taken for granted in much the same way film music is. Yet music's role in live performance is crucial to the way community rituals function. In his article "Mind over Music," Raj Parsaud concludes:

> The need for music to celebrate a victory over an enemy or to mourn the loss of a fellow hunter killed in the chase implies that music has a power beyond words to communicate mood and indeed to co-ordinate emotional states. This is why music is such a vital part of our rituals and ceremonies. Music at a funeral or a wedding helps to ensure we reach the equivalent emotional highs and lows at the same time.[7]

Implicitly my role in the company is to "co-ordinate emotional states" not only for the actors and the storyteller but for the audience as well.

The process of anticipation and preparation mirrors the function of music itself in playback theatre, which is to prepare and anticipate the moods and feelings of actors and audience alike. Music does not merely accompany the action. It is the role of the music to open and close the scenes within a story or statement. It must provide the prelude, scene setting, transition, and closure.

Even as the actors warm up, the music provides this preparatory role. It anticipates the needs for a starting point, a transition, a shift of rhythm, an intensification of feeling, a closure: it rolls out a carpet of sound under the actors' feet as they move forward. The music also suggests an ambience (intimate, public, sinister, warm) or an imagined environment—a fantasy forest, a dance club, a walk in the open air, heavy traffic.

My job here is to "co-ordinate the emotional states," to borrow Parsuad's term, of the varieties of improvisation going on in front of me. This can be paradoxical: at the same time I must both follow and lead; to be both a presence and be invisible; allow for diversity, diffusion, even anarchy, yet suggest unity, cohesion, resolution. Coming from both a jazz and folk-pop tradition, I have learned to express feelings from a spontaneous but semi-structured base: chord patterns, melodic ideas that might make someone want to sing, exciting bass riffs that inspire the feet to explore a new dance.

Unlike the jazz performer who must impress with the inevitable improvisatory solo, I have embraced the team experience of the Bonfire Company to move away from outstanding solos. In the words of Bonfire's director Paula Kingwill in her "Notes to the Performers":

You are in a team. You are held and holding. No one individual carries too much. Everyone is wide-awake to the offers and emerging stories. Allow it to unfold. Experiment and support. Enjoy what you are good at. Enjoy what others are good at. Let the fabric be woven. Fall in love with the teller. Open you heart and ears to them. Celebrate the fact that they are alive and here to transform you with their story. Call on God, your Ancestors and your Totem Animals to help you to be true to yourself and the story. We don't do this work without them. We are engaging with something larger than ourselves.[8]

BEYOND THE PERFORMER'S EGO: "THE BONFIRE OF THE VANITIES"

The name "Bonfire" was collectively agreed on by the company members when it was founded as a name that honored the tradition of fireside storytelling. While writing this essay, however, the title of Tom Wolfe's novel *The Bonfire of the Vanities* came to mind as a useful phrase to connect the Bonfire Theatre Company to the shedding of their ego-performance tendencies, that need for attention that is common to all performing artists.[9]

In his critique of playback theatre's potential excesses in his book *Playing the Other: Dramatizing Personal Narratives in Playback Theatre,* Nick Rowe warns that "the performers can become dazzled by their desire to create a spectacle; they can use the freedom they have to show off at the expense of the teller's story."[10]

Over many rehearsals we have weaned ourselves from this need to perform from an egoistic agenda, the conventional "star performer" model. Our aim, as both musician and actors, is to offer the performance as a gift that honors the storyteller. It reverses the notion of stardom and fame by bringing the focus onto the receiver rather than the giver, onto the audience rather than the performer. This work differs from other theatre performance rituals in that there is a different order of giving and receiving.

THE SHOW

The show starts. The audience also needs to warm up. It needs to familiarize itself with this unique situation of reflecting on current and remembered feelings and communicating them to the cast. Some members of the audience prefer to remain silent throughout. Yet they support the telling and the enactment simply by being witnesses. Others may feel their hearts beating with the insistent message: "Say it!!"

To help reduce the audience's anxiety, the actors walk randomly about the stage to my jazzy walking bass while Paula the conductor asks members of the audience to give her just one word to describe their day, how they feel about living in South Africa at the moment, about their work, or about their lives generally. In response to each word thrown at them by the audience the actors freeze into postures that reflect its meaning in a variety of ways, often humorous. This is the part of the show where most laughter is heard. Humor is the icebreaker that helps the audience to relax into this unexpected world where the private is becoming public.

Next comes the "one-sentence story." The conductor asks the audience: "Give us a one-sentence story about something that happened to you, maybe today, maybe recently, maybe when you were a child." Those who tell one-sentence stories get a taste, along with the rest of the audience, of how economically theatre can summarize life situations, moods, experiences. When members of the audience tell their one-sentence stories in a detached manner, the conductor challenges them with the key words: "And you felt . . ?"

By now audience and actors are sensing the electricity and potency of the material that is very much "of the moment." A collectively unrehearsed expression of grief or joy accompanied by improvised music and animated props can have an immediacy that nothing rehearsed can match. The tension, vulnerability, and impact of "in-the-moment telling" is potentially stronger and more "resolving" or healing precisely because it is unrehearsed and is being created in real time. This is why we spent a year in rehearsal familiarizing ourselves with the skills and dynamics specific to improvised playback and allowing the "chemistry of the situation" to reveal the unexpected. It is often the unexpected that provides the tension that makes the difference between mere telling and transformative revelation.

Whereas in conventional theatre the function of music tends to be *incidental,* to be bridging or referential, in improvised playback the music is relied upon for its capacity to be *interventive.* The music evokes specific feelings, suggests ambience or environment, and above all focuses on and sustains the more unconscious feelings that the actors may not easily be able to express without musical support. Music is thus a crucial holding form: it gives relief to the audience's uncertainty when witnessing an improvisation.

As former playback musician Niels Hamel puts it: "Music is there to fill the *empty space of uncertainty* with sounds with which the audience can connect on a subliminal level."[11] Paradoxically, it is the risk that is shared by both performer and audience in what Fox calls "nonscripted theatre"[12] that makes that theatre more immediate, more present, more heroic even, than prepared theatre. It can make the difference between merely being told and being moved.

THE FIRST STORY: LET'S BUILD

By now the audience is warmed up and ready for the more demanding process of listening to more extended stories. There will be a chance for three members of the audience to step up and sit in the teller's chair to the right of the performance area where the conductor will assist in the telling of a more lengthy and detailed story.

A middle-aged Xhosa speaker is the first to put up her hand. The actors applaud, celebrating her courage as she walks to the teller's chair. Her name is Nomhle,[13] and she speaks in clear and confident English: "My story is about how we women built the first brick houses in Masiphumelele." The statement is so dramatic the audience burst into applause.

Nomhle tells how she called a meeting of the mothers in her area over a concern about health problems. The drains were bursting. The children were playing in the sewage. She knew that they needed to build brick houses in order to access plumbing and better sanitation. She had the idea that women should help each other build their own houses by starting up a fund and making their own bricks. She was elected to organize the making of the first bricks, and the women built their houses together.

Nomhle has grasped the potential of this storytelling event to provide a story with a vivid metaphor for community building and self-reliance: the making of bricks and the building of new houses. She is invited to choose an actor to represent her in the story and, interestingly, she chooses Chuma Sopotela, the youngest actor on stage, to be her.

In Peter Brook's groundbreaking book on theatre practice written over forty years ago, *The Empty Space,* he throws an interesting light on how an audience watches a play.

> In the French language amongst the different terms for those who watch, for public, for spectator, one word stands out, is different in quality from the rest. *Assistance*—I watch a play; *j'assiste à une pièce* .... The audience assists. With this assistance, the assistance of eyes, and focus and desires and enjoyment ... the word representation no longer separates actor and audience, show and public: it envelops them: what is present for one is present for the other. It has come from a life outside the theatre that is essentially repetitive to a special arena in which each

> moment is lived more clearly and more tensely. The audience
> assists the actor, and at the same time for the audience itself
> assistance comes back from the stage.[14]

This is particularly true of the kind of *assistance* demanded by playback. Throughout Nomhle's narration, the audience has been listening to a fellow member. The telling has been raw and unpackaged in a way that is distinctly different from television. While television and other media claim to tell the stories of our lives back to us, here an audience engages directly in the creative process in which they witness their own stories on their own terms. Our empathy is automatically demanded, and our sense of community is appealed to by the simple fact that we are witnesses to a story told by one of us here tonight. Equally this includes the audience's attitude to the actors and musician. They must bring their *assistance* to help make it a success.

It is now my job to play a prelude while the actors go to the back of the stage and select costumes and props while indicating to one another what roles they intend to adopt. Because the story has been so inspiring and joyfully told I want to play something upbeat. Reggae and the line from Bob Marley, "Let's get together and feel all right" from his song "One Love" come to mind. I trust that and slide into an improvisation that negotiates its way toward a statement of the familiar theme. As I repeat the melody on the keyboard a young girl in the front row starts to sing the words. She is undaunted by the fact that she is singing alone. I smile encouragingly at her so that she will not lose her nerve. The music has implicitly invited her to cross the boundary between performer and audience. There is a naturalness to her voice. She sings alone and I do not indicate to the audience to sing along, since the mood is evidently not there so early in the show. Yet like the storyteller, she is singing from and for the audience without showing off. I am excited that the message of participation without vanity is manifesting here. At the same time, for me this is a unique experience of *assistance*. The music ends as the actors take up their positions.

"Are we ready?" asks the conductor. "Let's watch."

To get the scene going I offer a lively melodic motif that suggests "let's get busy." What sometimes makes the initial musical idea not only acceptable but even compelling for the audience is the mere fact that it is an improvised musical response. It as if the conductor had said, "Let's listen" instead of "Let's watch." For the actors, the opening music is certainly helping by filling the "empty space of uncertainty" mentioned earlier.

Chuma, the teller's actor, steps forward and cues her fellow actors to take on the role of neighbors by shouting: "Look at this sewage! Let's call a meeting! Come to my house! It's time to build our own houses and get proper plumbing!"

The music adjusts itself to the rhythm of the actors' movements. They can skip about to it, dance to it, or interrupt it with dialogue. If they do the latter, the music will become quiet or more punctuated so as to avoid acoustic competition.

As the activity of brick making and building grows on stage, so the music builds on its own energy to suggest a simple perpetuum mobile, a continuous pattern of notes that are repeated without interruption to suggest an unstoppable force. The motif drops in volume but sustains itself with a sense of energetic lightness that will not need to stop until the scene or maybe even the whole story ends.

Suddenly the teller's actor has an idea. She beckons to the children in the front row. "Come, children. Help us build the houses." The children gleefully leap on stage and join in, to the laughter of the audience.

I am conscious of the need for a finale in the form of a song as the actors are shouting "Let's build the houses!" and "Let's build together!" I convert these into a simple chorus and sing:

> Let's build the houses
> Masimabane

Fortunately the actors pick up on it so it gathers into a lively musical finale. The audience claps wildly and by doing so itself brings closure to the performance. In a community that has recently experienced the destruction of homes and lives, this has been a cathartic event.

The Second Story: Personal Trauma

It is time for another story. Tentatively a young Xhosa woman puts up her hand. She is applauded as she steps up to the teller's chair. Her name is Zinzi, and with the conductor's help she is able to tell her story of how she was recently harassed on a station platform by two threatening young men who tried to involve her in their criminal activities.

While Zinzi speaks I listen to the shifting timbres, melody, rhythm, and dynamics of her voice. My job will be not only to mirror but to transform these essentially musical elements of speech. Depending on the tone and energy of the teller's voice, I, along with the actors, will try to transform not only the story but also the individual voice of the teller. This may mean emboldening the quiet voice, honoring the melodic or rhythmically engaging voice with equal quality, and perhaps expressing the hidden vulnerability of the "pathologically normal" neutral voice with a more dramatic musical language.

"Let's watch!"

In this playback, the teller's actor is standing on a station platform feeling uneasy at the approach of two dangerous-looking young men. She remains calm and handles the situation well. But it is the music, with its discordant piano bass chords punctuating the action even as the characters talk, that must suggest the ongoing underlying fear of sudden potential violence the narrator felt. It's up to the music to sustain this feeling of menace: a sustained discord on an organ literally sustaining the feeling of unease throughout the scene. In such a situation where the unexpected is about to happen, the music can represent that very disruptive force, playing uneasy or tension-building sounds that conflict with the apparent comfort-zone scene we are watching.

The music, as in film, appears to "know" what is going to happen. Robert Spande in "The Three Regimes: A Theory of Film Music" points out that

> film music paradoxically really does know what's going on. It knows when Freddy is going to jump out of a closet; it knows when any supposedly contingent event is about to transpire. The music infuses all that goes on the screen with the knowledge of an Other.[15]

This "knower," music, is an almost godlike reader of situations. It "knows" when and what will happen. It "knows" when things begin or end: in the enactment of an accident, for example, it anticipates the build-up and actually *becomes* the crash at the moment of impact.

Here too the music is the omniscient "knower." It "knows" the conflicting feelings going on inside Zinzi as well as "knowing" exactly how dangerous these men are. Unlike film, where the action and music are recorded separately, here we have a live tension of synchronized action. (Actors and musician are not always miraculously in tune. Opening with gloomy music to a scene intended to show naïve joy can force the musician to grind to a halt and wait. Misreadings do occur, and the musician's task is to remain alert to the offers made by the actors and not to override them with a clever but inappropriate musical cue.)

Meanwhile things have become static on stage. The men have run out of things to say or do and the woman has turned her back on them. The music must intervene somehow. I abruptly stop. The sudden silence changes everything. The actors are obliged to move the scene on. The woman turns slowly and dramatically and looks them in the eye, unflinching and holding her ground. The men have the wind taken out of their sails and are unable to act. They are outfaced. Uncomfortably they slink away and give us their backs.

The music returns with a bold resolving chord, symbolizing the woman's courage and resolve. It also cues the audience to provide closure by clapping and for the actors to freeze-frame the action at this point.

A SIMPLE FORMULA

In playback, the music is thus less like theatre music and closer to film music, where its function has often been described as "telling you what to feel." In playback, as in film, music often works best when it is subliminal for both actors and audience. Paradoxically, while the music is not the focus of a performance, it can be crucial to the effectiveness of a scene.

A formula for how music can express and resolve conflict in a given playback story might work as follows. The equilibrium of the opening situation is disrupted by the unexpected, a conflict ensues and the narrator finds a way through that brings closure to the story.

Musically, this might be simplified as follows: An initial musical motif, A, captures a mood that enhances the opening scene the actors are building. So here motif A is saying "Things are moving along in a consistent and predictable fashion." Enter the unexpected element or event. Now enters countermotif B. Sometimes it's the musician's job to actually cue such an intervention if only with a sudden silence. The countermotif tells the actors and the audience that we have moved on and that conflict, the essence of drama, now holds the stage.

There are situations where the conflict sets up a protracted struggle. In such an instance motif B can have a very interesting role: it can actually engage in a musical fight with motif A. This naturally invites the use of discords, clashing atonalities, and arrhythmic statements, building tension that implicitly wants resolution but has to wait until the action is ready for it. It is up to the actors to provide this before the music can move on to a resolving idea, motif C. If the improvisatory musical chemistry is trusted, this motif C may suggest itself as a totally unexpected new musical idea. It may, on the other hand, be a repeat of the opening motif but in a new way, perhaps actually incorporating some of the energy, tempo, or shape of countermotif B. Hence we have an exciting resolution of the two motifs, a compound of both motif A and motif B, suggesting an integration or digestion of the disrupting experience. Alternatively, motif A—a reminder of how things were—is repeated in its original "innocence" while an element of motif B lingers to create a shadowy tension. This way the unresolved can have its say.

Although such a formula is not obvious in tonight's show, aspects of it are present in much of the music that is made.

THE THIRD STORY: COLLECTIVE TRAUMA

There is time for one more story. As if waiting for this moment, a man boldly stands up. He is invited to take the teller's chair and immediately begins the saga of his life. His name is Matthew. He is from Somalia, and as a refugee it may be a risk for him to speak publicly in a place where foreigners have been recently attacked and chased out. He has been living in Masiphumelele for some time. Once seated in the teller's chair, he speaks slowly and carefully but with determination.

It is a very long story about growing up with fourteen years of war in Somalia; of his burning desire to escape the violence; of his moving across borders and having to pay bribes to do so; of the constant search for work; of traveling right through Africa; of his determination to get to the new South Africa where he knew many had found a new home; of the arduous journey to get here and the difficulty of finding work and a place to live once he did get here. His story ends not only in the disillusionment of a "promised land" turned xenophobic, it ends with a plea for peace and understanding.

In assisting the teller of such traumatic events as these the conductor will not focus on the trauma itself as this can be too re-stimulating. Instead she will focus on the difference between before and after and what has been learned from the experience. The actors themselves are trained to represent a traumatic event only symbolically, never graphically. They focus on the here and now of survival and hopes for the future.

While the actors huddle and sketch an outline of their performance, I play a prelude that attempts to convey in music the symbolic meaning of Matthew story. I interpret it as essentially a shift from danger and struggle to a place of peace and hope.

The way my improvisation moves is not as schematic as it might appear, however. Musical improvisations in playback work best when they allow a motif to develop by its own chemistry over time and to supply its own transformation and resolution. As Niels Hamel puts it: "The music is not composed *for* the performance but *from* the performance."[16]

I am conscious of offering the music to the teller as a kind of gift in the same way as the actors will offer their interpretation as a gift.

When someone narrates a story from their own life, according to Peter Brooks, it is

> an act of generosity to which the receiver should respond by an equal generosity, either in the telling of another story . . . or in the commenting on the story told, but in any event by the proof that the gift has been received, that the narrative has made a difference.[17]

What I play is not a clever display or solo recital but a meditation on aspects of the teller and his story. Were I to play a rehearsed piece (which can of course be resorted to when no inspiration comes) it would come across as slightly formulaic: music therapy by prescription. It is an exposing experience for the musician yet it mirrors the exposing experience gone through by the teller. It can be an intense moment of transfer where the personality of the teller enters the musician and comes out in the music, possibly unrecognizable except to the musician himself.

But I trust that in the process the music will have its own multivalent meanings, for the audience as well as for the teller. While the conductor's words may sum up the content ("This is a story about one man's struggle to find peace"), the music explores, meditates, dreams on both the teller and the tale and may inspire the actors and the teller to see new things in the story. At the very least, like the actors, the musician has the power to turn the teller's story into legend, to turn the storyteller into a hero. The music can also deepen the compassion of the audience for the experience of the teller, who is implicitly supported by their attendance and their attention, their *assistance.*

The conductor says "Let's watch" and the performance begins.

I start with a low throbbing drone. The opening music is perhaps the equivalent of lights: bare, essentially a blank slate. It signals the unknown as well as the known. A drone is itself a challenge to silence. It also acts as a platform on which the actors must provide the first offers. The bare drone itself is tonally ambiguous: as bare fifths it could go in either direction, major or minor, light or dark. Drones can also suggest the timelessness of "once upon a time." Ananda Coomaraswamy describes the *tanpura,* the droned string instrument of much raga music that is heard before, during, and after the melody, as "the timeless and whole which was in the beginning, is now and ever shall be."[18] At the same time its peaceful spaciousness can be tweaked to suggest a menace or threat by doubling the octave below, which adds more darkness to its presence.

The actors move into position and mime a series of tableaux representing war, struggle, and escape. They set out a row of plastic crates and hold scarves symbolizing barriers. The teller's actor negotiates these "barriers" that confront him and climbs along the row of crates in slow motion.

It is evident we have moved into physical theatre here to portray the epic nature both of Matthew's story and the plight of refugees globally as well as in Masiphumelele. Some of the dark, slow rhythmic chords of my prelude return but these are transformed by the constant movement on stage as the actors circle and confront the hero in his long and arduous journey.

To represent his final arrival in South Africa the actors crouch in positions of humility and receptivity that suggest I need to play something elegiac. I play quiet high piano chords with lots of silences in between, inspired by the simplicity of the piano music of Arvo Pärt. This allows both the teller and the audience to put the rawness of the traumatic experience at a distance. There is no place for a feel-good Hollywood ending. The plea for peace he concluded with is musically implied simply by allowing the ending to move into a gradual silence.

The show ends with the conductor asking the audience "What themes did we witness in these stories tonight?" Voices from the audience call out: "Building a future!" "Caring for one another." "Peace." "Journeys." "Standing together." What was held privately has been given into the public domain. The audience has had the chance to offer "the proof that the gift has been received, that the narrative has made a difference."

The actors step forward in slow motion in a group mime known as a "fluid," where each actor provides a repetitive movement that collectively provides a summing up. It is allowed to build to a climax where all end together. The music provides bold cadences, an affirmative closure with just a hint of unresolved tension to the harmony to avoid a simplistic "feel-good" conclusion. Many tensions are unresolved in this community, and the music has the privilege to be able to state that too.

POSTLUDE

After the show we debrief together. Standing in a circle around our imagined fire we acknowledge how we felt about the show as a whole. We congratulate one another on what worked and we celebrate our success. At the same time we speak of what is unresolved: the unfinished building in Nomhle's story, the ongoing threat of abuse against women in Zinzi's tale, and the ongoing xenophobia in South Africa Matthew's story touched on.

In a final ritual we brush off all the trauma we have carried during the show along with our disappointments with aspects of our own individual performances. All that is unhelpful to us and the continuity of our work is thrown into the bonfire like so many vanities, and then we symbolically put the fire out.

NOTES

[1] Masiphumelele is an African township in Cape Town, South Africa, situated between Kommetjie, Capri Village, and Noordhoek. Initially known as Site 5, the township was renamed Masiphumelele by its residents using the Xhosa word for "we will succeed."

[2] Jonathan Fox, *Acts of Service: Spontaneity, Commitment, Tradition in the Nonscripted Theatre* (New Paltz, NY: Tusitala Publishing, 1986).

[3] Bonfire Theatre Company, "What We Do and Why," available at http://www.bonfiretheatre.co.za/whatwedo.htm.

[4] Bonfire Theatre promotional document, September 2006.

[5] Paulo Freire, *Pedagogy of the Oppressed* (London: Penguin, 1970).

[6] Erene Kaptani and Nira Yuval-Davis, "Participatory Theatre as a Research Methodology: Identity, Performance and Social Action Among Refugees," *Sociological Research Online* 13, no. 5 (2008), available at http://www.socresonline.org.uk/13/5/2.html.

[7] Raj Persaud, "Mind over Music: How Your Brain Dictates Your Musical Tastes," *BBC Music Magazine,* July 2001, p. 36.

[8] Paula Kingwill, "Notes to the Performers," April 2008, unpublished memo in author's possession.

[9] Tom Wolfe's novel *The Bonfire of the Vanities,* one of the great satires of the 1970s and 1980s, or the "me age," was written during the same period that Playback Theatre emerged in the United States.

[10] Nick Rowe, *Playing the Other: Dramatizing Personal Narratives in Playback Theatre* (London: Jessica Kingsley Publishers, 2007), p. 181.

[11] Niels Hamel, "Music: The Integrative Element in Playback Theatre," unpublished paper in author's possession, p. 6. My italics.

[12] Fox, *Acts of Service.*

[13] All the names of the storytellers have been changed.

[14] Peter Brook, *The Empty Space* (1968; repr., London: Penguin, 1972), p. 156.

[15] Robert Spande, "The Three Regimes: A Theory of Film Music," *50 Film,* 17 March 2008, available at http://50film.blogspot.com/2008/03/three-regimes-theory-of-film-music.html.

[16] Hamel, "Music: The Integrative Element in Playback Theatre," pp. 7–8.

[17] Peter Brooks, *Psychoanalysis and Storytelling* (London: Blackwell, 1994), p. 87, quoted in Nick Rowe, *Playing the Other.*

[18] Ananda K. Coomaraswamy, *The Dance of Šiva* (New York: Dover, 1995), pp. 77–80.

15

Abandonment, Wish, and Hope in the Blues

WILLIAM WILLEFORD

Often deeply moving, subtle, complex, and mysteriously condensed and ambiguous, the blues is a form of musical folk poetry that originated around the turn of this century and developed through various phases and styles to the present day. Geographically, it encompasses the Mississippi Delta, the Texas panhandle, Georgia, the Carolinas, Tennessee, New Orleans, Memphis, and Chicago. The notable singers of this performance art have included Skip James, Mississippi John Hurt, Charles Patton, Blind Lemon Jefferson, Blind Willie McTell, Ida Cox, Ma Rainey, Bessie Smith, Leroy Carr, Memphis Minnie, Robert Johnson, Joe Turner, Jimmy Rushing, Robert Pete Williams, Lightning Hopkins, Muddy Waters, and John Lee Hooker, each of whom has an instantly recognizable musical and poetic voice. This individuality is manifest for the most part in variants of a simple musical form.

The lyrics of a blues performance may be drawn from a vast stock of traditional "floating" verses, may be improvised to fit the occasion, or may take the form of set compositions, usually reworking traditional materials. Highly formulaic, the blues is a world patterned in accordance with characteristic themes, images, and symbols; a world familiar yet mysterious, public yet subjective and idiosyncratic, offering deep satisfactions to be had in no other way than through one's imaginative habitation of it.

In principle, blues lyrics can be about virtually any subject that strikes the interest of the blues singer or composer. Blues may celebrate good times, feeling good, partying, and sexual pleasure. But most blues are about "troubles," in the form of thwarted love, abandonment, infidelity, death, murder, poverty, hard work for little pay, homelessness, natural disasters, drunkenness, drug-taking, gambling, prostitution, and jail. While the overtly joyous blues boast or revel in grandiose fantasy or in prospects of sexual pleasure, there are no blues about wildflowers or beautiful sunsets. And though a few blues artists (such as J. B. Lenoir) have dealt with such subjects as racial violence, social protest is rare in the blues.[1] Indeed, the most characteristic attitude of the blues is a noncommittal one, which is far from a simple hopelessness.[2] The broadest subject matter of the blues is *having* the blues, so that overtly joyous blues, too, usually refer at least indirectly to having the blues as a deplorable and probably inevitable condition.

Though noncommittal treatment of such themes as I have listed reflects a fatalism well justified by the real-life experience of many blues performers and much of the blues audience, I will focus on another reason for the inclination of the blues to leave problems unsolved or to temper any solution with at least the hint of further problems. Emotional life in general is predicated on the certainty of uncertainty, and feeling, as a special dimension of emotional life, is also so predicated: a mother must read and relate to the feeling-state of her infant, whom she must comfort even under adverse circumstances and even in the certainty that circumstances now ameliorated will become adverse again. And the mother's feeling relationship with her infant is the basis of further developments of feeling, which at the deepest level are concerned with survival. In its exploration of such themes as what it is like to be on the "killing floor," the blues draws us back to this level of feeling.[3]

In its concern with knowing what to feel and with feeling what is proper to be felt, the blues is an extraordinary development in the education of the heart. The blues shows with special clarity things of importance about the relationship between individuality and community, the need for the whole person to remain open to the world with its contingency and pain, the emotional force and restraint necessary to differentiated feeling, and the ways in which the mother-infant dyad may be potently implicit in the artistic or, more broadly, the spiritual transcendence of real-life frustrations and conflicts. Further, despite the frequent bleakness of its subject matter, the blues is a comic art that celebrates the triumph of both individuality and community. The blues shows with special clarity things of importance about the transformative workings of imagination—about imaginative transcendence—and about the interrelations between imagination and feeling.[4]

A blues performer does not need to have the blues at the moment in order to sing the blues well, though deep feeling is one of the valued qualities of a blues performance. Muddy Waters has been described as leaving the bandstand after a strong performance in a state of near-trance lasting about half an hour; in contrast, another blues artist has been censured for "phoning in" his blues message as though it were an order to a business firm. And Texas barrel-house and saw-mill pianist Buster Pickens observes:

> The only way anyone can ever play the blues—he's got to have them. . . . Nach'al blues come directly from a person's heart: what he's experienced in life. . . . Whether he's been troubled, whether he's ridden freight trains, where he's been put in jail; been beaten up by railroad dicks and everythin' else you understand— pushed around in life. . . . You have a tough way in life—that makes you blue. That's when you start to sing the blues—when you've got the blues.[5]

It is not necessary for the audience to have the blues at the moment to appreciate a blues performance. But it is essential for performer and audience to know at least tacitly what it is to have the blues.

Both performer and audience are present because the blues remains a potentiality to be faced now in the hope that it will not be actualized in an incapacitating way but will instead be converted to something else, to self-enhancing feelings and states, beginning with the vital, bodily good times of the performance. Thus, the blues performance assumes the present or available reality of not having the blues. This is as much the point of departure of the blues experience as is knowledge of having them.

The condition of having the blues is the emotional frame of reference that the blues performance attempts to bring to imaginative awareness. Some sort of prior knowledge of the condition is necessary for that awareness (though one need not have been beaten up by railroad dicks to know it).

One function of the blues performance is to articulate the not-yet-articulated, even though what is thus expressed is in some sense already tacitly known. What is it to have the blues? How do we know what it is to have the blues? And what does having the blues have to do, even if indirectly, with performing the blues?

Actually, the blues as musical poetry is an ongoing process of trying to define what having the blues is. Much of the blues is about "the blues," often, importantly, in such a way that it is not possible to draw a clear distinction in a blues text between the blues as having the blues and the blues as musical poetry. The lack of distinction is important; the ambiguity is calculated and deliberate. Thus Otis Spann, the splendid pianist with the Muddy Waters blues band for many years, sings: "When you in trouble, blues is a man's best friend. . . . Blues ain't goin' to ask you where you goin', and blues don't care where you been," and later: "We can't let the blues die, the blues don't mean you no harm. . . . I'm goin' back to the lowlands, that's where the blues came from."[6] The blues that "we can't let die" is probably (mostly) the consoling, soul-strengthening music. Going back to the lowlands implies a return to poverty, the poverty of lower-class southern farmers that Spann and countless other blacks had moved to Chicago and other northern cities to escape. The blues of the lowlands is perhaps partly the music but surely also the toil and pain out of which it was born. The line says ironically, "The blues as music and as an imaginative world view makes having the blues harmless, so let us pay tribute to the music and the world view by going back to the real misery, to the condition of having the blues, that made the music and the world view necessary."

If we did not, at least tacitly, already know the unwilled condition of having the blues, the blues performance would not work to free us from the condition by offering us a provisional definition of it. Although map is not territory, in lived experience the ambiguity between them is as important as the distinction between them, and the blues exploits this ambiguity in ways that have rich implications for the psychology of feeling and imagination.

In emotional life we map the territory in order to gain the distance from it that we have lost or feel ourselves in danger of losing. Feeling is never final: feeling is process, feeling always begins again. Even habitual feeling-judgments must be continually enlivened by being experienced as part of feeling-as-process. If the best solution Spann can offer to the problem of having the blues is going back to where the blues was born, the problem is exposed as unsolved and new imaginative maps will have to be devised to reveal the nature of the territory of having the blues. More blues will have to be played and sung; continuation and repetition are as necessary to the blues party as they are to solemn festivals.

By offering a specious solution to the problem, Spann is in a sense pushing his audience further in the direction of having the blues. But the nature of the emotional issue changes significantly in the process. The issue is no longer the direct danger of having the blues, it is the disintegration of the defense against having the blues as the implications of the specious argument come to awareness.

Though it is useful, a "normal" defense against having the blues may result in an impoverishment of inner life and an increase in the danger that the defense will fail. In general, in psychic life, letting in a defended-against force—any energy-charged psychic content—is a first step in arriving at a more adequate conscious attitude toward it.

The kind of defense I have in mind is well illustrated, along with its failure, in a film about the blues, *Bottle Up and Go,* in which a black hat salesman describes circumstances that make one have the blues. Grinning and laughing nervously, his hypomanic manner is a striking instance of what psychiatrists call "inappropriate affect," denying the pain of the familiar realities he is enumerating. But his jollity disappears and his eyes look troubled as his account proceeds and he allows himself to feel the import of what he is saying. The letting in of such a force generates emotion, which, if it is to remain ego-syntonic, demands a new distancing in the form of a more alert and precise reading of the emotional situation—in our case, that described in the blues verses. Emotion thus motivates imaginative engagement in which distancing plays a necessary role. It is this distancing that allows the emotional situation to be read in the mode of feeling and allows the literal to open out to the metaphorical, the symbolic, the ironic. The distance thus achieved is, however, variable, and the process by which it is increased or decreased is subtle.

Indeed, though the blues is concerned with issues of pathos, blues verses and the blues performance as a whole are ironic in the sense that what is said is always at some distance from what is meant. Occasionally the irony is clear cut, as when Howlin' Wolf ("three hundred pounds of comfort and joy") sings that he "ain't superstitious" and then lists his superstitions one by one.[7] Usually, though, the irony is more subtle, as in Spann's verses already considered or in another piece in which he declares that he has a wonderful feeling everything is going to be all right, a feeling deep down in his soul, a feeling that he is going to love his woman every day and every night. The confidently loping melodic line and driving, charged rhythm totally fit this joyous and hopeful sentiment. Still, his declaration that she "done came back home" to him implies conflict and separation, and in admitting to being worried that she might leave him again, he hardly offers cause for feeling all that wonderful.[8]

Sometimes the clues to how ironic the tone is are unspecifiable. For example, if a blues performer sings about leaving his present woes and going somewhere else to begin anew, his message and manner may partly inspire our confidence. And yet we might have reason to wonder whether he really does have any new place to go or if he will do anything other than find himself in a new version of his old situation if he does go or if, indeed, flight is not also a form of defeat. Such ambiguity, forcing one to reach through the semantic text to the expressive features of the overall performance, is fundamental to what could be called the blues aesthetic.

Verses sung in 1983 by guitarist-singer Johnny Copeland offer a striking example of ironic distancing. In high spirits he sings, at a brisk tempo:

> When the rain starts fallin',
> My feet start to itchin';
> I know that it's time to go.
> You know, I promised myself
> It ain't gonna rain in my life no mo'.
>
> When you all out of money,
> Things get funny;
> Look like everybody know.
> I'm gonna pack my bag, and down the road I go.
>
> Well, the rain keep a comin', and I keep a runnin';
> I'm movin' like the wind.
> You know, when the rain catch up,
> I'm on the move again.
>
> When you hear from me again,
> I'll be somewhere down the road.
> I'm gonna ride that train
> Just as far as my money goes.
>
> When the rain starts fallin',
> My feet start to itchin';
> You know, I promised myself
> It ain't gonna rain in my life no mo'.[9]

Having the blues is the rain the singer wants to escape. And his joyously imagined flight is predicated on certain defeat: If he is out of money, he cannot pay for a train ride. Having the blues is ultimately no more controllable than the weather.

When a blues singer sings the traditional line "The sun's gonna shine in my back door someday," he is expressing hope that things will get better, and he knows, and we know, that he is speaking metaphorically when he sings with wistful resignation about the wind and the rain. The expressive features of Copeland's voice and music, with their soaring, charging energy, their brash exuberance, convince us that he takes his fantasy literally. He sounds utterly delighted to be actively not understanding the implications of what he is saying.

Our pleasure in the singer's self-confident delight is derived from our tacit awareness of the condition of having the blues. That awareness is affirmed even while its tacit character is insisted upon. We know what we are looking away from even while we are looking away from it. The artistic persona of the singer denies painful reality; the performance as a whole does not. Its irony serves the interrelated functions of detaching us from that reality while keeping us in touch with it. In the imaginative world view of the blues, joy is born of pain; pain is not to be denied. Joy is not simply the denial of pain but represents an order of value in its own right. Irony assures that pain is not denied, is taken into account as the value of joy is affirmed.

One could regard the fictional persona's swaggering denial of reality as a form of what psychoanalysts call manic defense against depression and the rage that may be latent within it. But regarding it in this way still leaves questions about the relations among, first, the reality-denying verbal content; second, the hints of ironic distancing in the presentation; and third, the tumultuous energy of the performance as a whole. By "ironic distancing" I mean that although the singer presents himself as not understanding the dissembling illogic of his own words, what we hear is precisely the self as thus presented, an artifact neither inviting nor allowing a response based primarily on identification with him. Rather, we are meant to register incongruities of which, in the artifact of his self-presentation, he is unaware. Is the energy of the performance simply that of wishful manic defense? Or is it rather the energy of a hopeful determination to survive and rejoice? Or does irony in the performance effect a transformation from the mode of wish to that of hope?

Ironic detachment can help one participate in life without being its mindless tool or victim. And this entails seeing illusion as illusion. Our appreciation of Copeland's posture as posture and as comic gives us the proper form of access to his energy. But this demands of each of us a reorientation of the ego.

Through the exercise and affirmation of its own discriminating powers the ego is persuaded and enabled to open itself to content, including emotional currents, that vary from its prevailing set. To deal with irony, to recognize illusion as illusion, is to master ambiguity without opening oneself up to it. Discrimination—holding separate things apart—allows imaginative sympathy based on an awareness of levels. We feel with the blues singer, while hearing, as part of a larger artistic whole, the details of the utterance that he or she offers as the expression of conscious intent and while assessing that conscious intent as illusory. Thus, ironic detachment may allow the ego of the audience to enter into a fictional representation of wish fulfillment in such a way as to find life-giving hope in it, through it, beyond it.

In general, the blues is radically committed to what has been called the blues ideology, which holds that real-life problems are not soluble in real-life terms, or that solving such problems will immediately lead to further problems. One must remain open to the reality of human misery. This openness is the price and the precondition of the artistic transcendence of misery offered by the blues.

The verses of Spann that we began with invite a process of reasoning that serves to maintain emotional distance. Some of the more raw and intense blues of the impassioned, short-lived genius Robert Johnson illuminate another aspect of the emotional engagement that is fundamental to the blues. Johnson begins "Preaching Blues" (recorded in 1936):

> I's up this morning, I got blues walking like a man.
> I's up this morning, my blues walking like a man.
> Well, the blues—give me your right hand.[10]

The singer states a problem forming in his awareness: "I's up this morning / I got blues walking like a man." Ambiguously and ominously, he either has blues walking like a man or it is he himself that he thus imagines. Seizing the initiative, the singer implausibly ascribes his own feeling to the presence by addressing it as "Worried blues." A man may have good cause to worry—how or why should the blues have anything to worry about? In any case, there is a question: Do I have the blues, or does the blues have me?

The singer proposes shaking its right hand like that of a newly met stranger rather than greeting it casually as the familiar visitor it more likely is. Still, the conciliatory action of shaking its hand would affirm his separation from it, while perhaps giving him a clearer sense of who and what the blues really are.

But such cautious bravado may fail. It is then exposed as having served to allay a disabling but justified fear that the blues may prove invasive and implacably alien. The singer rises to the difficult occasion of focusing on this prospect: "Blues fell, mama-child, and they tore me all upside down." And he predicts that they will go on ravaging within him like heart disease or consumption. Addressing grim prospects works better than pretending they are not there, so feeling his way into the reality of such defeat marks an advance toward a realistically life-affirming view of the problem he has raised.

For example, "Denise," who dislikes her businessman father and who has shaped her life to honor values he does not appreciate, sometimes clearly exercises valuable traits she "has" from him when she is working at her best as the artistic director of a theatre. Moreover, from time to time, usually unbeknown to herself, she overtly manifests in her behavior this or that of the traits for which she dislikes him, including his contentious willfulness. Or "Charlotte," who had a dissolute, sadistic, neglectful mother, is an excellent psychotherapist in her work with disturbed children. The process by which she has become disidentified from her family background has given her a rich understanding of its psychodynamics, and this understanding enables her to identify with her young clients and to use that identification on their behalf. Occasionally however, the image of her mother possesses her as she bursts out in rage at her husband or a female co-worker.

Denise's moments of willfulness and Charlotte's moments of rage raise an important point: Just as for separation to be overcome there must be separation, so for identification and, in turn, disidentification to take place, there must be a prior knowledge of oneness. Identification and disidentification presuppose and work with vestiges of archaic identity.

In speaking of archaic identity, I am not assuming that the original psychic state of the infant is one of nondifferentiation and nondiscrimination and that this state is prominent in the psychic life of so-called primitive people. Rather, I find the phenomenological psychologist Stefan Strasser persuasive in remarking about interaction within the mother-infant dyad: "The most elementary of all human experience—we together in the surrounding world—is not at first perceived, thought, or sought after; it is primarily lived, through feeling."[11] We are first and always, though we forget this, "we together in the surrounding world."

Archaic identity is, then, the form of experience that prevails when the distinctions implicit in Strasser's phrase are annulled; for example, in sleep or in states of fusion. Though the capacity for union, in which boundaries are relaxed but preserved, is essential to psychic maturity and mutuality, fusion, in which boundaries are negated, also plays an important role in psychic life.

Fusion is a process of dedifferentiation in which sameness is emphasized at the expense of difference, an emphasis that is basic to the identifications that make the human person a member of society and to the workings of the imagination. To one's felt sense of who and what one is, emotional currents that arise sometimes do and sometimes do not—like the hellhound on one's trail—seem to belong to oneself. Especially owing to the bodily immediacy of such currents—as close to me as my body is to myself—they can largely overwhelm all sense of "me" and "mine" as representing a secure center of appropriate and responsible action. Yet the ambiguity occasioned by this weakening of ego-reference can bring with it a gain, since precisely in not knowing what I know in the way I usually know it, I may surmise the activity of the Self as it makes itself known in its own manner, like the wind that bloweth where it listeth. This experience may revitalize and modify in a clarifying way the ego's capacity for appraising value. And this brings us to "Mama-child."

To speak of "secure" ego functioning is to recall that the first security is that of "Mama-child." The archaic identity of "Mama-child" might well be thought to refer, on the one hand, to the security, the loss of which has delivered the blues singer up to having the blues, and, on the other, to the emotional frame of reference offering him the hope that he will be able to maintain sufficient emotional distance to endure his present state.

Although blues music is potentially dangerous, one may yield to the danger much as one may yield to the bittersweetness of certain experiences of love. Thus, blues artist John Lee Hooker speaks of "feelin' very normal, nothin' on your mind, period" but then hearing a blues record that so threatens you with "hurt" and "heartaches and things" that you take a walk or go for a ride in your car:

> Because you'd rather *not* hear it than to hear it. Because there's some places in them records, there's somethin' sad in there that give you the blues; somethin' that reach back in your life or some friend's life of yours, or that make you think of what have happened today and it is so true, that if it didn't happen to you, you still got a strong idea—you know those things is goin' on. So this is very touchable, and that develops into the blues.[12]

Still, though blues music may cause the condition it is supposed to relieve or cure, blues music will sooner or later do its healing work. In the blues as in life, feeling always begins again, regardless of how forbidding the emotional territory to be mapped. And so, in his charged encounter with man-like blues, Robert Johnson celebrates the courage to feel even what is emotionally harrowing.

Though some blues verses describe love as thwarted by death or abandonment, poverty or alcohol, it is highly characteristic of the blues to find the cause of one's loss of love in a rival and, for example, to contemplate the image of a stranger's muddy shoes next to the bed of one's woman.

BLUES TALK

Still, in the community of which the mother-infant dyad is the protoform, individuality must be affirmed in a cooperation with others that withstands and resolves rivalries. Speech among individuals—"talk"—facilitates such cooperation. "Talk," both as an activity and as a metaphor, is important in the experience of blues music. Various features of "talk" in blues performance provide a perspective on the ambiguities in the blues between twos (the mother-infant dyad) and threes (the oedipal triangle), between the verbal and extraverbal, and on ways in which the mother-infant dyad is implicit in the transcendence the blues offers—also when the blues one has or might have as a soul condition is caused by some form of triadic tension. Breaking down the distinction between twos and threes, the blues also breaks down the distinction between the verbal and the extraverbal. Ambiguities in the blues between twos and threes and between the verbal and the extraverbal are interrelated.

A sub-genre of the blues is "talking blues," a blues monologue with musical accompaniment. One blues scholar who conducted hundreds of interviews with blues performers was struck by how often the person interviewed would begin accompanying himself on an instrument such as guitar or piano, so that his verbal utterance was partly transformed into a blues performance.[13] For verbal meaning has its limits: painfully trapped within our words, we may find that music serves to revive verbal meaning or to reach beyond it.

The verbal content of the blues is concerned with emotional situations in stories that are not usually told explicitly; instead, the personal, subjective reactions of the singer or fictional persona are made the center of attention. That is, the blues, unlike the ballad, is nonnarrative and often even anti-narrative in its suppression of the story line. For example, Johnny Copeland, in another blues, sings about his daddy's telling him not to stop by the creek to swim on the way to school, advice the singer had to ponder. The incident is treated in isolation from other incidents, and the significance that made the incident seem worth relating to the singer is left undeclared. One might imagine that the incident was fatal in the sense of initiating a process of dropping out of school, leading to other forms of dereliction that ended by shaping his life in a particular way. But no such story is told.[14]

Incidentally, the same blues by Copeland suggests something of the way that the nonnarrative or even anti-narrative tendency of the blues is sometimes clearly related to the nonspecifiable irony common in it. After singing, "'Don't stop by the creek, Son,' that's what my daddy said," the singer remarks that he "almost didn't obey"; but after elaborating on his daddy's advice, he admits that that was where he "went astray," only to fall back thereafter to claim that he "almost didn't obey." The interest of the account centers in the fictional persona's wavering between maintaining and dismantling an edifice of lies about the course of his life and about the extent of his responsibility for it. Since it is essential in the blues, as an art of survival, not to sentimentalize and to see to it that false hopes are treated ironically, bravado and other forms of apparent wish fulfillment are to be heard in a double perspective. Bravado in the blues often asks to be heard as: "This grandiose posture is fun and an ego-strengthening exercise in courage and in demanding what I want but it is nonetheless make-believe, a form of tall-tale-telling."

The anti-narrative tendency of the blues is related to its tendency to develop its material more in an associative than in a linear or logical fashion. Indeed, the verbal content of the blues and its development sometimes seem dreamlike. As one writer about blues lyrics comments, perhaps consoling himself for fruitless efforts at comprehension, "It's not that what [blues singers] sing is trivial exactly. It's just that it does not entirely reflect what they are singing about."[15] Indeed, often in the blues performance only snatches of the verbal content are intelligible. Often fragmented, blues verses give glimpses and clues inciting associative processes in the listener—much as one may make up a meaning for what one is hearing in an unknown language. Though it is a relief when we come to understand blues verses that had baffled us, it is in keeping with many other elements of the blues aesthetic that a blues performance does not necessarily stand or fall on the basis of the intelligibility of the words. Just as the blues tends away from the linear, rational, or explicit toward the diffusely global, irrational, and suggestive, so it tends to press through the semantic altogether toward extraverbal expressiveness.

In the blues, everyday speech is expressively altered in various ways. A syllable might be prolonged or divided or be given a stress it would not have in conversation or be rendered falsetto or as melisma (the ornamental elaboration of a syllable as a succession of notes). In the singing of blues verses, words may be replaced by expressive but nonsemantic sounds, such as moans, humming, and musical figures played by guitar or piano or harmonica. A special case is presented by such blues artists as Mississippi John Hurt and Fred McDowell when they sing only part of a verse line or do not sing it at all when the singing of it is expected, so that the listener must "hear" the words in the guitar part. In this case it would not be quite true to say that words are being replaced by nonsemantic but expressive and communicative sounds, since the listener does, in a subliminal way, "hear" the expected but unsung words. By such devices the blues performer blurs the distinction between the verbal and extraverbal or creates and explores ambiguities between them. Just as making expressive sounds into words is transcendence, so the decomposition of words into expressive sound may be transcendence of another kind.

In this extraverbal transcendence, words are reabsorbed into gestural, postural, proprioceptive, sensory, and emotional currents of the body. These currents are basic to one's experience of oneself as having a personal vital core. And attending to these currents is a means both of acknowledging (from the side of the ego) the value of that core (as the Self) and of making its vitality manifest.

I have been suggesting that for activation of the dyadic level in later life to have salutary effects, feeling, in its concern with gradations, transitions, continuities, and coherence, must take up into itself and must contain potentialities for disruptive emotion. Though the real-life problems described in the blues are often triadic, dyadic elements juxtaposed with the triadic are essential to the larger artistic effect of the blues. As we have seen on the level of verbal content, the mother-infant relationship is suggested by the frequent epithets of "mamma" and "baby" as expressions of yearning for security and warmth, though the epithets are heard as highly metaphorical and though the yearning is expressed in such a way as strongly to imply that it will not find concrete fulfillment. The double elements— the instances of "two"—do not themselves directly refer to the mother-infant relationship, but they do suggest the mirroring and the active mutuality characterizing that relationship. And this is basic both to individuality and community as abiding concerns in the blues.

The most usual blues form consists of stanzas, each consisting of twelve measures (bars) of 4/4 time, based on a characteristic blues scale (which is most often thought to correspond to the Western diatonic scale), with the difference that the third, seventh, and sometimes the fifth intervals are treated with considerable—and important—expressive ambiguity, so that it has been proposed that these intervals be called not tones but tonal areas.[16] Each stanza repeats variants of a simple harmonic progression (I-IV-V-IV-I) and is divided into three sections. The first verbal line (A) is repeated, sometimes with a slight variation, and the stanza closes with a different line (B) that is either assonant with or rhymes with the first. Thus the AAB structure itself suggests the subsuming of the triple (the three lines of the stanza) to the double AB, with the B line being, in effect, the "response" to the "call" of the A line. Further, the words of each line fill slightly more than two bars and are followed by an instrumental response to the voice. Indeed, this instrumental answering to the voice is so important as a structural principle that it may override the convention of twelve bars, so that some performers may produce stanzas of thirteen or thirteen and a half bars. The instrumental line, too, amounts more to a second voice than to a musical accompaniment subservient to the verses, and some performers succeed by various devices in keeping multiple melodic lines going, either successively or simultaneously.

The bass guitarist of the Robert Cray band, Richard Cousins, sometimes expresses his own felt relation to the music being sung and played. His facial expression is an unsettlingly ambiguous response to what Cray is singing. Sometimes Cray will sing a verse infused with deep pathos and Cousins will respond with an expression that mockingly exaggerates the pathos to absurdity. Or he will seem to be responding to Cray's pathos with sly and detached bemusement. He performs the function of forcing the audience to ask itself again and again, "How, exactly, should we be taking what Cray is right now singing? Is it sad, funny, or both—or what?" This disorientation helps us get beyond half-hearted taking-for-granted and find our own wholehearted felt relation to the music.

I have observed that the AAB verse structure most common in the blues creates an ambiguity between two and three, related to the ambiguity between the three verse units in the twelve-bar stanza and the vocal part and instrumental answering within each unit. Further, though I said that the blues are basically sung in 4/4 time, because of the ways some blues artists use syncopation and triplets, musicologists have often puzzled over when a blues performance should be categorized as some version of modified 4/4 time and when it should be categorized as some version of a triple rhythm. These ambiguities between two and three are related to ambiguities in the ways blues artists treat verbal content. Often, as we have seen, conflicts described in the blues are triadic in character (the singer agonizes over the stranger's muddy shoes he has seen next to his woman's bed). But the resolution of conflict in this noncommittal art is performed through an opening to feeling, which tacitly draws on its model in the mother-infant relationship. This amounts to an affirmation of individuality, including the ability to be alone with oneself and to commune with oneself.

The capacity of blues to help listeners and singers differentiate feeling is an important means of maintaining and restoring coherence despite envy and thwarted desire. In the world of disorder and trouble represented in the blues, proper modes of feeling are necessary for survival, and the art of the blues celebrates them. When the blues performer calls his "mamma" Baby or calls his "baby" Mamma, he is acknowledging where proper modes of feeling begin.

The focus of the blues on abandonment enhances the grounding of ego in self, since focusing on what is wrong instead of sensing it dimly is an important part of making it right. This is a matter of feeling. The kind of feeling cherished and cultivated in the blues is the product of emotional heightening; a focusing on issues of emotional import, especially abandonment, and an evocation of the emotional response appropriate to those issues. Feeling-judgements implicit in the prevailing ego attitude are modified as a result.

Distrust of what I have come to call the self that knows what is good for itself is on one level a reexperiencing of early abandonment—it is distrust that the self has capacities for making things right when Mother fails to do so. Indeed, as much of blues music demonstrates, knowledge of abandonment (when it is not overwhelmingly sustained and severe) may be an important part of trust, or what the philosopher Franz Brentano calls "right loving"—a realistic opening to the good.

A person's claiming of his or her aggressive energies is surely important. But with experiences of abandonment and loss, one might think that a measure of *both* grief and hostility would be indicated as part of a clarification of the feeling issues that life has so far left him or her to deal with. And hostility needs to be focused, in the sense that he or she needs to know what it is most truly about. May it not ultimately be about experiences to which grief would also be an appropriate response?

Whereas one may find the prospect of rage less disquieting than that of grief, the predilection of the blues—as the name *blues* implies—is for sorrow that might become grief. Still, in the blues, rage sometimes comes to expression with a fine edge—for example, in blues lyrics depicting the vengeful actions of the spurned lover, as when Alberta Hunter sings "I'll crack his skull and drink his blood like wine."

A song that the old-time bluesman James Butch Cage (born in 1894) learned from his mother, the daughter of a slave, expresses hostility as part of a clarification of feeling bearing upon survival.

> Black nigger baby, black feet and shiny eyes,
> Black all over to the bone and india-rubber thighs,
> Turn that nigger round and knock 'im in the haid,
> Cause white folks say, "We're gonna kill that nigger dead." . . .
> Black nigger baby gonna take care of myself,
> Always carry a great big razor and a pistol in my vest,

Turn that nigger round and knock 'im on the haid,
Cause white folks say, "We're gonna kill that nigger dead."[17]

This song is a complex expression of what psychoanalysts call identification with the aggressor. The song takes identification with the aggressor as its starting point, but it does so in an ironic way; the singer is clearly playing a role. The singer's ironic detachment from the identification with white aggressors is so strong that it amounts to *dis*identification. Because of his detachment, the singer is able to clearly describe the persistent pattern of injustice that creates new generations of victims even though slavery has ended. And though there is no way to spare the black baby the unjust situation into which it has been born, the singer endows it with a strong ego—to the point that it seems almost indestructible. This child will need meanness and determination to survive, and these qualities will make it a dangerous victim.

The irony of the song obviates self-pity, which would detract from a clear perception of the pattern of injustice and the baby's plight. Still, its irony serves a feeling-judgment that includes a tacit awareness of the grief—the cause for grieving—that is implicit in the story. It is possible to grieve—to know grief—with a detachment that holds sorrow open to joy—joy that we, like the baby, are alive and intent on living. Irony allows this detachment.

Ironic detachment may be rejecting, even disdainful, as in much satire. But ironic detachment may also create the distance that allows measured engagement with issues of emotional import, including occasions for grief. That is, pathos and irony are interrelated in such a way that ironic detachment can offer the distance necessary for feeling and can thus help revivify feeling, both as process—the activity of feeling—and as feeling-judgment. Such revivifying of feeling is the restorative, life-affirming gift of the blues.

The irony of the blues is pervasive, complex, and often highly ambiguous. Blues pathos draws upon experiences of attachment and separation within the mother-infant relationship. While insisting that we know the painful reality of abandonment, deprivation, and constriction, the blues ironically plays with wish, for the delight of play and with the goal of mocking the delusions to which wish may lead. Through their beauty and the energy they generate, the blues reawaken the joy in survival that is the basic form of hope and draw the listener into the blues community of survivors.

Note from the Author: To locate recorded blues, consult Gary Graf, *Musichound Blues: The Essential Album Guide* (New York: Schirmer, 2002.) It includes biographies, ratings of records, and classifications and lists of various kinds.

NOTES

"Abandonment, Wish, and Hope in the Blues" was originally published as an article in *Abandonment* in the Chiron Clinical Series (1985) and was later incorporated as a chapter in *Feeling, Imagination, and the Self.* Permission to use this article in this slightly abridged form was graciously given to us by Chiron Publications and the author.

[1] See especially Lenoir's albums *Alabama Blues: Rare and Intimate Recordings,* LP, 1965; reissued as a CD by Snapper UK, 2004/2007; and *Down in Mississippi,* LP, L + R, 1966.

[2] In David Evans, *Big Road Blues: Tradition and Creativity in the Folk Blues* (Berkeley: University of California Press, 1982), pp. 19–22.

[3] "Killing Floor," on *Chester Burnett, AKA Howlin' Wolf,* LP, Chess 60016-2, 1972. The theme is explored by many other blues artists.

[4] C. G. Jung, *The Structure and Dynamics of the Psyche,* vol. 8 of *The Collected Works of C. G. Jung* (Princeton, NJ: Princeton University Press, 1968), pp. 67–91. My use of the word "transcendence" here is meant to imply Jung's account of imagination as the "transcendent [or more properly, transcending] function" bridging consciousness and unconscious psychic regions in ways that are responsive to the Self.

[5] Quoted in Paul Oliver, *Conversations with the Blues* (New York: Horizon Press, 1965), p. 170.

[6] Otis Spann, "The Blues Never Die," on *The Blues Never Die!* LP, Prestige 7719, 1969; re-released as a CD in 1991 by OBC.

[7] Howlin' Wolf, "I Ain't Superstitious," on *Howlin' Wolf: His Greatest Sides,* vol. 1, LP, Chess CH-9107, 1984; reissued as a cassette tape in 1990 by MCA.

[8] Otis Spann, "I Got a Feeling," on *The Blues Never Die!*

[9] Johnny Copeland, "When the Rain Starts Fallin'," on *Texas Twister,* LP, Rounder 2040, 1967.

[10] Robert Johnson, *Robert Johnson: King of the Delta Blues Singers,* recorded in 1936 and 1937, issued as an LP by Columbia (CL 1654) in 1966; reissued as a CD in 1998 by Sony.

[11] Stefan Strasser, "Feeling as Basis of Knowing and Recognising the Other as an Ego," in *Feelings and Emotions: The Loyola Symposium,* ed. Magda B. Arnold (New York: Academic Press 1970), p. 306.

[12] Quoted in Oliver, *Conversations with the Blues,* p. 164.

[13] Quoted in *ibid.,* p. 9.

[14] Johnny Copeland, "Don't Stop by the Creek Son," on *Texas Twister.*

[15] Peter Guralnick, *Feel Like Going Home: Portraits in Blues and Rock 'n' Roll* (New York: Vintage, 1981), p. 41.

[16] Evans, *Big Road Blues,* p. 24.

[17] James Butch Cage and Willie Thomas, "Kill That Nigger Dead," on *Songs of Complaint and Protest,* LP, vol. 7 of *Folk Music in America,* Library of Congress LBC-07, 1977.

Mercy: The Unbearable in Eigen's Writings and John Tavener's *Prayer of the Heart*

Stephen Bloch

Developmental and linear models, which characterize many approaches within psychoanalysis, rarely match the actual experience of psychotherapy. In classical Jungian theory the individuation process describes a psychological development that integrates shadow and then the contrasexual archetype, such as the anima or animus. Classical Freudian theory posits a movement from id- to ego-functioning as well as a developmental sequence through the psychosexual stages. Although Klein regarded her positions as fluctuating and therefore not as discrete stages, her thought includes the idea of a movement from the paranoid-schizoid constellation to the capacity for depressive functioning. These concepts of psychological development are seldom helpful in patients struggling with experiences of abuse, trauma, loss, or deprivation. Here an understanding of the difficulties in bearing unbearable experience is more important and the therapist plays a crucial role in helping the patient work with these overwhelming, unendurable states. A theoretical stream in psychoanalysis that incorporates aspects of Winnicott, Bion, and Eigen explores the nature of unbearable states of mind. From this perspective, the creative integration of a previously unendurable experience is the achievement, rather than the attainment of a specific stage in one of the sequential models.

On listening to John Tavener's *Prayer of the Heart* for the first time, I was struck by how the work seemed to be expressing a terrain similar to that which Michael Eigen explores in many of his writings.[1] In rendering a universal plea for "mercy" Tavener seemed to express a yearning that is implicit within Eigen's articulation of the struggle to creatively work with experience that is inherently overwhelming in nature. The word "mercy" seems an unusual word to use in psychoanalytic discourse. It does, however, link Tavener's evocative composition with Eigen's urgent and central concern.

In this essay I intend to discuss this link as well as demonstrate how music plays an essential role in these states of mind and their resolution. I will suggest that both Eigen's work and Tavener's composition are concerned with the experience of mercy and its role in the psyche.

The Unbearable in Eigen's Writings

Michael Eigen's prolific writings cover a wide range of clinical and existential concerns, including psychic deadness, faith, mysticism, rage, and lust. His work is notable not only for its areas of interest but also for the striking poetic style of his writing.

There is, however, one concern that runs as a leitmotif through his work. This is his exploration of experience that is unbearable and the problems individuals encounter in dealing with this. He approaches this issue repeatedly from different angles but always seems to be wrestling with our capacity to productively interact with the unbearable, the unendurable, and the catastrophic. In *The Psychoanalytic Mystic* he states this directly: "The psyche lacks the equipment to bear what it produces."[2]

It is the complexity and struggle of this process that he emphasizes, often providing insight into how the psychic digestive system can itself be damaged or function imperfectly.[3] Eigen emphasizes the need for individuals to keep finding ways that experience can be rendered useful and not overwhelming and mentions art and music as ways creative attempts can be made to work with experience that would otherwise be unprocessed.

The basis of his concerns lies in the work of Bion and Winnicott. Indeed, Eigen suggests that despite their differences one area of commonality may be their concern with unbearable experience. In particular Bion's work on dream-work and alpha functioning is significant to Eigen. This refers to the processes whereby "we take experience in, attend to it, work with it, grow with it, allow it to become part of unconscious creativity."[4] Eigen explores the difficulties and vicissitudes involved in psychic digestion and the sense that the dream is always failing, always struggling to fully digest what it has to. His writings explore these two aspects: first, the incapacity to fully digest what has to be processed; and second, the more pernicious state in which "dream-work gets damaged by the dream it tries to dream."[5]

BION

An early expression of this theme in Eigen's work is in his key paper "Between Catastrophe and Faith," subtitled "Towards Bion's Starting Points."[6]

In his introduction to the paper, Eigen comments that Bion may be difficult to read because his conclusions are so difficult "to hear or bear or believe." Bion is describing a psyche that has its origins in catastrophe. This is a "Big Bang" image where "primitive" and "incoherent" beta elements explode outward. The struggle of the nascent psyche is to transform these disintegrative experiences into psychologically manageable experience in symbol or representation. This is the operation of alpha function (or, as Bion put it later, dream-work alpha) on the undigested beta-elements.

Bion is describing the psyche at its point of origin and in its primal experience of space, time, and, indeed, sound. As in contemporary descriptions of the origins of the physical universe, Bion's psychical universe begins in "an intense catastrophic emotional explosion O,"[7] where parts of the personality are flung out. There are vast distances between these parts and their originating point.

The infant's cosmology is of a disintegrative explosion into infinity. To Bion, this is the originating Big Bang, which has to be worked with through rudimentary alpha functioning. The maternal container's own alpha functioning is a vital element in this process. As will be explored later, much of this containment happens in an acoustic medium.

This is not a developmental model where progressive stages are sequentially negotiated. It is a picture of an immature psyche struggling to integrate inchoate experience. This is in the context of the essential helplessness of the infant. To some these descriptions appear dramatic and overstated. Questions may be raised as to whether this occurs only in drastic failures of maternal containment or whether Bion can justifiably extrapolate universal from psychotic experience. Moreover, Bion may be describing the phenomenology of his own primitive, infantile, and, indeed, later traumatic experiences. Some subsequent writers, for example, have commented that his traumatic World War I experiences may have been a formative and crucial element in his theorizing.[8] However, Eigen suggests that whatever issues may arise from Bion's description, the "governing vision" is this:

> The self is born, evolves and dissolves with a sense of catastrophe. . . . Bion's account of human psychic life begins with catastrophic beta elements, whether pristine pre-thoughts requiring a birth process or the perverse dendritis [*sic*] of psychic collapse.[9]

Catastrophe to Bion is an "invariant" that can be mapped into specific contexts—for example, death, castration, disease, falling, and so on. An important aspect of his description is that it articulates the struggle of dream-work alpha to perform its role. The outcome is uncertain, as there are forces operating against its successful operation. Psychic catastrophe and the unbearable, are, in the Bion-Eigen view, at the core of the psyche. Human experience develops within this, and the need to make overwhelming experience workable is the fundamental task. The model becomes relational because it is the mother's alpha reverie that contains and digests raw and unprocessed experience and facilitates its becoming part of the infant's own psyche.

In Bion's terms the essential root of these states of mind are the turbulent impacts of O. Bion's O occupies a range of possible meanings, from the emotional reality of an analytic session to a sense of infinite, unknown, and unforeclosed openness. The dream-work alpha process filters and detoxifies the raw beta elements whose origination is in O. Again it is the impact of this that Eigen picks up on:

> the shock of impact that sets off waves of feelings, sensation, presentiments. . . . O is a mark or utterance, a signal or notation for something it can not contain, perhaps not even represent. We try with language to point to the unrepresentable.[10]

The originating root of what is metabolized is essentially beyond what can be understood or thought, even though there is a continuous attempt to filter the effects of the unfolding of O.

WINNICOTT'S UNTHINKABLE ANXIETIES

Another source of Eigen's concern with unbearable states is Winnicott's work on unthinkable anxieties. Winnicott describes primitive terrors that occur at the origins of the personality.[11] These are states where the infant is "overstrained" by gaps in environmental provision, specifically containment, by the "good-enough" mother. The infant at this point struggles to use his immature and barely formed resources to deal with these experiences. The "overstrain" points to the unbearable agonies that the primitive psyche has to process. The use of the word "overstrain" is significant in itself because it implies that some measure of strain may be part of ordinary infantile experience. It is when too much is demanded of the infant that damage occurs.

The good-enough mother facilitates the infant's ego-integration; failures here lead to unthinkable primitive breakdown, "specifically the stuff of psychotic anxieties."[12] These are about:

1. Going to pieces
2. Falling forever
3. Having no relation to the body
4. Having no orientation[13]

Winnicott writes of the baby as an "immature being who is all the time *on the brink of unthinkable anxiety.*"[14] The infant's personality forms around overwhelming, unthinkable, and unbearable experience. It is the mother's empathic management of the baby that allows these unthinkable anxieties to be "kept away."[15] Moreover, although the extent of damage at this point varies in degree, Winnicott writes, "It is impossible to think of a child who was so well cared for in earliest infancy that there was no overstrain in the personality" and that therefore "some experience of madness" (psychotic anxiety) is "universal."[16]

Eigen's reflections on Winnicott highlight the fate of these primitive agonies at the origins of the personality. Eigen uses language such as "before the infant could manage it,"[17] "the intensity was too much to bear,"[18] "unmanageable,"[19] and "states too much for it."[20] He concludes that this can lead to a deadening and loss of ability to experience. There may be an underlying despair and resignation in the individual, a sense that one can never deal adequately with the intensity that is endlessly produced from within.

Defensive organizations form around these places of disintegrative breakdown[21] and "original madness," which, because they are "inexpressible" and "beyond experience" are, in fact, unreachable.[22] Later anxieties in the individual link with early points of breakdown that cannot be remembered but remain residually as fears of breakdown. Eigen emphasizes that maternal failure leads to the infant's terror of its own incapacity because of the immaturity of its psychological resources. Thus, "dread of environmental failure is the outer shell of a deeper dread of failure of one's own equipment."[23]

Here again, as in Bion's sense of the catastrophic core of the personality, Eigen regards Winnicott's unthinkable anxieties as depicting "a cataclysmic failure of the psyche to live through its inability to sustain dire agonies."[24]

THE UNDREAMABLE OBJECT

Eigen's exploration into the nature of unbearable experience reaches its full intensity in the excoriating vision he articulates in "The Undreamable Object," a chapter in *Damaged Bonds*.[25] His principal theoretical base here is Bion's concept of dreaming or damaged dream-work. Bion's use of the term "dreaming" focuses on the digestion and processing of emotional experience. This is the action of alpha function on raw beta experiential elements. Dream-work alpha operates in waking and sleep and allows feelings to be metabolized and psychological work to be carried out on experience. Dream-work alpha digests raw material, allowing it to be recalled, stored, and evolved into imagery.

In this regard Ogden writes:

> Dreaming . . . must involve unconscious psychological work achieved through the linking of experience in the creation of dream-thought. This work of making unconscious linkages— as opposed to forms of psychic evacuation such as hallucination, excessive projective identification, manic defence and paranoid delusion—allows one unconsciously and consciously to think about and make psychological use of experience.[26]

It is this process that allows one to "dream undreamt dreams and interrupted cries."[27]

The intersubjective field in which this occurs is symbolized by the idea of the container and the contained. Ideally the mother is a container into which the infant can project its raw, undigested emotions. The maternal reverie and the processing of the infant's emotional states involve the mother's absorption, detoxifying resonance, and reflection.[28] The interactive container-contained field is where the infant's material is "borne," absorbed, and transformed. Similarly, in the analytic session, the analyst dreams the patient, thereby metabolizing raw emotional affects.[29]

However, Eigen explores a state of mind where what needs to be dreamt is corrupted dream-work or the difficulties in tolerating experience. The process is foreclosed and "dreams cannot do their dreaming work if what

they are compelled to do is digest a state of affairs that damages digestion."[30]
He is describing a state of mind where unendurable emotional content
overwhelms and "jams" the ability to process it. He writes:

> The patient is terrified to assemble a dream in which the
> dreaded object or object beyond dread may appear. . . . Yet
> it is precisely the depths of death and shards of madness and
> the mad/maddening object that dream-work must endure,
> or at least express.[31]

In Bion's language one could understand these states as a corroding
attack on containment and meaning. However, Eigen emphasizes the
essential indigestibility of the experience, which blocks digestion
because of its severity. Unbearable experience overwhelms dream-work
ability, or dream-work alpha is insufficient to metabolize all that needs to
be integrated. Thus, Eigen writes of breakdown in dream-work and the
need to continually restart the process in an ongoing attempt to find
ways of psychic digestion. This "anti-dream" object subverts the ability
to dream and the experience becomes unbearable. Dream-work alpha is
avoided or malfunctions because the state of mind to be dreamt is too
painful or overwhelming.

In summary, both Bion and Winnicott are describing unnamable,
unthinkable experience at the origins of the personality. The extent of
damage at this level varies in individuals. Unbearable experiences may be
ameliorated or intensified by the containing ability of the mother and other
environmental figures. Both suggest that these unbearable states are at the
core of the psyche and that there is something universal and elemental about
them. They are indicating that while these unbearable states may vary in
intensity, even in their negotiation they are significant. The infant is in
close and sensitive relationship to the possibility of failure in the
environment and aware of its own immaturity and incapacity. Eigen holds
that there are always traces of anxiety because even when it goes well
enough, the infant is aware of the psychic precipices and possible
catastrophes that have been avoided.

BION, MENTAL PAIN, AND PSYCHIC SUFFERING

Manuela Fleming's significant recent work complements Eigen's
writings.[32] Fleming revisits the notion of mental pain and the course of
this concept in psychoanalysis from Freud to Bion. Freud described psychic
pain, which in German is called *Seelenschmertz*, and viewed this primordial
pain as related to the infant's helplessness regarding separation from the

mother. This mental pain, a universal human condition, is experienced, according to Freud, "in the radical absence of the Other."[33] Freud regarded frustration tolerance as a key factor in the handling of pain and in the development of the individual's ability to symbolize in the face of mental pain. But it was Bion who extended this trajectory and developed a nuanced picture of the difficulties in managing mental pain and of how mental pain develops into representation and symbolization.

Bion is asking the essential question of what mechanism in and capacity of the psyche "allow the unbearable to be accepted by the mind . . . for it to be elaborated and to acquire meaning."[34] Many of Bion's conclusions derived from his work with psychotic processes, but he regarded these processes as applying to the roots of psychic life in general. Indeed, Bion regarded pain as an irreducible fact in psychic life. He stated "pain cannot be absent from the personality," and "I will consider pain as one of the elements of psychoanalysis."[35]

Bion suggests a number of interwoven and interacting processes that allow mental pain to be tolerated and metabolized. Fleming summarizes the following interrelated factors as operating in the mother-infant interaction:

1. Innate tendencies toward "destruction, hatred and envy"[36]
2. The nature of self-object links
3. The containing capacity of the mother
4. The nature of the containing alpha function and reverie in the digestion of beta elements in the infant[37]

Bion (1970) described patients who experienced "pain but not suffering"[38] and commented on how this intensity leads to a "fear of suffering pain." Fleming takes these reflections further and distinguishes mental pain from psychic suffering.

Fleming describes mental pain as "undefined sensations of longing, helplessness and distress."[39] It is a static, stuck experience that cannot be communicated in words or representations. Mental pain is "deprived of sense"[40] and the possibility of explanation. By contrast, psychic suffering can be communicated and, indeed, this communication is accompanied by feelings of relief. Mental pain, however, is beneath communication and experiences of pleasure or displeasure.

Those suffering from mental pain lack a sense of self or the presence of a responsive other. Nobody seems to be in relation to the pain. By contrast, psychic suffering refers to and involves a sense of self ("I suffer") and an other who can respond to it.

Psychic suffering can be elaborated through mourning and develop into mentalizing, representation, and symbol. In contrast, mental pain has an unyielding, indigestible quality to it. Fleming also suggests that the mental and emotional aspects of pain occur at the intersection of psyche and soma, where "undefined" and "unnameable" sensations reside. Emotional experience can either be transformed into imagery or verbalization or moved into unmentalized somatic states.

Two processes are essential in the movement of mental pain to psychic suffering:

> 1. The pain must be tolerated by an other who absorbs and contains the sufferer's experience. Without containment and tolerance, an experience remains undigested and incommunicable. The mother or analyst plays an essential role here. The processes can then be carried out internally by the infant/patient.
>
> 2. The interaction between the container and the individual in mental pain involves metabolizing by "alpha function." Alpha function refers to processes whereby raw affect and impacts are digested and metabolized so as to make it possible for them to be represented and then symbolized.

To summarize, Fleming proposes that mental pain refers to experiences that are not tolerated and that cannot be expressed or named. They are made manifest in silences, impressions, or bodily gestures. Psychic suffering refers to the result of negative experience that has been absorbed and tolerated and therefore rendered communicable. The movement into the communicable allows abstraction and symbolization. As will be seen, musical aspects of communication may be essential to this process.

Indeed, in discussing how mental pain can be worked with, Fleming emphasizes the musical sensitivity of the therapist:

> The analyst shall ideally be open to semiotic dynamics, i.e. to dream what the analysand is not able to dream, open . . . to the musical dimension of communication, thus developing his or her "negative capabilities" of tolerance for doubt, for incertitude and for novelty.[41]

MERCY

The infant lives through and around the primitive terrors and agonies Bion, Winnicott, and Eigen have described. Within these experiences there is a reaching out to an other who will hold, contain, and therefore ameliorate the states of mind the infant undergoes.

I suggest that this reaching can be understood as a need and as a plea for mercy. It is merciful for an unthinkable anxiety to be soothed, for an unbearable agony to be met and contained. The scream, yearning, and tropism within a primitive anxiety are toward the merciful lessening of its intensity. A terror that is endured and metabolized rescues an infant back from shocks that can deaden its psyche. Mercy is the experience of the unbearable being rendered bearable, the unendurable rendered endurable. Mercy is the felt sense of the movement from catastrophe to faith,[42] from mental pain to psychic suffering. Mercy softens the savage super-ego and immobilizing shame.

The word "mercy" may seem too archaic, anachronistic, and theologically based to be used to understand primitive psychological experience, and the word also has overtones of justice, punishment, and traditional notions of sin. However, mercy has much to do with the modulation of persecutory guilt, rendering it tolerable.

The word itself also seems unsayable, as though the emotions behind it are too raw and innocent. Yet many of the infantile states of mind described in psychoanalysis and experienced by patients implicitly involve a plea for the quality of mercy. The mother's containment (dream-work alpha) of an infant's overwhelming terror or a therapist's alpha dreaming of a patient's experience is a gesture of mercy and is experienced as such.

This second part of my essay will explore how a contemporary musical setting of an ancient petition, the "Kyrie Eleison," deepens an understanding of the concept of mercy.

THE *PRAYER OF THE HEART* BY JOHN TAVENER

Prayer of the Heart was composed by the contemporary British composer John Tavener (b. 1944). His work, as a whole, is written with religious conviction and reflects his involvement with the Orthodox Church. He explores minimalism in order to bring out the sacred quality of his concerns.

The work to be explored is a setting of the ancient "Prayer of the Heart." This is the classic prayer to God or Jesus for mercy. The form and amount of syllables may vary, but the core petition is for mercy, as in "Christ have mercy" or "God have mercy." Although the "Kyrie Eleison" is essentially Christian in use, it has roots in the Old Testament psalms and, indeed, may even have earlier roots.

The "Kyrie Eleison" is often chanted in litany, particularly in the Eastern churches. This practice is close to mantric practices. Because it is part of the construction of the Christian Mass, many different composers have set it to music, from the ninth century to the present day. There were early music settings by, for example, Johannes Ockeghem, Guillame de Mauchaut, Josquin des Prez, and Giovanni Pierluigi da Palestrina. Later composers such as Bach, Mozart, and Beethoven composed works incorporating the "Kyrie," as did twentieth-century composers such as Faure, Berlioz, Stravinsky, Vaughan Williams, and Benjamin Britten. This work by Tavener reflects the influences of early music and his contemporary, Arvo Pärt.

The words of the Jesus Prayer in Tavener's work are sung in three languages—English, Greek, and Coptic. A taped heartbeat sounds throughout the work. Rob Cowan, in his review, comments on the work as "raw (and) rapturous" and describes Björk's vocalizing as suggesting "by turns childlike awe, ecstasy, intimacy and—occasionally—savage confrontation."[43] Vargiu perceptively describes the "austerity" of the music and the sense of it "taking place in a dream as if deep sleep were soothing and muffling the tragedy of the human soul."[44] Vargiu also comments on the raw intensity and range of Björk's evocative singing and feels that, at one point, one has access "not only to the core of her voice but also to the core of the human voice itself."[45]

Tavener composed the work specifically for Björk, the Icelandic "avant-pop" singer.[46] He talks about this process in the following way:

> I'd heard her voice. . . . It was quite a raw, primordial sound, and I was very attracted to this sound. I thought of the ejaculatory prayer called the "Jesus Prayer"—"Lord Jesus, have mercy on me" and I set it in three languages, in Coptic, in English and in Greek. I thought the way she sung it was quite wonderful, and it couldn't possibly be sung by anybody else but her, or someone with a voice very, very similar to hers. It had nothing of a Western trained voice about it. In fact, it wasn't trained at all, and this is why I liked it so much, because it had a savage quality, an untamed quality. . . . These are qualities that I like. . . . I liked the simplicity of her, I liked the spontaneity of her, and I liked the result that came forth in "Prayer of the Heart."[47]

Tavener emphasizes the primordial because he is reaching into an experience that is primal and elemental. He is finding the sound that carries a universal plea and he chooses a voice that because it is not classically trained is also not contrived. Björk sounds undefended and innocent. The experience of the listener is of the psyche in extremis reaching for a containing presence.

My concern in this essay is not with the manifest Christian content of the "Kyrie Eleison"; I am suggesting that the significance of the plea for mercy is a plea for unbearable states of mind to be rendered tolerable and bearable. In this way Tavener expresses a movement from the unendurable to the endurable, from mental pain to psychic suffering. The primordial plea evokes the psychological encounter between primitive terrors and their containment as Bion, Winnicott, and Eigen have described it.

The following analysis illustrates how the musical techniques in the composition allow an experience of the merciful dreaming of unbearable states of mind. The use of the drone and harmony carry a very literal resonance of the earliest relationship between mother and infant and reminds us palpably of how this interaction is, fundamentally, played out in an acoustic medium.

BJÖRK'S SINGING

Björk's singing is resonant of the plea that an infant makes to its mother or containing figure. The reply of the string quartet is one of reverie and absorption. The dream atmosphere that Vargiu describes suggests the unconscious reverberations of the interaction between container and contained.

Björk's voice begins tentatively and vulnerably as though she is trying to find the sound that most captures her experience. The sounds of an infant can sometimes be expulsive, but at other times the infant may search for the sound that communicates his/her emotional state and listen for the empathic response, often in sound, that means that he/she has been held and contained. As Björk's singing is responded to in the acoustic reverie of the string quartet, she is encouraged and strengthened and her singing becomes stronger and firmer. Her plea is heard and believed, and we know this by the soundscape that Tavener creates.

Her singing moves between different emotions. Sometimes it is tentative and uncertain, at other times urgent and uncompromisingly insistent. Toward the end her voice conveys a sadder resignation or acceptance. She has been through a crisis and has come through.

At points in the work, her vocalizing of the words emphasizes certain syllables. There is a focus and penetration here—she is quite sure of the honesty and force of her plea. However, one can conjecture that the emphasis also illustrates something else. It points to a compensation against a competing force that is taking her away from sound, an impulse that is anti-sound or an experience that feels to be beneath sound, that cannot be captured in sound. Dreads that feel too overwhelming for expression in sound are carried below and outside sound. Perhaps "the undreamable object" is an unsoundable object. Munch's *The Scream* is often referred to in analytic sessions and is an image that captures specific dreads and emotions. It seems to express an experience that overwhelms sound and that is communicated through non-sound. The emotion that needs to be expressed is too much for sound. Sound fails to express the intensity of the agony of what needs to be communicated.

When an experience finds its way into sound, it is raw, unprocessed, and unredeemed. Bion's phrase "nameless dread" refers to an infant who is thrown back on itself by an impenetrable maternal container who cannot or refuses to "dream" the infant's experience. Reflecting on experiences beyond sound, one can consider that the concept of the "nameless" is already too sophisticated and precocious. There are "soundless dreads" before names can be given, states of mind where an infant can be thrown back on itself and fall forever because its experience cannot be met acoustically. Although the infant's responsiveness to words is remarkable, the essential primal reverie is held in a preverbal sonorous interactive field.[48]

At various points Björk's sound overwhelms tonality, again as though the intensity is too much for containment in sound. Her unbounded emotion strains the usual scales, the melismatic singing moving in and around the notes. There is a scream behind this singing, a point where the unbearable moves into sound. This sound moves around and into the listener.

The scream is significant because it is at the intersection of the unbearable and sound. As Winnicott points out, a scream can be the last sound before hope is abandoned. The loss of the ability to scream may result from the mother's not responding to the infant's distress. The extinction of hope and a sense of futility is a consequence. It is in therapy, as Eigen emphasizes, that the scream can be retrieved and a split between mind and body can be healed. The integrating function of the scream is explicit in Winnicott and implicit in Bion's description of the explosive and disintegrative origin of psychic experience.[49]

THE DRONE

Tavener makes use of the extended and sustained tone of the drone in his composition. Its use is widespread, especially in religious and traditional world music. In Indian classical music, for example, the drone is sounded before any other rhythmic or melodic expression, and in Irish and Scottish traditional music the drone (often piped) underpins and stabilizes a vocal or instrumental melody.

Tavener has placed lengthy drone notes in his other compositions (for example in "Song for Athene," *My Gaze Is Ever Upon You,* and *The Veil of the Temple*). The use of drones in *Prayer of the Heart* is not as prolonged as in other works, but the sustained fundamental and fifth is decidedly a drone. In this work, after the harmonic chord shifts, the drone sounds throughout each section. Its tonality is based on a newly introduced chord.

There are three aspects of the drone I wish to discuss in relationship to this composition. In reflecting on his music, Tavener is quite emphatic that the drone(or "ison," as Tavener terms it) is the representation of spiritual reality and is, in fact, the acoustic counterpart to silence. This is clear in the following excerpt from an interview with Brian Keeble:

> Tavener: The ison represents for me the divine presence and somewhere I suppose in every piece I write this eternity note must be present—the presence of God, as it were.
>
> Keeble: Let's be very specific here: metaphysically the drone is the acoustic representation of silence?
>
> Tavener: The silence of God. The silence of eternity. Yes.[50]

For Tavener, the drone represents a transcendent reality. It is tempting, however, to understand the drone in another way. According to Nakkach, the origins of the French word for drone—*"bourdon"*—is "seam," implying that which "weaves together and holds together."[51] The drone, therefore, links with the psychoanalytic concepts of holding and containment. The drone sound grounds and holds the other aspects of the music, whether they are sung or instrumental. It collects the other dimensions around a base that provides a solidity and security.

Ann Belford Ulanov writes that "to heal an early agony we must depend on someone present" and of the importance of someone "holding the situation, the journey back to where we fall apart."[52] The drone sound evokes that "someone present" and, in the sense that so much of the sense of the mother's presence is mediated through sound, is an essential aspect of that experience. It is the acoustic correlate of the enduring and sustaining presence of the mother.

The drone therefore opens to a transcendent reality at the same time that it reaches into the containment of infantile states of mind. In holding the transcendent and the infantile, it expresses acoustically the human condition of "the ever necessary confrontation of a mystical core with suffering, degradation, annihilation, and an endless play of destructive forces that exert deforming pressures."⁵³ The drone, in combining these opposites, becomes a symbol despite its apparent simplicity. It may be this symbolic effect that explains its extensive use, especially in more spiritual and traditional genres.

Listening to the simplicity and lack of adornment of the drone leads to an emptiness that must be confronted and engaged with. Something important happens in the lack of complexity and the boredom that an individual may experience. There is no possibility of manic denial through intricate sounds and rhythms. An encounter with a drone, especially an extended one, is an exercise in tolerance and frustration. It may be that this connects with the links between frustration, tolerance, and thought that allow the transformation of mental pain in the early mother-infant relationship. The drone mother holds and suffers experience and bears the infant's experience, living through places of non-excitement. Walter Benjamin highlights the importance of tolerating nonstimulating environments: "Boredom is the dream bird that hatches the egg of experience. A rustling in the leaves drives him away."⁵⁴

One's relationship to a drone varies. At times the sound is foregrounded, making it the essential communication. At other points it disappears and becomes the background, barely noticed and tacit. Yet without it, the essential wholeness of the work would be lost and the other aspects would be abandoned. The drone is the sonorous expression, then, of the mother who is the infant's base—sometimes more directly present in awareness, at other times more in the background.

The drone, finally, reminds us also of the surviving maternal object. The drone mother survives movements away and back to her just as the root tonality "survives" various intervals along the scale.

Winnicott's description of this aspect of the early infant-mother relationship involves the interaction of an "aggressive subject and surviving object."⁵⁵ The infant in essence is saying to the mother, "You will be loved because you survived."⁵⁶ Winnicott's sequence captures the nuances of this interaction and functions as a psychoanalytic sutra, which, as in the original Sanskrit meaning of the word, stitches aspects of consciousness together:

> The subject says to the object: "I destroyed you", and the object is there to receive the communication. From now on the subject says: "Hello object!" "I destroyed you." "I love you." "You have value for me because of your survival of my destruction of you." "While I am loving you I am all the time destroying you in (unconscious) *fantasy*."⁵⁷

The object's survival allows object constancy to be established. It facilitates an embodied aliveness based on primitive excitement and a loving that is indistinguishable from destructiveness in the infant. Crucially, the survival of the object establishes an externality of the other outside the area of "omnipotent control."[58] The enduring and resilient drone survives destruction and reassures the listener on a visceral level. It is a crucial component of Tavener's composition and gives rise to a core experience in the movement from unbearable pain to tolerable psychic suffering and therefore is a merciful, elementally soothing sound.

An Acoustic Mandala

Björk's singing is responded to by a shifting harmonic pattern. The chords move through a full circle of the different keys.[59] It is as though the melody needs to be contained by the full range of harmonic responsiveness, and the keys move stepwise from major to relative minor. The complete harmonic cycle therefore forms a harmonic mandala, containing the prayer in a circular structured whole.

The harmonic accompaniment can be imagined as performing holding and containing functions with regard to the melody. It resonates, deepens, and gives an empathic context to the notes of the melody. Harmony is to melody as container is to contained.

The full cycle in this work gives a sense of how the essential plea needs to be dreamt in the acoustic reverie of the different keys. Here is the counterpart of the containing mother/analyst finding different ways of responding to the impact of the infant's/client's communication. The full cycle of keys reflects different textures of this reverie, or perhaps only the complete cycle is capable of absorbing and containing the depth of the plea.

The chordal progression moves from major to the relative minor and resolves in the dominant major (I to VI minor to V). The alternation of major to minor is also a to and fro movement from strength and resilience to vulnerability and mourning. These shifts are a further harmonic feature of the work. It reflects a movement between destruction and repair, wounding absence and reassuring presence.

The Heartbeat

The composition begins with a percussive heartbeat and the repetitive sound continues throughout the work.

At one level, the heartbeat may refer to Tavener's own suffering with Marfan's syndrome and therefore to the composer's own vulnerability and finitude. However, the composition goes further than Tavener's own individual angst and is more concerned with essential human concerns. The significance of this sound is more likely to lie in the most archaic roots of psychic experience—the sounds of the womb environment. There is growing evidence of the existence of prenatal sound memories. Neurophysiological research suggests that the human can hear from the fourth month of development.[60] The higher frequencies may be of the mother's voice. Lower frequencies would be the sounds of the mother's heartbeat, breathing, and digestion. An embodied sense of these low-frequency sounds may be experienced earlier than hearing.

Suzanne Maiello suggests that some form of introjection may exist at this point and that this may have sound qualities, particularly when it is of the mother's voice. Maiello comments:

> The alternation of the sound of her voice and her silence may give the unborn child a very first experience of both presence and absence, and thus becomes the basis for the constitution of a pre-natal proto-object, which I tentatively called "sound-object."[61]

This may involve early differentiation between "me" and "not me."

If this is true of the mother's voice, it may well be also true in the case of "unconscious somatic associates"[62] of the mother that the unborn child has. Music can be experienced in the body as much as aurally, in the same way that the infant experiences the uterine environment. The heartbeat could be therefore one of the earliest roots of the "sound-object."

Maiello notes (following Isaacs) that "auditory phantasies could be located somewhere half-way between the primary concrete somatic experiences present already before birth"[63] and latent visual experiences that are present in the womb. It is these primary concrete somatic experiences that I wish to emphasize. One can imagine the mother's heartbeat not only as a sound but also as a primal somatic experience. Here the rudimentary sense of self and other occurs in a soundscape that is inseparably both aural and embodied.

The presence of the heartbeat in Tavener's work therefore evokes embodied memories of the earliest roots of sound, roots that later develop into a sense of rhythm, music, and language. It may also be evoking the earliest origins of the sense of self and other and the alternating experience of the presence and absence of the other. Across this oscillating beat of silent void and surviving presence, Björk's voice expresses a plea for this experience to be made bearable.

My analysis of the musical techniques that Tavener uses can be summarized as follows:

> A plea for mercy exists on the border of what is endurable and dreamable.

> An acoustic mandala harmonizes and holds the experience in reverie and containment.

> Drones provide a sustaining and surviving presence, both relativizing the unbearable in the transcendent and containing the infantile.

> A percussive heartbeat viscerally reminds us of the earliest sound object and the most primitive experience of presence and absence.

CONCLUSION

This essay has brought Eigen's exploration into the nature of unbearable experience together with Tavener's composition *Prayer of the Heart*. I have suggested that in the core of the unbearable is the reaching out for and pleading for mercy. Mercy is the quality and gesture that allows the dreaming of a state of mind that is indigestible, or as in the "undreamable object," that overwhelms one's ability to endure or bear an experience. An elemental, primordial prayer, the "Kyrie Eleison," articulates such a plea. It expresses and sounds the psyche in extremis and the need for an other to help endure that which is unendurable and therefore facilitate its integration. John Tavener's contemporary setting of the "Kyrie" gives expression to this state of mind and reveals a movement from indigestible mental pain toward tolerable psychic suffering. It allows musical access to core processes in the primitive psyche. The work also facilitates an acoustic imagining of the early mother-infant relationship.

The play between the Hebrew words for "womb" and "mercy" allows a final insight into these themes. *Rachamim,* the Hebrew word for mercy, is based on *rehem,* meaning "womb." A womb is merciful in its containment. Mercy is also a womb, in that by rendering experience bearable it allows psychic growth. Music, and especially this music, involves both these aspects—a containment of psyche and a way for it to evolve.

Notes

[1] John Tavener, *Prayer of the Heart,* performed by Björk and the Brodsky Quartet on *John Tavener: A Portrait,* CD, Naxos, 2004.

[2] Michael Eigen, *The Psychoanalytic Mystic* (London: Free Association Books, 1998), p. iv.

[3] Michael Eigen and Aner Govrin, *Conversations with Michael Eigen* (London: Karnac Books, 2007).

[4] *Ibid.,* p. 52.

[5] *Ibid.,* p. 53.

[6] Michael Eigen, "Between Catastrophe and Faith," in *The Electrified Tightrope* (Northvale, NJ: Jason Aronson, 1993), pp. 211–225.

[7] Wilfred R. Bion, *Attention and Interpretation* (1970; repr., Lanham, MD: Rowman & Littlefield, 2001), p. 12.

[8] See Kay M. Souter, "The War Memoirs: Some Origins of the Thought of W. R. Bion," *International Journal of Psychoanalysis* 90, no. 4 (August 2009): 795–808; and Joan and Neville Symington, *The Clinical Thinking of Wilfred Bion* (London: Routledge, 1996).

[9] Eigen, "Between Catastrophe and Faith," p. 217.

[10] Eigen, *The Psychoanalytic Mystic,* pp. 39–40.

[11] Donald W. Winnicott, *The Maturational Process and the Facilitating Environment* (New York: International Universities Press, 1965); and D. W. Winnicott, "Fear of Breakdown," *International Review of Psycho-Analysis* 1 (1974): 103–107.

[12] Winnicott, *The Maturational Process,* p. 58.

[13] Winnicott, *The Maturational Process*; D. W. Winnicott, *Babies and Their Mothers* (London: Free Association Books, 1988), p. 58.

[14] Winnicott, *The Maturational Process,* p. 57. Winnicott's emphasis.

[15] Donald W. Winnicott, "Ego Integration in Child Development" (1962), in *The Maturational Process.*

[16] *Ibid.,* "The Psychology of Madness: A Contribution to Psychoanalysis," in *Psychoanalytic Explorations,* ed. C. Winnicott, R. Shepherd, and M. Davis (Cambridge: Harvard University Press, 1992), p. 126.

[17] Michael Eigen, *Toxic Nourishment* (London: Karnac Books, 1999), p. 172.

[18] *Ibid.,* p. 174.

[19] *Ibid.,* p. 172.

[20] *Ibid.,* p. 171.

[21] Eigen, *The Psychoanalytic Mystic,* p. 96.

[22] Michael Eigen, *The Sensitive Self* (Middletown, CT: Wesleyan University Press, 2004), p. 79.

[23] Eigen, *The Psychoanalytic Mystic,* p. 97.

[24] *Ibid.,* p. 97.

[25] Michael Eigen, *Damaged Bonds* (London: Karnac Books, 2000).

[26] Thomas H. Ogden, *This Art of Psychoanalysis: Dreaming Undreamt Dreams and Interrupted Cries* (Hove, UK: Routledge, 2005), p. 47.

[27] *Ibid.*

[28] James S. Grotstein, *A Beam of Intense Darkness: Wilfred Bion's Legacy to Psychoanalysis* (London: Karnac Books, 2008).

[29] Wilfred R. Bion, *Cogitations* (London: Karnac Books, 1992), p. 120.

[30] Eigen, *Damaged Bonds,* p. 5.

[31] *Ibid.,* p. 38.

[32] Manuela Fleming, "Towards a Model of Mental Pain and Psychic Suffering," *Canadian Journal of Psychoanalysis* 13, no. 1 (2005): 255–272; Manuela Fleming, "Distinction between Mental Pain and Psychic Suffering as Separate Entities in the Patient's Experience," *International Forum of Psychoanalysis* 15 (2006): 195–200; Manuela Fleming, "On Mental Pain: From Freud to Bion," *International Forum of Psychoanalysis* 17 (2008): 27–36.

[33] Fleming, "Towards a Model of Mental Pain and Psychic Suffering," p. 249.

[34] *Ibid.,* p. 259.

[35] Wilfred R. Bion, *Elements of Psychoanalysis* (London: Heinemann, 1963), pp. 61–62.

[36] Wilfred Bion, "Attacks on Linking," in *Melanie Klein Today: Developments in Theory and Practice,* vol. 1, *Mainly Theory,* ed. Elizabeth Bott Spillius (London: Routledge, 1988), p. 98. Bion's essay was originally published in 1959.

[37] Fleming, "Distinction between Mental Pain and Psychic Suffering," p. 196; and Fleming, "On Mental Pain," p. 31.

[38] Bion, *Attention and Interpretation,* p. 19.

[39] Fleming, "Towards a Model of Mental Pain and Psychic Suffering," p. 251.

[40] Fleming, "Distinction between Mental Pain and Psychic Suffering," p. 198.

[41] Fleming, "Towards a Model of Mental Pain and Psychic Suffering," p. 269.

[42] Eigen, "Between Catastrophe and Faith," pp. 211–225.

[43] Rob Cowan, "The Compact Collection," *The Independent* (London), 23 February 2004, available at http://www.independent.co.uk/arts-entertainment/music/reviews/the-compact-collection-757117.html.

[44] Riccardo James Vargiu, music reviewer, personal communication, 10 April 2010.

[45] *Ibid.*

[46] Alex Ross, *The Rest Is Noise: Listening to the Twentieth Century* (New York: Farrar, Straus and Giroux, 2007).

[47] CD booklet notes for *John Tavener: A Portrait,* p. 9, Naxos Rights International Ltd, 2004.

[48] Johan Norman, "To Talk with Infants: Using Words in Psychoanalytic Practice with Children Who Are Not Yet Able to Speak," 1997, unpublished paper available at www.sicap.it/merciai/bion/papers/norma.htm.

[49] Michael Eigen, "Screaming" in *Rage* (Middletown, CT: Wesleyan University Press, 2002), pp. 151–155.

[50] John Tavener, *The Music of Silence, A Composer's Testament,* ed. Brian Keeble (London: Faber and Faber 1999), p. 154.

[51] Silvia Nakkach, "Devotional Music Therapy: Contemplative Vocal Music and the Passage," n.d., unpublished paper available at www.voxmundiproject.com/pdf/Music_Therapy.doc.

[52] Ann Belford Ulanov, *Finding Space: Winnicott, God, and Psychic Reality* (Westminster: John Knox Press, 2001), p. 60.

[5354] Michael Eigen, *Ecstasy* (Middletown, CN: Wesleyan University Press, 2001), p. viii.

[55] Walter Benjamin, *Illuminations* (New York: Schocken Books, 1968), p. 91.

[56] Ulanov, *Finding Space,* p. 29.

[57] Donald. W. Winnicott, "Children Learning" (1968), in D. W. Winnicott, *Home Is Where We Start From: Essays by a Psychoanalyst,* comp. and ed. Clare Winnicott, Ray Shepherd, and Madeleine Davis (New York: W.W. Norton & Co., 1986), p. 148; D. W. Winnicott, "The Use of an Object and Relating through identifications," in D. W. Winnicott, *Psycho-Analytic Explorations,* ed. Clare Winnicott, Ray Shepherd, and Madeleine Davis (London: Karnac Books, 1989), p. 222.

[58] Donald W. Winnicott, *Playing and Reality* (London Tavistock Publications, 1971), pp. 105–106. Winnicott's emphasis.

[59] *Ibid.,* p.106.

[60] I am indebted to Chris Wildman for his assistance in helping me understand the harmonic pattern in "Prayer of the Heart."

⁶¹ A. Tomatis, *Der Klang des Lebens* (Reinbeck bei Hamburg: Rowohlt Verlag, 1987); H. F. R. Prechtl, "Fetal Behaviour," in *Fetal Neurology,* ed. A. Hill and J. Volpe (New York: Raven Press, 1989).

⁶² Suzanne Maiello, "Interplay: Sound-Aspects in Mother-Infant Observation," in *Developments in Infant Observation: The Tavistock Model,* ed. Susan Reid (London: Routledge, 1997), p. 158.

⁶³ Susan Isaacs, "The Nature and Function of Phantasy," in *Developments in Psychoanalysis,* ed. J. Riviere (London: Hogarth, 1952), quoted in Suzanne Maiello, "Interplay: Sound-Aspects in Mother-Infant Observation," p. 105.

⁶⁴ Maiello, "Interplay: Sound-Aspects in Mother-Infant Observation," p. 158.

17

Song and the Psyche: Whispers of the Mind

Nóirín Ní Riain

I
n this chapter, I explore some of the dimensions behind the relationship between song and the psyche. I will consider aspects of the three essential dimensions of song: the voice, hearing and listening, and the source and destiny of every song and sound, the realm of silence.

Vocal sounds are heard by both the maker of the sounds and the listener; hearing and the voice are closely related both in the psyche and in one's encounter with the external world of things and people. Rilke, writing about his composition of the *Sonnets to Orpheus*, defined this distinctly aural experience as "the most mysterious, most enigmatic dictation I have ever endured and achieved . . . written down in a single breathless obedience . . . without one word being in doubt or having to be changed."[1]

VOCAL DIMENSIONS

This delicate little Aeolian harp that nature has set at the entrance to our breathing is really a sixth sense, which followed and surpassed the others. It quivers at the merest movement of metaphor; it permits human thought to sing.—Gaston Bachelard[2]

Given sound by the life-giving breath, which never rests in life, the voice bursts forth out of the silence and arrests both the voiced one and the listener. The timbre is always in flux; register changes in the voice are directly in the control of "the voicer" and can be manipulated according to the shape of the voice's resonators in the chest, the larynx, the mouth, the nasal cavities, and the skull. Just as a cathedral space or a concert hall has a fundamental timbre, so too every voice possesses its own unique vocal resonance. This timbre is the grain of the voice. According to French semiologist Roland Barthes,

> The *grain* of the voice is not indescribable (nothing is indescribable), but I don't think that it can be defined scientifically, because it implies a certain erotic relationship between the voice and the listener. One can therefore describe the grain of a voice, but only through metaphors.[3]

When the voice ceases to affect in a profound way, it is imaged by Barthes to be white and cold without fulfilling its innate capacity for love and eroticism. Every human voice is connected to desire; every act of the voice is an act of the erotic.

> There is no human voice which is not an object of desire. . . . There is no neutral voice—and if sometimes that neutrality, that whiteness of the voice occurs, it terrifies us, as if we were to discover a frozen world, one in which desire was dead.[4]

The word "voice" also means "sound" in many languages: Hebrew *qol* and Greek *phone* are each a single word that means voice, sound, and noise. In ancient culture, according to Thomas Allen Seel, *phone* "could be made by animals, nature, humankind, and by the Godhead."[5] In other words, this one word for voice could mean a voice of nature, a human voice, or the voice of God. The Irish word is *glór,* which also carries that trilogy of meanings. The timbre of your song is therefore the vibration of your psyche that defines and identifies you. The eighteenth-century Silesian poet Eichendorff values the sound, the song, in all things: "*Schläft ein lied in allen Dinger die da träumen fort und fort. Und die Welt hebt an zu singen trifft du nur das Zauberwort*" (There is a song in all things which keeps on dreaming. And the world starts singing if you only hit the magical word).

The voice is a virtuoso player in the orchestral work of the ear. It is all sounds, particularly articulate sounds, uttered through the mouth of sentient beings. In human beings, these sounds, which are naturally emitted in speech, shouting, and singing, are characteristic of the utterer, even though the timbre of the voice is naturally dynamic and in flux.

Classical Western singing technique has often tried to work against the natural voice. Paul Newham, a voice therapist, suggests that in European classical singing, "the aim . . . has always been to reduce or even eliminate the changes in timbre between one register and another."[6] My own experience of classical singing is a proof of this. Two weeks before my final singing diploma examination in 1969, I felt, painfully, that the voice I was singing through was not real and did not have the timbre that was natural to my being. There were four of us doing this examination and we all had an identical timbre and technique that directly reflected the ideals of our vocal teacher. I consulted her about this, suggesting that the true grain of my voice was a symbiosis of plain-chant timbre, *sean-nós* (traditional Irish) style, and of course, classical technique.[7] She not only refused to dialogue but forbade me to enter the examination and withdrew access to the appointed accompanist. However, having procured my own accompanist, I proceeded to take the diploma examination in my own voice and was awarded the highest marks of all four of us!

Only the sounds that the human brain can imagine, create, and make sense of can be physically birthed through the articulatory system that is the voice. The brain controls all sounds made by the human voice, and in this sense it is the voice; it controls both the production and understanding of the organized sounds that create language. Musicologist Victor Zuckerkandl has said that "the singer or player cannot help hearing what he sings or plays: the circle must be closed."[8]

You can hear the echo of your soul or imagine its full capacity only vaguely, but the sound of your voice has been sculpted and refined for thousands of years. It was fine-tuned long before you were in the womb. "Truly you have formed my inmost being; you knit me in my mother's womb. I give you thanks that I am . . . wonderfully made. . . . My soul also you knew full well" (Psalm 139).

THE BIOLOGY OF THE VOICE

The sound-producing organ of the voice is the larynx. This is a cavity at the upper end of the windpipe containing the vocal cords. It forms part of the air passage to the lungs. There are two pairs of membranous folds in the larynx called vocal cords. The upper pair, called false vocal cords, is redundant for the production of vocal sound; it is the lower pair, called the true vocal cords, that is activated to produce sound when air from the lungs passes between them. The edges of these true vocal cords are drawn tense, and the breath from the lungs makes them vibrate, producing sound. Breath is essential for giving birth to the sound or sounds uttered through the mouths of living creatures. Breath is the life-giving force of humanity;

your breathing is the pulse beat of your nature. We can survive for three weeks without food; three days without water is not life threatening; but three minutes without breathing is a time-trinity that one can never be resuscitated from.

The voice is in constant intimate conversation with the ear. No sound coming from the vocal cords can escape unnoticed by the ear. Although the word for eye sounds like "I," the word for "me," it cannot see itself without the help of a mirror. However, the ear is always alert to the dulcet tones of its sister, the voice. The valuable research of French Canadian physician Dr. Alfred Tomatis has shown that this relationship between the ear and the voice is almost constantly providing and supplying the brain with sensory energy. "The ear provides the nervous system with almost 90 per cent of its overall sensory energy," he claims.[9]

In girls between ten and fourteen years old, the vocal cords increase from about fifteen millimetres to seventeen millimetres. This lowers the pitch of the voice. Women's voices change in timbre during menstruation, pregnancy, and menopause. Here again the larynx increases in size, which allows access to lower sounds. The vocal cords of a boy increase to up to twenty-three millimetres. His larynx not only extends but also drops in position, and the resonating cavities in the chest and pharynx enlarge. For the voice to live and speak, a miraculous coalition must be evoked. The lungs create the breath, which glides between the vocal cords in the larynx, and sound lands on the tongue, which molds the sounds into verbal sculpture.

The mysterious physical functions of the ear have inspired awe throughout the ages. Victor Zuckerkandl devalued the many attempts to describe these adequately: "Far from accounting for the efficiency of our organ of hearing, [these attempts] make it appear all the more miraculous."[10] Music educationist David Elliott marvels at how the listening process "proceeds with an ease and an accuracy that are nothing less than miraculous."[11] Joachim-Ernst Berendt goes even further by suggesting that to hear accurately is to be fully alive because the entire "world is sound."[12] To be in the world is to participate in the conversation with that sound. To put it another way, an actual sound is unrealized until it engages with the auditory sense. To birth sound means, for most people who are blessed with hearing, to hear it. To listen is to take in and entertain sound. The power of meaning is in the actual sound, but with every sound, the first task is to hear the original murmuring. The ear never rests, even in sleep; it is always receiving welcome and unwelcome sounds. There is so much sound in the world that it is reasonable to propose that the aural sense is paramount. The silent, written word keeps physical things at a distance, but what arrives through the ear penetrates to the core.

HEARING AND LISTENING: DIFFERENT LOGICS

Sounds, voices, noises, surround most of us blessed with hearing. A sound is the sensation produced by the organ of hearing when certain vibrations are caused in the silence of the surrounding air. In the words of T. S. Eliot, "by the delicate, invisible web you wove / The inexplicable mystery of sound."[13]

Hearing and listening are inherently human activities that affect our biological, emotional, cognitive, and spiritual responses. How and what we listen to is, was, and always will be crucial. Victor Zuckerkandl says that at "the magical stage [of early man's relation to the world] the crucial organ was the ear, the crucial sense the sense of hearing."[14] This primitive primacy of the aural still exists; memories, after all, are profoundly elusive, but they are full of sounds. English psychiatrist and author Anthony Storr writes: "At an emotional level, there is something 'deeper' about hearing than seeing; and something about hearing other people which fosters human relationships even more than seeing them."[15]

It is crucial to differentiate between hearing and listening. Roland Barthes first articulated this distinction: "Hearing is a physiological phenomenon; listening is a psychological act."[16] *Hearing* is a biological process that refers to aural experiences pertinent to the earth and the universe. This is "mundane" or worldly hearing.

On the other hand, *listening* pertains to the psychological. It is through language that one hears, but what one hears in the listening is more than language itself can impart. The phrase "reading between the lines" means to understand or to discover an implicit meaning in addition to the explicit one. Listening with the psyche is precisely "hearing between the words." However, to do this properly, we must listen with discernment and detachment, because, as philosopher Peter Kivy suggests, "what we expect has a great deal to do with what we 'hear.'"[17]

It is a spiritually wholesome thing to simply listen. As the contemporary Italian philosopher Gemma Fiumara suggests: "It is possible that evolving humans tend to speak out at their best because they are listened to—and not vice versa."[18] Listening is being present when the sound or word is spoken. The notion of being on the alert at the moment of someone speaking describes an omnipresent feature of our lives. This is the sense of hearing at its most precise. "I'm all ears" means so much more than "I'm listening" or "I hear you." Something critically important is about to be heard in the present and its meaning must not go unnoticed. A key sentence that will express the soul of our being is about to be spoken. We must be at hand, and in the particular moment, we must really listen.

EVER ANCIENT, EVER NEW: SOCRATES

This is nothing new. Here we are echoing the ancient Athenian philosopher Socrates who lived, according to Plato, on two very audiocentric planes of existence. He worked orally and aurally to act as midwife, to birth an intellectual conversion in his hearers. His inner voice, the personal power or discernment with which he was graced to bring this about, he could only vaguely describe as his *daimonion,* an elusive inner figure that constantly prompted him aurally. (This *daimonion* suggested an approach to his very existence when it advised him "Socrates, make music." Music holds the ultimate existential key to life.)

Socrates was the son of a midwife. His own art of midwifery was very selective and distinct from the common art of midwifery on two counts: first, it attended only to men; and second, it was concerned only with the delivery of the psyche. Its relevance here is that his philosophy was audiocentric. In other words, what was important was that the process or technique of Socratic midwifery was essentially accomplished through the voice and listening. Socrates asked questions out loud and felt that the human ear was to be trusted and would not mislead. He outlined a taxonomy of voices.

> As for introducing "new divinities" how could I be guilty of that merely in asserting that a voice of God is manifest to me indicating my duty? . . . Will any one dispute either that thunder utters its "voice," or that it is an omen of the greatest moment? . . . But more than that, in regard to God's foreknowledge of the future and his forewarning to whomsoever he will, these are the same terms, I assert, that all men use, and this is their belief. The only difference between them and me is that whereas they call the sources of their forewarning "birds," "utterances," "chance meetings," "prophets," I call mine a "divine thing." . . . I have revealed to many of my friends the counsels which God has given me, and in no instance has the event shown that I was mistaken.[19]

VISUAL VERSUS AURAL ONTOLOGY

The eye is impatient. It wants to see everything within and beyond the horizon. The ear can take in only one thought at a time, and each meaningful thought takes its place in a pattern of what went before and what is coming next. This is what Gaston Bachelard intimates in the mixed metaphor of the following quote: "Sight says too many things at one time. Being does not see itself . . . it listens to itself."[20] The visual is a babble of image; the auditory is being itself—an auditory ontology. Since listening is so preciously bound to the origins of being, it must be revered and treasured. Zuckerkandl's articulation of this kind of listening wins the day.

> A world of the purely audible opens a domain in which the ear is lawgiver. . . . The existence of such a domain confers an entirely new dignity upon the audible world as such. . . . We should speak rather of the gift the Creator bestowed upon the visible world—the gift of sharing in the audible, in the dignity of being audible. . . . The phenomenon is unique.[21]

The eye can revisit its object endlessly—it can look again and again—but the ear generally gets one chance to listen. Therefore the ear has to be much more industrious and active in this mortal life. The act of conversation is a temporal act, of the moment. It is aural and only now. The ear is the only real connection between the past and the present; with eyes closed, ears attuned, we say, "I'm just trying to think back." The truth is in the very sound, according to Bachelard:

> At times the sound of a vocable, or the force of a letter, reveals and then defines the real thought attached to a word. . . . All important words, all the words marked for grandeur . . . are keys to the universe, to the dual universe of the Cosmos and the depths of the human spirit.[22]

Transcendent listening is an act of imagining new possibilities, not just by looking beyond one's own horizon but by an imagination that hears sounds above and below the threshold of the ear. Each divinely created and gifted ear has its own threshold of soundscape; a threshold attuned to cosmic, nonhuman sound, to the communicative sounds of human speech, and to an aural sensibility that reaches beyond both the human and nonhuman. All keen listening is metamorphosing; through the aural, one is completely changed in character and in form. From the act of choosing to listen in the first place, the change takes place. The rapid transformation, the metamorphosis from the chrysalis to the butterfly, is aural. It is the "how," not the "that," that is the birthing process of what is really heard, understood, and ultimately communicated. The artist Bridget Riley counsels the observer: "You will have to learn to listen, because it is through a special sort of listening, a sort of 'listening-in,' that one learns how to speak."[23]

Silence: The Third Member of the Psychological Sonic Family

*Give yourself the opportunity of silence and begin to develop your
listening in order to hear, deep within yourself, the music of your
own spirit.*—John O'Donohue[24]

*Words, after speech, reach
Into the silence.*—T. S. Eliot[25]

Originally, the world was a silent mass waiting for the visitation of its
near relative, sound. Humanity came after and was an expert hearer and
obedient listener. But in that same landscape of sound and silence, we have
forgotten how to attend. We must relearn how to hear; we need to retrieve
the mystery, the miracle that is the sound and the silent signal of everything
in creation and surpassing it. The Danish philosopher Kierkegaard, in a
much-quoted statement, urgently called for the establishment of silence in
the noisy world of his society.

> If I were a physician, and if I were allowed to prescribe just one
> remedy for all the ills of the modern world, I would prescribe
> silence. For even if the Word of God were proclaimed in the
> modern world, how could one hear it with so much noise?
> Therefore, create silence.[26]

Sound and silence are in a close relationship. Silence is the positive ground
or horizon of sound. Within the realm of the silent, the meaning of a sound
is processed long after the sound has ceased. The ancient Chinese
proverb "The sound ceases but the sense goes on" summarizes true
silence. Poet Seamus Heaney has written, "The silence breathed / and could
not settle back."[27]

Sound is nourished and nurtured by silence. The only reason that a
sound can resonate is because there is silence. There can be no sound
without silence and no true silence without there having been sound. Silence
is the natural milieu of sound, and sound is unimaginable without silence.
Silence and sound are not opposites but are paradoxically and fundamentally
correlatives, bound together in a complementary relationship. They form
the two sides of the coin of human listening and being.

Silence and the sounding word are inextricably linked. John
O'Donohue summarizes this point: "All good sounds have silence, near,
behind and within them."[28] Speech is patterned, structured, verbal sound.
Any act of speech breaks the silence and resurrects it again on cessation.
Speech is in relationship with the silence that gives rise to and contains it.
Silence keeps discourse balanced. Silence is a contradiction in terms; to

try to define or articulate it, one has to break it, interrupt it, and surprise it. The paradox is that silence is both near and far off. America's most famous spiritual poet, Emily Dickinson, wrote:

> Then Space—began to toll,
> As all the Heavens were a Bell,
> And Being, but an Ear,
> And I, and Silence, some strange Race
> Wrecked, solitary here.[29]

There is an innate sacredness in every silence, as in every sound. Max Picard (whose wonderful little book *The World of Silence* is still a classic) insists on both the interconnectedness and the sacred nature of all silence and sound.

> When one is silent, one is like someone awaiting the creation of language for the first time. . . . In the silence, one is as it were ready to give the word back to the Creator from whom one first received it. Therefore, there is something holy in almost every silence.[30]

Picard also makes the connection between *listening* and silence: listening is only possible, he claims, "when there is silence in man: listening and silence belong together."[31] They create an inseparable duality. Thus, stillness and its corresponding resonance simply "are." Silence is the *cantus firmus* of life; all sound merely interacts with the constant vibrating silent hue of nature.

Silence is the source and the destiny of every *sound* as well as every listening. Silence is an original, primary event like birth and death. To be in this still inner world is to listen and hear. Out of listening silence, an obedient response emerges. Silence always listens; listening is always in a state of silence. Silence, like the phenomenon of listening, is always obedient, waiting for sound to set it in motion. William Wordsworth describes the poetics of his own solitude: "Obedient as a lute / That waits upon the touches of the wind."[32] Silence waits obediently and freely for the touch of sound. Silence is not simply a spectator; it participates in the work of the ear.

Pythagoras, the pre-Christian founder of a religious and political order, acknowledged the importance of the discipline of silence by imposing on new disciples five years of total silence. The primacy of sound, its definition and organization, is an important aspect of the Pythagorean legacy. The discovery of the numerical basis of all musical concordances is attributed to him. He was probably keenly aware of the symbiotic relationship between silence and patterned sound, which is music.

The realm of poetry can suggest these interactions of dynamic sound, listening, and silence, interactions, according to George Steiner, that "are actions of the spirit rooted in silence. It is difficult to *speak* of these, for how should speech justly convey the shape and vitality of silence?"[33] A poem is a metaphor for silence. O'Donohue puts it simply yet emphatically: "Poetry is the language of silence."[34]

Silence and listening to sound are inseparable. Silence is the shore of the ocean of sound. All speech (the heart of which is in the listening) and sounds are born from and into silence. There is a pre-speech, pre-sonic state from which heard speech and sound emerge. This silence waits expectantly for the arrival of its near relation, sound.

In the deep space of silence, the inner contradictions that work against well-being are addressed and healed. Stillness is a positive reality that is a powerful means of self-expression. An intimate knowledge of silence is integral to human meaning and is synonymous with human existence. Quietness brings self-understanding back to the being who chooses and creates it. The hush of stillness is the great self-challenger. In the great space of stillness, limitations and expectations are exposed and confronted. Theologically speaking, an awareness of God puts silence to the test; silence nourishes the possibility and potentiality of God for humanity that has long since lain like a dry, withered leaf.

Silence is the positive ground or horizon of sound. It is an infinite commodity in that it surrounds all sounding. Silence is the womb of listening and hearing; silence is also the midwife assisting at the birth of sound. Within the realm of the silent, the meaning of the sound is processed long after the sound has ceased. "Heard melodies are sweet but those unheard are sweeter," in Keats's memorable lines.[35] It is a definitive, albeit difficult state of activity. Ambrose of Milan cautioned 1,600 years ago that "it is more difficult to know how to be silent than how to speak." For the disciple who submits to or chooses this discipline of yearning, it carries its own infinitely creative risks.

Words once spoken out of the silence fade into another silence from out of which meaning and understanding gradually emerge. T. S. Eliot's lines "Words, after speech, reach / Into the silence" imply dynamism, movement, and success in establishing communication.

My Song Is Everyone's Song

And deep things are Song. It seems somehow the very central essence of us, Song.—Thomas Carlyle

The strange power of song over the psyche is difficult to decipher because it is always exceptional, elusive, and different for each one of us. But the amazing, free, and beautiful fact is that singing is, was, and always will be good for the psyche of both singer and listener. The Roman poet Horace observed this phenomenon over 2,000 years ago: "*Minuentur atrae, Carmine curae*"(Dark worries will be lessened by song).[36]

How we sing, even the song we choose to sing, reveals the essence of our psyche. The very act of singing and listening to song unites people's stories and cultures. If you want to know me, listen to my song. One ancient proverb from the Irish tradition rightly claims *Mo scéal féin—scéal gach duine* (My story is everybody's story). A song is simply a story, so my song is everyone's song; your song is my song. Listen keenly with the ear of the heart to mine, and I, in turn, will listen to yours. A singer is not simply entertaining: a singer is converting his or her listeners through the sound of the story to the sound of the soul. There is something mythological about the singer, the vocal musician. "Myth" and "music" are close relatives in the Greek tradition. *Muthos* is the sound for word, speech, story, or legend, the heart of all song. *Mousiké,* the source of "music," refers to any of the nine sister goddesses, the Muses, who are experts in all areas of song. The words come first, the imaginative powers of the listener follow. In the space created by synergistic imagination, the story is carried and convincing. Here in the song of the psyche is "a music you would never have known to listen for."[37]

When Rilke wrote about having "written down [the *Sonnets to Orpheus*] in a single breathless obedience," he was surely talking about submitting to the silence out of (or in which) God's voice can be heard. God's voice, whether as a voice that thunders or as a Whisper of the Mind, bubbles out of that silence and is audible to those who listen. And the role of the singer of this sacred song is to amplify God's voice and give to it a musical presence. In this way, what has variously been called "The Voice from the Cloud" or "A Feather on the Breath of God" may, through Song, expand the consciousness of each Psyche that belongs to those individuals who are willing and able to hear; even to hear what they had not expected.

NOTES

Track 28 on the CD that accompanies this volume is a recording of "The Song of the Wandering Aengus" by Nóirín Ní Riain.

[1] R. M. Rilke to Xavier von Moos, 20 April 1923, quoted in W. Barnstone, *To Touch the Sky: Poems of Mystical, Spiritual and Metaphysical Light* (New York: New Directions Books, 1999), p. 194.

[2] Gaston Bachelard, *The Poetics of Space* (Boston: Beacon Press, 1969), p. 197.

[3] Roland Barthes, *The Grain of the Voice: Interviews 1962–1980* (London: Jonathan Cape, 1985), p. 184.

[4] Roland Barthes, *The Responsibility of Forms: Critical Essays on Music, Art, and Representation,* trans. Richard Howard (Oxford: Basil Blackwell, 1985), pp. 279–280.

[5] Thomas Allen Seel, *A Theology of Music for Worship Derived from the Book of Revelation* (Metuchen, NJ: Scarecrow Press, 1995), p. 95.

[6] Paul Newham, *The Singing Cure: An Introduction to Voice Movement Therapy* (Boston: Shambhala Publications, 1993), p. 125.

[7] *Editors' note:* This is beautifully demonstrated in Nóirín's rendering of "The Song of the Wandering Aengus," Track 28 of the CD. This recording is part of the album *Sanctuary,* sales of which support victims of domestic violence. See www.myspace.com/sanctuaryalbum.

[8] Victor Zuckerkandl, *Man the Musician,* vol. 2, *Sound and Symbol* (Princeton, NJ: Princeton University Press, 1973), p. 12.

[9] Alfred Tomatis, *The Conscious Ear* (Barrytown, NY: Station Hill Press, 1991), p. 186.

[10] Zuckerkandl, *Man the Musician,* p. 85.

[11] David J. Elliott, *Music Matters: A New Philosophy of Music Education* (New York: Oxford University Press, 1995), p. 81.

[12] Joachim-Ernst Berendt, *The Third Ear: On Listening to the World* (Dorset: Element Books Ltd., 1988), p. 3.

[13] T. S. Eliot, "To Walter de la Mare," in *The Complete Poems and Plays of T. S. Eliot* (London: Faber and Faber, 1969), p. 205.

[14] Zuckerkandl, *Man the Musician,* 2:73.

[15] Anthony Storr, *Music and the Mind* (New York: The Free Press, 1992), p. 26.

[16] Barthes, *The Responsibility of Forms,* p. 245.

[17] Peter Kivy, *Music Alone: Philosophical Reflections on the Purely Musical Experience* (Ithaca, NY: Cornell University Press, 1990), p. 7.

[18] Gemma Fiumara, *The Other Side of Language: A Philosophy of Listening* (London: Routledge, Chapman and Hall, 1990), p. 187.

[19] Quoted from "Xenophon on Socrates; Defence to the Jury," in *Philosophers Speak for Themselves: From Thales to Plato,* ed. T. V. Smith (Chicago: Chicago Press, 1954), p. 107.

[20] Bachelard, *The Poetics of Space,* p. 215.

[21] Zuckerkandl, *Man the Musician,* 2:87.

[22] Gaston Bachelard, *The Poetics of Space,* trans. Maria Jolas (1958; repr., Boston: Beacon Press, 1964), p. 198.

[23] Bridget Riley, *The Eye's Mind: Collected Writings 1965–1999* (London: Thames & Hudson, 1999), p. 211.

[24] John O' Donohue, *Anam Cara: A Book of Celtic Wisdom* (New York: HarperCollins Publishers, 1997), p. 72.

[25] T. S. Eliot, "Burnt Norton," in *Collected Poems 1909–1962* (London: Faber and Faber, 1974), p. 194.

[26] S. Kierkegaard quoted in Peter Kreeft, "How the Sea Can Help You Pray," n.d., available at http://www.peterkreeft.com/topics-more/sea-prayer.htm (accessed 19 August 2009).

[27] Seamus Heaney, *Station Island* (London: Faber and Faber, 1994), p. 61.

[28] *Ibid.,* p. 70.

[29] Emily Dickinson, *The Complete Poems of Emily Dickinson,* ed. Thomas H. Johnson (London: Faber and Faber, 1970), p. 129.

[30] Max Picard, *The World of Silence* (Chicago: H. Regnery, 1952), p. 174.

[31] *Ibid.*

[32] William Wordsworth, "The Prelude," in William Wordsworth, *The Prelude: A Parallel Text,* ed. J. C. Maxwell (Middlesex: Penguin Books, 1971), p. 108.

[33] George Steiner, *Language and Silence: Essays 1958–1966* (London: Faber and Faber, 1967), p. 30.

[34] O'Donohue, *Anam Cara,* p. 67.

[35] John Keats, "Ode on a Grecian Urn," lines 11–12, in *John Keats: The Complete Poems,* ed. John Barnard (Middlesex: Penguin Books, 1973), p. 344.

[36] The Latin text is from Horace, "Q. Horati Flacci Carminvm Liber Qvartvs," section XI, lines 35–36, in *The Works of Horace,* ed. Thomas Chase (Philadelphia: Eldridge and Brother, 1881), p. 106.

[37] Seamus Heaney, "The Rain Stick," in *The Spirit Level* (London: Faber & Faber, 1995).

List of CD Tracks

Track 1: Nicholas Abbott, "The Golden Key," private recording by Nicholas and Simon Abbott, Cape Town, South Africa.

Track 2: Excerpt from Movement 3 of Mahler's *Symphony No. 9*, on *Mahler: Symphony No.9. Richard Strauss: Metamorphosen, Tod und Verklärung*, Simon Rattle conducting the Vienna Philharmonic Orchestra, 2 CDs, Angel Records, 1998.

Track 3: Excerpt from Movement 1 of Mahler's *Symphony No. 9*, on *Mahler: Symphony No.9. Richard Strauss: Metamorphosen, Tod und Verklärung*.

Track 4: Excerpt from Movement 1 of Mahler's *Symphony No. 9*, on *Mahler: Symphony No.9. Richard Strauss: Metamorphosen, Tod und Verklärung*.

Track 5: Excerpt from Movement 1 of Mahler's *Symphony No. 9*, on *Mahler: Symphony No.9. Richard Strauss: Metamorphosen, Tod und Verklärung*.

Track 6: Excerpt from Movement 1 of Mahler's *Symphony No. 9*, on *Mahler: Symphony No.9. Richard Strauss: Metamorphosen, Tod und Verklärung*.

Track 7: Excerpt from Movement 1 of Mahler's *Symphony No. 9*, on *Mahler: Symphony No.9. Richard Strauss: Metamorphosen, Tod und Verklärung.*

Track 8: Excerpt from Movement 2 of Mahler's *Symphony No. 9*, on *Mahler: Symphony No.9. Richard Strauss: Metamorphosen, Tod und Verklärung.*

Track 9: Excerpt from Movement 2 of Mahler's *Symphony No. 9*, on *Mahler: Symphony No.9. Richard Strauss: Metamorphosen, Tod und Verklärung.*

Track 10: Excerpt from Movement 3 of Mahler's *Symphony No. 9*, on *Mahler: Symphony No.9. Richard Strauss: Metamorphosen, Tod und Verklärung.*

Track 11: Excerpt from Movement 3 of Mahler's *Symphony No. 9*, on *Mahler: Symphony No.9. Richard Strauss: Metamorphosen, Tod und Verklärung.*

Track 12: Connee Boswell, "Isle of May," on *Connee Boswell: Heart and Soul*, Living Era CD, 1997.

Track 13: Lee Wiley, "Memphis Blues," on *A Touch of the Blues*, BMG CD #7478, 1998. Courtesy of Universal Music Enterprises.

Track 14: Ludwig van Beethoven, "Recitative" of *Piano Sonata No. 31 in A-Flat Major*, on *Piotr Anderszewski Plays Bach: English Suite BWV 811/Beethoven: Piano Sonata Op. 110/Webern: Variations Op. 27*, EMI Classics, 2004. Courtesy of EMI Records Ltd./Virgin Classics.

Track 15: Ludwig van Beethoven, "Arioso dolente" of *Piano Sonata No. 31 in A-Flat Major*, on *Piotr Anderszewski Plays Bach: English Suite BWV 811/Beethoven: Piano Sonata Op. 110/Webern: Variations Op. 27.*

Track 16: Ludwig van Beethoven, "Fuga" of *Piano Sonata No. 31 in A-Flat Major*, on *Piotr Anderszewski Plays Bach: English Suite BWV 811/Beethoven: Piano Sonata Op. 110/Webern: Variations Op. 27.*

Track 17: Excerpt from Robert Schumann, *Humoreske*, recorded for *Music and Psyche* by Steven Masi, New York City.

Track 18: Excerpt from Robert Schumann, *Carnaval*, recorded for *Music and Psyche* by Steven Masi, New York City.

Track 19: Excerpt from Robert Schumann, *Carnaval*, recorded for *Music and Psyche* by Steven Masi, New York City.

Track 20: Excerpt from Robert Schumann, *Novelletten*, recorded for *Music and Psyche* by Steven Masi, New York City.

Track 21: Excerpt from Robert Schumann, *Novelletten*, recorded for *Music and Psyche* by Steven Masi, New York City.

Track 22: Excerpt from Robert Schumann, *Novelletten*, recorded for *Music and Psyche* by Steven Masi, New York City.

Track 23: Excerpt from Robert Schumann, *Novelletten*, recorded for *Music and Psyche* by Steven Masi, New York City.

Track 24: Excerpt from Ludwig van Beethoven, *An der ferne Geliebte*, recorded for *Music and Psyche* by Steven Masi, New York City.

Track 25: Excerpt from Ludwig van Beethoven, *An der ferne Geliebte*, recorded for *Music and Psyche* by Steven Masi, New York City.

Track 26: Excerpt from Robert Schumann, *Fantasie*, recorded for *Music and Psyche* by Steven Masi, New York City.

Track 27: Excerpt from Robert Schumann, *Fantasie*, recorded for *Music and Psyche* by Steven Masi, New York City.

Track 28: Nóirín Ní Riain, "The Song of the Wandering Aengus," on *Sanctuary: Acoustic/Celtic/Roots Music,* New Voice, 2007.

Contributors

Helen Anderson is a music therapist in private practice who has lectured widely. Her most recent publications are "A Concerto of the Heart," which appeared in Paul Ashton, ed., *Evocations of Absence*; and "Music, Image and Psychic Transformation," *Mantis* 20, no. 1 (2009). Under the name Helen Henderson, she has published "Sound and Symbols in Childhood Pathologies," in *Proceedings of the World Congress on Infant Mental Health* (University of Cape Town Press, 1995), among other papers.

Paul W. Ashton is a psychiatrist and Jungian analyst in private practice in Cape Town, where he lives with his wife and youngest daughter. He is the author of a monograph *From the Brink: Experiences of the Void from a Depth Psychology Perspective* (Karnac, 2007), and editor of and contributor to *Evocations of Absence: Multidisciplinary Perspectives on Void States* (Spring, 2007). He has published various reviews and articles and lectured about music, art, literature, and the Void. He is a member of the Southern African Association of Jungian Analysts and is the editor of *Mantis,* the journal of the Southern African Association of Jungian Analysts.

John Beebe, a widely published Jungian analyst, editor, and lecturer in practice in San Francisco, has had a lifelong interest in the arts, particularly American popular entertainment. Some of this is expressed in his 1981 article "The Trickster in the Arts" and his 2008 book (co-authored with Virginia Apperson), *The Presence of the Feminine in Film.* He dates his fascination with popular and jazz singing to age six, when Tony Martin's cover of "Flamingo" was his favorite record.

Stephen Bloch is a clinical psychologist and Jungian analyst in private practice in Cape Town, South Africa. He has published the chapter "Music as Dreaming" in *Evocations of Absence* (2007) and given seminars on other aspects of music and psychoanalysis as well as on ethics. He is a founding member of the Southern African Association of Jungian Analysts (SAAJA) and has served on SAAJA's Executive Committee as well as on its Assessment and Review, Ethics, and Library Committees.

Michael Eigen is the author of eighteen books, including *Flames from the Unconscious: Trauma, Madness and Faith*; *Feeling Matters*; *The Psychoanalytic Mystic*; and *The Sensitive Self.* He has led a seminar on Bion, Winnicott, and Lacan for over thirty years. He is on the faculties of the National Psychological Association for Psychoanalysis and the New York University Postdoctoral Program in Psychotherapy and Psychoanalysis.

Melinda Haas, LCSW, is a Jungian analyst in private practice in New York City and Woodstock, Vermont. She is a graduate of the C. G. Jung Institute of New York. Melinda studied at the Dalcroze School of Music as a young child. After gaining a BA in Comparative Literature, Melinda began teaching the Dalcroze method, accompanying modern dance classes, teaching piano and improvisation, and composing for dance. Most recently she has been engaged in exploring the intersection of these two areas of study. She is president of the board of the Archive for Research in Archetypal Symbolism.

Mario Jacoby, Ph.D., is a lecturer and a supervising and training analyst at the International School of Analytical Psychology (ISAP) in Zürich, Switzerland. For many years (until 1997) he was a member of the Curatorium (Board of Directors) at the C. G. Jung Institute in Zurich. He is also a guest lecturer at the Alfred Adler Institute and at the Burghölzi, the psychiatric clinic of the University of Zurich. He has been invited on lecture tours and training courses in major cities all over the world. He has a private analytical practice in Zurich. His first interest was in music, and at a young age he studied under Georges Enesco at the Ecole Normale in Paris and under Max Rostal at the Guildhall School of Music and Drama in London. He became a professional violinist, touring with the Zurich Chamber Orchestra to the United States and Canada.

Mario Jacoby has published several books on analytical psychology, including *The Analytic Encounter* (1984), *Individuation and Narcissism* (1990), *Shame and the Origins of Self-Esteem* (1994), and *Jungian Psychotherapy and Contemporary Infant Research* (1999). He has also published more than fifty articles on analytical psychology in various psychological journals.

Laurel Morris is a Jungian analyst in private practice in New York City. She was trained at the C. G. Jung Institute of New York. She has been involved in Jungian training as both teacher and supervisor at the C. G. Jung Institute of New York and, currently, at the Jungian Psychoanalytic Association. She has taught and presented on many topics, particularly studies related to Jung's work on alchemy and the imagination as related to analytic methodology. She is also engaged in ongoing study of music and art as related to psyche. She has served on the boards of the C. G. Jung Institute of New York, the Archive for Research in Archetypal Symbolism, and the National Association for the Advancement of Psychoanalysis, and she participated in the founding of the Jungian Psychoanalytic Association.

Nóirín Ní Riain, Ph.D., is an internationally acclaimed singer of spiritual songs from many traditions who has given concerts and workshops worldwide. A theologian and musicologist, she was awarded the first doctorate in theology from Mary Immaculate College, the University of Limerick. Her thesis subject was "Towards a Theology of Listening," for which she coined a new word—"Theosony"—from the Greek *Theos* (God) and Latin *sonans* (sounding). She has recently published an auto/auro biography that tells the story behind Theosony: *Listen with the Ear of the Heart* (Veritas, 2009). It was selected as one of the Great Irish Books of the Year by Publishing Ireland in 2009. Her theological observations are to be published in 2010.

Kevin O'Connell studied music at Trinity College Dublin and holds his Ph.D. in Composition from Dublin City University. He completed his first chamber orchestral commission for BBC Radio 3 at the age of 25. He has since been commissioned by many leading arts organizations, including the Ulster Orchestra, the Irish National Symphony Orchestra, the Lotus Quartet of Stuttgart, and the Opera Theatre Company and by cellist Raphael Wallfisch. In 2008 he toured China with pianist Archie Chen, who played his piano work *Céimeanna.* He holds an Arts Council major bursary to work on his first symphony. He is head of composition at the Royal Irish Academy of Music and a member of Aosdána, Ireland's academy of creative artists.

Patricia Skar, BMus, MFA, is a Jungian analyst in private practice in Beatenberg and Thun, Switzerland, and a senior analyst in the Independent Group of Analytical Psychologists (London). Having performed piano and violin from an early age, she began writing on music and analysis in her diploma thesis for the C. G. Jung Institute Zurich, "Music and Analysis: Contrapuntal Reflections" (1992). Since then, she has practiced analysis in Ireland and England and lectured widely in a variety of clinical and academic settings, including Trinity College Dublin and Oxford University. Her published articles focus on the relationship between music and analytic processes and the connections between Jungian psychology and the new sciences.

Lawrence Wetzler is a clinical psychologist and psychoanalyst in full-time private practice in Manhattan and Long Island. He is on the faculties of the Adelphi Postgraduate Program in Psychotherapy and Psychoanalysis, the Institute for Expressive Analysis, and the Object Relations Institute. An aspiring concert pianist, he gives yearly piano recitals in the area and writes on the relationship between music and psychoanalysis.

Chris Wildman is a music therapist who works with a variety of
Cape Town populations. These include child burn survivors,
children and adults affected by HIV and AIDS, and patients
suffering from TB. He graduated from King's College London
in 1970 and moved to Cape Town in 1974, where, after
working for a decade in education and development, he
completed a postgraduate music therapy diploma at the SA
College of Music. He is both musician and musical director
of the Bonfire Theatre Company.

William Willeford is a Jungian analyst practicing in Atlanta, Georgia.
He is the author of *Feeling, Imagination, and the Self:
Transformations of the Mother-Infant Relationship* (1987) and *The
Fool and His Scepter* (1989).